More Praise for *Cowboy & Wills*

"*Cowboy & Wills* is the very best kind of memoir: a quietly profound story that reminds everyone of the power of simple acts of love. Holloway and her remarkable son are bound to inspire and transform many lives."

—Hope Edelman, *New York Times* bestselling author of
The Possibility of Everything

"Monica Holloway had me laughing *and* crying within the first five pages. She crafts artful and, so often, hysterical observations of everyday life, while also revealing the many dimensions of heartache that come with being a mother."

—Jennifer Lauck, *New York Times* bestselling author of *Still Waters*

"An intimate, loving, funny look at the heartbreaking relationship between one mom, one dad, their very special little boy, and the puppy that was heaven-sent to love them all."

—Leslie Morgan Steiner, *New York Times* bestselling author of *Crazy Love*

"Monica Holloway has written one of the most extraordinary memoirs I've ever read. Tender, loving, and heartbreakingly intimate, it chronicles her struggle to coax her son, Wills, out of the shell of autism. I highly recommend this gorgeous and frank book about family, connections, and the ephemeral state of belonging."

—Barrie Gillies, senior editor, *Parents* magazine

This title is also available from Simon & Schuster Audio and as an eBook

Cowboy & Wills

A REMARKABLE LITTLE BOY

AND THE DOG THAT CHANGED HIS LIFE

Monica Holloway

5/10/14

Dearest Katie —

Sending you tons of love + support!

Marie Holloway

GALLERY BOOKS

NEW YORK   LONDON   TORONTO   SYDNEY

Gallery Books
A Division of Simon & Schuster, Inc.
1230 Avenue of the Americas
New York, NY 10020

Note to Readers
Names and identifying details of some of the people
portrayed in this book have been changed.

First Gallery Books trade paperback edition June 2010

For information about special discounts for bulk purchases,
please contact Simon & Schuster Special Sales at
1-866-506-1949 or business@simonandschuster.com.

The Simon & Schuster Speakers Bureau can bring authors
to your live event. For more information or to book an
event contact the Simon & Schuster Speakers Bureau at
1-866-248-3049 or visit our website at www.simonspeakers.com.

Select scenes from chapters 1, 2, and 13 appeared in different form
as "Red Boots and Cole Haans" in *Mommy Wars,* edited by Leslie
Morgan Steiner, published by Random House, Inc., in 2006.

Interior designed by Kyoko Watanabe

Manufactured in the United States of America

10 9 8 7 6 5 4 3

Library of Congress Cataloging-in-Publication Data

Holloway, Monica.
  Cowboy and Wills : a remarkable little boy and the dog
  that changed his life / by Monica Holloway.
    p.   cm.
  1. Price, Wills—Mental health.   2. Autism spectrum disorders—
Patients—United States—Biography.   3. Golden retriever—
Therapeutic use—United States.   I. Title.
  RJ506.A9P75   2009
  618.92'85882'0092—dc22
  [B]   2009030422

ISBN 978-1-4165-9503-8
ISBN 978-1-4165-9504-5 (pbk)
ISBN 978-1-4165-9996-8 (ebook)

For Jessica

Wills Price is exceptional.

If you happen to meet him walking down our street, you'd see a lanky boy in red baggy sweatpants. His thick black eyelashes frame enormous, cornflower blue eyes and he has freckles that march across the top of his tiny turned-up nose. When he lets loose with a belly laugh, his dimples deepen and he throws his head back while twisting the front of his shirt. He prefers wearing stripes—T-shirts and turtlenecks mostly. He's very particular about this. There have to be stripes.

He has just a hint of a lisp, the result of a slight overbite, just like his dad's. His ears stick out at the top just like mine, and his thick bangs blow straight up in the air when he runs. Wills is always polite and articulate—his voice clear and his speech sophisticated. He hits every sound perfectly.

He collects things: fossils, heart-shaped rocks, sea glass, packets of flower seeds that lie in neat rows on his bookcase, old rusty railroad spikes he picks up when we're train watching, and dusty bottle caps.

Wills knows the parts that make up a Boeing 747 engine, as well as every state capital by heart. In kindergarten, he built the Las Vegas strip on a piece of plywood, yet he has trouble buttoning his shirt or balancing on a small bicycle with training wheels.

He cries in crowded or noisy rooms, but is right at home in the heart of New York City.

There is no doubt about it. Wills is an extraordinary kid.

The main thing you need to know if you happen to meet Wills is that Cowboy will be there, too—Cowboy Carol Lawrence, to be precise. And Wills is nothing if not precise—that's all part of being exceptional. Cowboy and Wills are inexplicably linked. They walk every day, boy and dog—dog and boy.

Cowboy is a girl and Wills is a boy. They're both blonds.

If you smile at them, Wills might not notice because he usually looks the other way when strangers pass, but Cowboy . . . well, if you smile at Cowboy, be prepared for instantaneous rip-snorting attention. She loves people. She loves to put both of her paws on your chest and lick you right on the lips. Wills loves people, too, he just doesn't know it yet.

Cowboy and Wills walk so close together that they lean into one another, attempting to walk in a straight line. Cowboy, ever so slowly, shoves Wills off the edge of the sidewalk so that he has to push his way back, onto the cement. Cowboy doesn't mind—she's an easy girl to get along with. But Wills doesn't like to get grass stains or mud on his shoes.

They walk on—Wills with his hand casually resting on Cowboy's head, Cowboy, holding her own leash in her mouth, walking herself next to Wills.

Today Wills is pulling his red wagon. He and Cowboy are searching for rocks to place around the perimeter of the pond Wills has begun digging in our backyard. Cowboy is more than happy to help with the excavation, but inevitably ends up unearthing the pansies over by the fence.

When Wills spies a rock that might be the correct size, he rolls it over a couple of times with the toe of his sneaker, making sure there aren't spiders or roly-polies underneath. Cowboy sniffs the place where the rock has been, and then plops down on the sidewalk, legs sprawled out behind her so that her tummy lies bare on the cool sidewalk. She's awaiting his decision.

If Wills places the rock in the wagon, that's Cowboy's cue to pull herself up and keep moving—her favorite thing to do. With that golden retriever perma-smile on her face, it seems she'd be happy doing just about anything as long as she's with Wills. If the rock is rejected, it takes Wills a minute to let it go. He doesn't like to leave things behind. Cowboy watches and waits.

Once Wills feels that the rock will survive without him, they journey on.

Often, these two are heading nowhere in particular, but wind up in that ambiguous place between bravery that only comes in pairs—and miracles that continue long after there is no one to toss the ball to.

Part One

It Takes a Zoo

CHAPTER ONE

The day after Wills was diagnosed with autistic spectrum disorder, I took him for a ride to Ben's Fish Store in Sherman Oaks to buy a large freshwater aquarium. We picked up all the equipment; a ten-gallon tank, a filter, multicolored rocks to spread on the bottom, an imitation pirate ship made out of clay, tacky neon plastic plants, a large rock with a hole in the middle for the fish to swim through, fish food, a small green plastic net, a special siphon with a clear hose on the end to clean the tank, and replacement filters. It totaled $462.84—a high price that I could barely afford to squeeze onto my overextended Visa. I didn't care; my three-year-old had autism.

We couldn't buy the actual fish that day because the entire aquarium needed to be set up, with the filter plugged in for at least a week before any fish could go into it.

"What would happen if we bought one fish for him to look at right away?" I asked Ben, the owner, more for myself than for Wills. I didn't want to face an empty aquarium.

"That fish would die," he said, at which point Wills began crying and cupping his hands over his ears to ward off the unsurvivable grief over the loss of a fish we hadn't even met yet.

"We'll wait," I said, picking up Wills and balancing him on my hip. Then Ben, in full Goth regalia, helped us carry our booty to the car. It took three trips.

Wills was elated, I could tell. His eyes were flashing that clear blue twinkle I only saw when he was really, really happy. Sometimes his eyes were more like mirrors, my image bouncing back at me. Those were the times I was most panicked, watching Wills recede so deep inside himself that I saw no way to grab hold of his tiny hand and pull him back to me.

But when Wills was present, the world tilted toward perfection.

I, like Wills, was thrilled with our fish store purchase. The aquarium would push back the grief I'd felt twenty-four hours earlier (and every waking and sleeping moment since), sitting in his therapist Katherine's office, hearing her say, "Wills has autistic spectrum disorder. He clearly possesses autistic traits, but at three years old, I hesitate to diagnose him more specifically. For now, we can assume he's under the autistic umbrella."

It wasn't that the diagnosis was a shock; we'd dreaded hearing it ever since we first took Wills to see Katherine a year and a half ago. Even before I'd called her that first time, autistic indicators had been lining up with shocking accuracy: he was a clingy, anxious baby who hadn't hit a single developmental mark. He was terrified of strangers, on sensory overload every time we left the house, and he refused to make eye contact. But still, the diagnosis struck with the velocity of Hurricane Andrew. And then, even more devastating, was when I learned later that day that autism was a "lifetime affliction"—no cure.

I placed the aquarium on a beach towel I'd spread out on the family room carpet and watched Wills pour the multicolored rocks into the bottom. He held the heavy plastic bag with both hands as the tiny stones pelted the glass, creating a huge racket—the kind that usually drove him to tears. He stopped for a moment and the noise stopped. He poured more rocks and the noise resumed. Wills looked at me.

"It's noisy, isn't it?" I said. He hesitated, but then kept pouring.

Already this aquarium was paying dividends. If Wills could ignore the clatter, then his overly tidy, more-than-slightly OCD mother could relax enough to tend an enormous fish tank with all of its gelatinous algae and floating poop ropes hanging from fish butts.

I was hoping for something reliable and alive in the house.

My husband, Michael, had no say in the fish undertaking because he wasn't home. He wasn't even in the same time zone.

Michael had been working as a writer on a television show in Chicago for the past six months and, even though he flew back every other weekend for a thirty-two-hour visit, during which he was exhausted and distracted, and even though we'd made the Chicago decision together, it created a huge support vacuum.

In my ugliest, most self-pitying moments, I clung, white-knuckled, to the notion that I was the helpless victim of a neglectful and absent husband. It was less devastating than placing my outrage and disappointment where it was warranted—on the gods who anointed my towheaded, blue-eyed boy with a life of autism—because the truth was, there wasn't *anyone* to blame. Still, thoughts of revenge ricocheted around in my head, looking for the culprit, worried, I think, that it just might be me.

It was a fact that with all of the therapies Katherine said Wills needed, it would take plenty of cash to keep him moving forward, and for the first time in both our lives, Michael and I had some.

When we first met, Michael was driving a taxicab while working on his writing career and I was a struggling stage actress, working as an office temp. Neither of us could afford health insurance, but we didn't spend much time contemplating that—we were enamored, consumed by each other, and *young*.

Our finances were slightly better once we married, and I was hired as assistant to the executive producers of a reality television show and Michael began writing for a small animation company. But right before Wills was born, Michael's career took off, and as it turned out, just in time.

So his job in Chicago was an enormous blessing. We had the money and insurance to help Wills, and I was free to be a stay-at-home mom, spending my days fawning over my darling son and trying to make him better. I knew how lucky I was.

The only problem was how isolated I'd become. In a cross between *Mommie Dearest* and *Girl, Interrupted*, my family and I had parted ways. Only my sister JoAnn, who lived four blocks from us, and I remained close. This lack of family presence put a lot of pressure on Michael. With the exception of JoAnn, he was my entire extended family—mom, dad, uncles, cousins, aunts, sibling. It wasn't fair, putting that much pressure on him, but I didn't know that then. I was attached to my six-foot-five pillar of calm like paint on a barn, so when he temporarily moved, it was like losing my family all over again—only this time, a family I really, really loved—one who took care of Wills and me and loved us right back.

JoAnn pitched in when she could, keeping us company and letting me out of the house once in a while, but she was extremely busy working in social services. Still, what a comfort it was having her so close.

I pulled the aquarium filter out of the box and read the directions aloud. Wills looked at me, hopeful. "Place the plastic shelter-cover onto the rotating mechanism . . ." I looked at Wills, "We'll have to wing it," I said. I was lousy with directions. He nodded.

Somehow we managed to get the filter working and for a week it hummed away in the fishless aquarium, the green and blue plastic plants sashaying in the current. Wills and I sat in front of it, admiring the cozy underwater environment we had created.

"It's beautiful," I said. He smiled.

"Daddy will like it," he said, watching the bubbles tumbling from the filter.

"Yes," I said, "when he comes home, he'll *love* it."

Michael had called to say that the show was a mess. He'd have to work on rewrites over the weekend and couldn't fly home. I was looking at another two weeks without a break, and still hadn't had a chance to process Wills's diagnosis, let alone discuss it in any depth with Michael. What would it mean for Wills's future and ours? Wills was autistic, and I couldn't change it. It was a fact, like the sun setting or the sum of two plus two. I'd let him down. Someone did.

"I ordered monkeys," I told Wills, attempting a lame joke that just might work on a three-year-old. Wills didn't "get" jokes due to his concrete thinking, but Katherine had suggested I try some out on him. "I hope they fit in there."

"Fish only."

"In the aquarium?" I asked.

"Fish." He looked at me confused, his eyebrows pinched together.

"Oh, that's right, fish," I agreed. He nodded, serious and focused. "Mommy's only kidding, honey. I didn't order monkeys." He looked directly at me. "But wouldn't it be funny if I did? They'd be so much fun."

"Monkeys don't live under there," he said, poking the glass.

"I know," I said, giving up. "I was joking." Bombing was more like it.

Wills had the misfortune of having silly parents. Michael and I were careful to keep our laughter under control, but nothing gave us more pleasure than cracking each other up. And this would send Wills into a screaming fit, pointing and yelling, "NO! NO!" The fact that laughter, such a vital part of life, was so disturbing to Wills was one of the cruelest ironies for this couple of born comedians.

The quiet, the lack of fun, made Michael's absence even more profound. Where were the Frank Sinatra songs he played while cooking Swedish meatballs in his underpants? What was a Sunday afternoon without Michael's Mets game muted in the background so that the cheering (or, given that these were the Mets, sobbing) fans wouldn't upset Wills? I sat down and wrote my husband a love letter—one of many—except that he wrote more frequently than me. His were often just a couple of sentences scribbled on the back of a script, but sometimes he wrote on his legal pad. Those were the keepers. The letters were something I could look forward to, but they didn't have green eyes and wavy brown hair like Michael. Today I was needing the real thing.

Still feeling fragile from Wills's diagnosis, the two of us stayed home all week with only the sound of the humming aquarium to keep us company—no weekly visit to the grocery store, no walks around the block, nothing. I didn't want to run into someone we knew who might ask how we were doing. I hadn't figured out an answer to that one yet.

We found plenty of things to do. Wills loved wetting down our sidewalk with the garden hose. I'd help him pull on his green boots with the frog faces molded into the toes, and watch as he stomped around in his boots and diaper soaking the place. With all of the water gushing, everything was drenched—me, the grass, the Adirondack chairs, his plastic banana scooter—but Wills didn't get a single drop of water on himself. He was always pristine: no water, no dirt, no paint, no clay ever touched him if he could help it. (There were lots of rubber gloves at our house.) If his hands accidentally got dirty or sticky, he'd stand with his fingers spread wide, frozen in place until I picked him up under his armpits and carried him to the bathroom, where we'd wash away the offensive filth.

Katherine and I hoped to make him more comfortable with messes. The only problem was, I needed the exact same help. My anxieties often manifested in my cleaning around the baseboards of our house at three in the morning, regrouting the bathtub while Wills napped, or obsessively picking up leaves in the backyard. Mindless, neurotic tasks, like lining up books on the shelves according to

the color of their spines, seemed to be the only thing that brought me relief.

The OCD had followed me through my teen years and had kicked into high gear when I began noticing that Wills wasn't holding his head up or crawling at the appropriate times. The longer the delay, the more I scrubbed. My son might not have been rolling over at nine months, but you could eat a four-course meal off my dining room floor.

When I dreamt of being a mother, I'd pictured a completely different scenario. I was sure that immediately upon delivering my child, I'd become a carefree mom, napping when my son napped and carrying him around parks and zoos in an organic cotton sling. Instead, I hung over the edge of his bassinette like a scientist monitoring a petri dish and never once used the sling for fear of suffocating him in the folds of the rose-printed fabric.

I was unsure about the difference between letting a child experience the world for himself and what constituted neglect. So I erred on the overprotective side. If JoAnn was over at the house and Wills cried, the two of us practically knocked heads together while rushing into his room and bending over his plushy blue-and-white crib with the *Cow Jumping Over the Moon* mobile to ease whatever excruciating pain he must have been experiencing—but it was usually just gas.

Finally, the week of waiting was over, and it was time to pick out our fish.

"We're ready," I told Ben as the bell on the front door of the fish store jingled. Wills was riding on my back with his soft, square hands tucked under my chin.

"Excellent," he said, cracking his knuckles. "Come with me." He walked us down a dark, narrow aisle where the freshwater tanks glowed infrared. "You can choose any of the fish on this wall," he said, with a sweeping gesture toward the incandescent tanks.

We peered inside each one, and Wills pointed to the fish he wanted.

Ben suggested we start out with ten fish. "You'll probably lose a few the first couple of weeks anyway as your tank is getting accli-mated. You don't want to overcrowd it."

We were disappointed. We wanted at least twenty. With my son's future at risk, I didn't think there were enough fish in the store to compensate for my grief and ten was certainly not going to do it. But we listened to Ben and bought three swordtails, four neon tetras, two black mollies, and one small sucker fish to keep the tank clean. Traveling home in two clear plastic bags filled with water, they had just enough air to get them down Ventura Boulevard and into the house. Wills crossed one leg over the other as he settled into his soft, blue car seat, a plastic bag resting in his lap. The other bag was balanced on the cup holder beside me. Leon Redbone sang "Shoo Fly, Don't Bother Me," and I felt relaxed for the first time since I'd given birth. In the rearview mirror, I saw Wills patting the top of his plastic bag.

We brought the fish into the house, took the lid off the aquar-ium, and floated them on top of the water for twenty minutes per Ben's instructions. "The fish have to acclimate to the temperature of the water," he'd warned us.

Just when we thought we couldn't stand it any longer, it was time to open the bags and release them. With each blur of color, our aquarium became more alive. Wills and I sat on cushions in front of the tank and watched the fish explore their new home. It was oddly satisfying to have ten living things dependent on us. And unlike our lives, we controlled it all—the temperature, the environment, and the population.

Wills checked the tank every morning to see how everyone was doing and fed them himself. When we found a fish floating on top—dead, slimy, and covered in white fuzzy death fluff—I'd lay it in a small cardboard jewelry box that Wills had decorated with colored sequins and bury it in the six-foot-by-four-foot garden we'd just begun working on behind our garage. The number of dead fish was directly related to the exorbitant amount of food Wills was dumping into the tank every day, so I began measuring it out for him into tiny teaspoons.

After yet another burial, I looked down at my miraculous child who was squatting in his garden, concentrating on the back of a fern leaf, his eye pressed a little too close to his plastic magnifying glass. His patience and concentration were unmatched for a three-year-old, and as I watched him, an enormous swirl of hope encircled me. Autism was just a word, and for that one moment, the abject terror that had struck, paralyzing me over the last week, vanished. I had good reason to hope. Wills had a habit of surprising us. Sure, he didn't walk until he was sixteen months old, but when he did, he just got up and strolled into the kitchen as if he'd just remembered it was happy hour and the glasses needed to be chilled.

I'd sat there dumbstruck. He padded back around the corner to see why I hadn't followed. I jumped up and hurried after him.

He looked different standing on his own two feet. His back seemed so long and his diaper, comfy and snug around his waist, was bunched up in the back, with pastel pictures of Mickey Mouse leading an imaginary parade across his butt. I'd never seen it from that angle.

After that, he walked everywhere, with me running around behind him, silently cheering.

Wills, who'd been completely silent—no babbling or cooing—began talking the exact same way. JoAnn and I were outside a piano store when Wills, at seventeen months, pointed to a spigot and said, "Water." We screamed so loudly that he started crying.

I picked him up immediately and said, "Yes, water. You are exactly right, that's where water comes from."

He pointed toward the sky. "Airplane."

I danced in place. "You want to see airplanes?" I asked him.

"Airplane," he said, again.

"Okay, let's go see some airplanes!" I would have taken him to Monte Carlo if he'd asked.

I couldn't have been more thrilled. What I didn't know was that Wills's first fixation had manifested with a single word, "airplane." From the moment he said the word, it was impossible to get Wills to focus on anything else. Almost every day, he and I sat alone in the lobby of the tiny Van Nuys airport, Wills's face pressed against the glass, watching airplanes come and go. He clapped when they landed and waved bye-bye when they took off. Although Wills was usually unable to tolerate loud noises, the roar of the jet engines didn't faze him. He was happy there.

I tried taking him to Balboa Park on the way home, where other children were running beside the lake feeding the ducks and playing on the jungle gym, but he was having none of it. It was either the airport or our house. He did like going to Barnes & Noble, where he'd pull out books with airplanes on the covers, and sit on my lap, mesmerized as I read about the construction of LAX or the Wright Brothers' first flight. His colorful board books with ducks and fire trucks on the cover sat in his blue bookcase, untouched. Soon after, his toy box began filling up with plastic airplanes complete with rubber wheels and tiny pilots with painted-on hats. Those were quickly replaced with miniature replicas of real airplanes. Wills wanted his toys to be authentic. Kiddie airplanes didn't cut it.

Michael and I focused on how smart he was—how advanced. Who'd ever heard of a toddler sitting still for a history lesson in aviation? We were astounded by his ability to recognize airline names from the logos on their tails. Michael would take Wills to Encounters, the funky-looking restaurant in the middle of LAX, where he'd point to approaching aircrafts and pronounce in his shy whisper, "Japan Airlines . . . Alaska . . . Lufthansa . . . Qantas . . ."

Wills was prodigious in other ways as well. He had an incredible facility for building things, creating forts, train stations, and airports (of course) out of stacks of videotape cassettes and blocks. He made himself a pair of glasses, just like Mommy's, asking me to cut the bottoms out of two Dixie cups so he could string them together using gardening wire. He sat on the front stoop, balancing them on his turned-up nose.

But still, it was getting harder to ignore Wills's idiosyncrasies. Aside from his obsession with airplanes, Wills was extremely sensi-

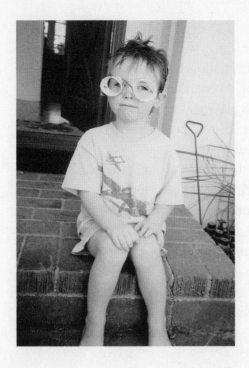

tive to textures and noises; a flannel shirt gave him "the goose bumps" and bubbles in the bathtub actually "hurt" his skin. The sudden bark of our neighbor's dog would send him running toward the back of the house, hands clamped over his ears, his face distorted in pain.

Probably the most worrisome development was what his pediatrician, Dr. Todd, described as his "profound stranger anxiety." If we strolled by someone in the park and they bent down and said, "What a gorgeous little boy," his thrashing legs and ear-piercing screams sent his admirer bolting in the opposite direction.

Still, there were times when he could experience new people and places without a fuss, like his first visit to Michael's parents' house. They lived in New Jersey and the five-hour flight to Newark went off without a hitch. Wills was unaffected by the other people stuffed into the narrow fuselage, the blast of the engines, or the sour smell of airplane food. He sat in his car seat, feet crossed, nibbling oyster crackers and telling us about the cooling system—as composed as Jack Benny delivering a joke.

Michael and I were heartened, thinking that maybe he was outgrowing some of his anxieties, but then someone would inevitably come up to us in the park beside Michael's parents' house to say hello, and Wills would scream and run in the opposite direction. We didn't know what to think. I spent nights pacing and fretting and my days bugging his pediatrician for reassurance.

* * *

One day when Wills was eighteen months old, my friend Jenn called and asked if she could drop off a book she had borrowed. I hung up the phone and looked at Wills playing with his blocks.

"Jenn's coming over," I said. He looked startled. "I know you don't like visitors but she's really great."

A few minutes later, the doorbell rang and Jenn was waving at me through the glass. I felt like the old me, the woman who yearned for company, throwing open the door to greet her; I couldn't wait for her to meet Wills.

I turned to introduce them, but he was gone.

"Hang on, Jenn, I have to get Wills," I said, following the trail of dropped blocks.

The trail ended near his closet, where two red leather boots were poking out the door.

"I see you," I teased.

When I pulled back the door, he was sitting there, arms wrapped around his body, rocking back and forth.

"Hey, buddy," I said kneeling down, "what's going on?"

I looked into two completely blank eyes. Wills was not there.

I tried to pick him up, but he scrambled farther back into his closet and clamped his hands over his ears.

"Hang on, honey, I'll be right back."

I ran out to the living room. "Jenn, I'm sorry, Wills isn't feeling well. Can we get together another day?"

"Sure," she said, heading for the door.

I forced a smile.

"Thanks for stopping by."

I closed the front door and ran back to Wills's room. He was behind a stack of boxes now, his soft blond head barely visible.

"Jenn's gone, buddy. Can you come out now?"

He couldn't.

I could live with the shrieking in public. I could humor his obsession with airplanes. I could minimalize his sensitivity to sound and texture. But I could not deny that he was vanishing from me. I knew if I let that happen, I might never get him back.

I sat in front of the closet with my hand stuck behind the boxes, touching his soft leg.

"It's okay, buddy. Come out when you're ready. It's okay."

The following morning I made an appointment to see Katherine. Michael and I told ourselves it was going to be okay. Katherine would say, "All children go through stages that are puzzling or not in sync with a doctor's expectation. There's nothing to worry about," but that didn't happen. It was both shocking and inevitable—my eighteen-month-old son now had his own therapist.

Over the next year and a half, we did every exercise Katherine suggested—narrating his feelings for him, structuring his day so that there were as few surprises as possible, helping him make eye contact. But here we were at age three, and the diagnosis had come—autistic spectrum disorder. The very next day, we bought the fish.

As Wills gazed at his new aquarium, the phone rang. It was Michael. I was in a wretched, I-have-cramps-and-am-going-to-explode-with-water-weight-gain mood; tired, flabby, and temporarily single. It had been more than a week since the diagnosis, and I was an emotional yo-yo. Depending on the day (or the hour), I'd go from thinking, *Wills is a genius and everything's going to be fine,* to *How could this be happening?* And the yo-yo-ing wasn't just centered around autism, it extended to my unsuspecting husband—a love letter from me one day/an emotional sock in the jaw the next.

"Our new neighbor asked me out on a date today," I told Michael.

"What?" he asked.

"I told him I was married and his response was, 'I've never seen anyone over there,' and I said, 'Exactly.' He thought I was divorced!"

"I hope you turned him down." Michael laughed.

"It's like someone snatched you away," I said.

"I'm right here." It was painfully obvious how dependent I was on this man who made me so happy and was by far the most reasonable of the three of us.

"You have no idea what's going on with your son."

"I know what's going on," he said. "I talk to you every day. You tell me exactly what's happening. I hear you. I'm not just blowing it off." He was right. I regurgitated our daily routine like a bulimic after a binge.

"Well, I'm glad you're listening," I said.

"Don't you know how hard this is on me?" he fired back. "I miss both of you so much," his voice rising in pitch. "I'm missing out on *everything.*"

"Not everything," I said, trying to defuse what I'd sparked. "I'm rarely bathed."

"I'd like to see you unbathed," he said, "I'd like to see you painted green—it doesn't matter how you look, Monica, I *always* want to see you and Wills. You know that."

"I do know," I said.

A long pause lay there, like a dead squirrel on the road.

"I'm scared," I finally admitted.

"I'm terrified," Michael said.

"What if we can't help him?" My lips started doing that involuntary shivering thing—and then the tears.

"We'll help him and, like Katherine said, he'll continue to improve," he assured me. "We love him so much. That's a good start."

"I wish love cured autism."

CHAPTER TWO

At our next session, Katherine suggested that Wills join a toddler group at The Early Years, a Santa Monica preschool where she was a consultant. This would be the first time that Wills would be among his peers and I would be among the motherset.

I tried on six different outfits, imagining what it would take to fit in. I combed my hair into a long ponytail, and then pulled that out. I clipped it up in the front and let it hang down in the back, and finally, I just let it flop down around my shoulders. My appearance wasn't going to make this any easier but still, I hoped.

I might as well have been wearing a burlap sack. Things went south for us within five minutes of entering the place.

The other children were sitting in a circle singing "Rags the Dog" and clapping, while Wills was under a reading table with his forehead pressed into the carpet and his hands pressed over his ears. I climbed underneath to be with him.

"Wills, do you think you can come out for a few minutes?" I asked, rubbing his back. There was no response. "We can sit outside if you'd like." Nothing. I was trying not to be embarrassed, but I felt it anyway, imagining that the other parents were looking at us and wondering what was wrong.

I wanted my son to sit in the circle and clap *his* hands. I wanted us to belong.

Tama and Joy, the preschool directors, welcomed Wills, despite his anxieties, and used everything they'd learned in their thirty-plus years of experience to help make him feel more comfortable. But Wills was too traumatized to relax or even eat a snack.

On our way home from that first awful day at The Early Years, we hurried to Pets of Wilshire to buy a hermit crab. The fish had helped distract me from the pain of Wills's diagnosis; maybe another small animal could ease the abject terror of seeing what other children Wills's age were capable of doing. Inside the store, they were holding a dog adoption. I put Wills on my hip so he could see into the pen.

"Puppies." He pointed with delight. These were actually full-grown dogs but they were just as beautiful.

"Aren't they great?" I asked, relieved to see Wills relaxed and smiling again.

"Yeah," he said, distracted by the number of people coming through the door to see them. "Let's buy Bluey and head out."

"Who's that?"

"The hermit crab," he said. "Hurry."

Wills took Bluey to Katherine's office in a small plastic carrying case and held him up for her to see. She looked as surprised as I was when Wills announced, "We're getting a new puppy."

"Are you getting a new dog?" she asked me.

"Not that I know of. . . . We just saw a dog adoption when we bought the hermit crab," I explained.

A puppy did sound sweet and very tempting, but if I wound up at the pet store every time Wills had a bad day, I'd work my way up to a backyard zoo to rival Neverland Ranch.

After that I began noticing dogs everywhere. How had I missed them all—trotting down Ocean Park Boulevard attached to rasta-style leashes, sleeping under someone's chair at the Coral Tree Café, or hanging out the window of a passing car? Michael and I had had an older dog, Hallie, whom we'd rescued. She was loyal, loving, and fiercely protective, but she wanted nothing to do with snuggling or children. Maybe a puppy was just what Wills needed.

While picking up hermit crab food at Elaine's Pet Depot, I began hanging out by the puppy pens in the back of the store. I even fingered the hand-sewn collars. This was getting serious.

On a long visit over Labor Day weekend, Michael nixed the idea. "Honey, you have enough to deal with right now. Let's just wait on the whole puppy thing." *A voice of reason,* I thought—but when it came to animals, even the "voice of reason" was hard pressed to stop me. A puppy . . . the seed had been planted. I'd wait it out.

During Wills's first year at preschool, there was a singalong at a park overlooking the Pacific Ocean. Beyond anxious, Wills bit his thumbnail, hid behind my leg, and cleared his throat again and again. When the whistle blew to sit down in the circle, Wills began screaming. Trying to climb up my body, he pulled down the back of my pants, exposing the thick band of my Jockey underwear to the Beverly Hills, thong-wearing crowd. The director of the school offered to let me sit in the circle with Wills and the rest of his class. My feelings of dread mounted as I awkwardly climbed over a field of small bodies with my thirty-two-pound son in my arms to a tiny spot on the quilt.

There was no room for crossing legs, so my size 9 loafers stuck out into the middle of the circle, giants among the tiny Stride Rites. Wills wrapped his arms and legs around my body, his face buried in my blouse.

He tried to soothe himself by rocking back and forth and making small whimpering noises to drown out the world. I patted his back and scanned the crowd, feeling intensely alone. There were twenty video cameras pointed in our direction, operated by smiling dads—none of them Michael, who was still in Chicago.

The children began to sing:

> *I can see clearly now, the rain has gone.*
> *I can see all obstacles in my way.*
> *Gone are the dark clouds that had me down.*
> *It's going to be a bright, bright, sunshiny day.*

I was mulling over the irony of the song when I felt Wills's hands slip away from his ears. His body relaxed for just a moment and I heard vibrations coming from his throat. I had never heard him sing or hum anything. Even in front of a huge group of people, his worst nightmare, Wills was finding his own way to be part of the singalong. Katherine was right. As anxious as Wills was, there was still a part of him that wanted to belong, to connect.

I put my cheek against his cheek. He squeezed my side, and I forgave the gods, a little, for everything they had put us through.

On the way home that afternoon, we stopped by Petco for fish food. Walking to the aquatics section, we peered into one of the glass cages along the wall and saw a ball of blond and white fur curled up like a cinnamon roll: "European Golden Hamster" it said on the side of the cage.

"He's so cute," I gushed. Wills's hands were entwined and tucked under his small chin. "Let's buy a book on hamsters and see what they're like," I said and off we went to find one. I read the book aloud in the car while he ate McDonald's French fries in his car seat. When he was done eating, we went back and bought that hamster.

The Petco clerk put him in a small cardboard box with air holes and Wills held it against his chest as he sat in the red plastic cart with his feet dangling down. As we rolled through Petco, we collected a Habitrail house, hamster food, hamster fluff for nesting, a plastic exercise ball, an exercise wheel, food, and a water bottle. I spent $314.00. Damn, this was really, really bad. I couldn't keep spending this kind of money; my credit card was completely maxed out.

Wills named the hamster Booner Schooner and took him *everywhere*. We bought a small wire traveling cage with a purple plastic lid that Wills carried around like a purse.

Booner rode next to Wills on a trip to Beeman Park and, as the hamster rolled his fuzzy body around in the sand, kids began gathering. For the first time in his life, Wills initiated a conversation with his peers.

"A hamster," he said, pointing to Booner Schooner.

"Can we pet it?" someone asked.

"Hamsters have very sharp and long teeth that are capable of biting through cardboard," he told them just as Booner Schooner yawned (on cue) and showed his elongated yellow teeth and jaw pouches. The kids were mesmerized.

Bursting with pride, I sat cross-legged in the sand, watching my son stiffly, but bravely, talk with other children. Wills had dipped his toe into the toddler social arena. It was, without a doubt, the baby steps Katherine, Michael, and I had been praying for.

The next time we brought Booner Schooner to the park, Wills refused to go toward the swings, choosing instead to play in the middle of the baseball field alone.

"Don't you want to show Booner to the kids?" I asked, sitting beside him.

"Booner's busy," Wills said. "He doesn't like the kids." He repeated this several times under his breath. This was new, repeating words and phrases over and over. Katherine called it echolalia. "It gives him time to figure out the meaning of the words," she explained. "Most of the time, he doesn't even know he's doing it." And yet it unnerved me. Of all the ups and downs of autism, the echolalia scared me the most and I wasn't even sure why. But the minute it started, I could feel the cold tingle moving up my spine. "Something's wrong with your son," the nagging voice in my head whispered. "Something's terribly wrong."

Booner was twisting himself around in Wills's hands. "Are you sure he doesn't like kids?" I asked. "He looked pretty happy to me last time," I encouraged. "I think he loves kids, but he doesn't know how to play with them. I think he's afraid they'll be too rough. What do you think?"

Wills didn't look up. "I touched a shark once," he said, changing the subject. He connected plastic Habitrail tubes to form a circle in the grass.

"Where?"

"At the Aquarium of the Pacific," he said, "Long Beach." Booner was eating mud.

"With Aunt JoAnn?" I asked. JoAnn was always taking him to the coolest places.

"Yes." He nodded.

"Were you scared?"

"You can hear them purring," he said, lifting Booner and offering him the open end of the tube.

"What do they feel like?" I asked.

"Your upper lip."

I hoped he wouldn't want a shark next.

Wills continued seeing Katherine, three times a week. She was our saving grace, tall with straight blond hair and freckles scattered across her smiling face. But I was constantly reminded that just because her appearance was delicate didn't mean that she couldn't kick my butt. She could and did.

In fact, she encouraged Michael and me to take Wills out in public as much as possible—restaurants, grocery stores, public restrooms. I understood why we had to do it, I'd read all the information and had listened to Katherine's logic, but seeing him kicking and sobbing because he didn't want to be seated at Denny's was devastating. He looked like a kid having a tantrum, instead of someone too traumatized to calm down. I would rather have jumped off a building than watch Wills go through this. It wasn't just the people who stared at us like we were torturing our son, it was the very fact that we *were* torturing our son. "Do not isolate him" echoed throughout every single book I'd read on autism, but I wondered if the authors of those books had had their hair yanked out by a petrified child.

I called Katherine one afternoon because Wills had just been invited to a birthday party—his worst nightmare.

Wills was terrified of birthday parties. Parties were unpredictable, with all of the unexpected shouting and horn blowing. Helium balloons sometimes flew away and disappeared *forever.* Parties also took place at other people's houses and Wills didn't know what might be waiting inside—the color of the walls, how many bedrooms they had, or what the backyard might look like. He *refused* to go to the bathroom, and, finally, the "Happy Birthday" song sent him running for the nearest exit. At one party, I didn't see a fire truck that was pulling up to take all of the children for a ride. Wills spied it first and charged through a screen door, knocking it and him onto the cement. I didn't think I could bear watching him trying to brave another one.

"You have to take him, Monica. I know you don't want to, but just like some of the other positive steps Wills has taken, he'll be capable of making it through a birthday party someday and that's the goal. It probably won't happen tomorrow, but if he's 'protected' from birthday parties and playdates, if he's isolated, he won't have the opportunity to practice his social skills. He needs other children to watch and learn from."

"Can't he watch kids at the park instead?"

"Birthday parties are part of our social culture," Katherine said. "He needs to experience them."

"I hope they'll be serving martinis," I said.

She laughed. "Let Michael drive."

Sunday afternoon, I was cursing Katherine's name as we walked up Jackson's sidewalk toward the helium balloon bouquet tied to the front porch and the shiny Happy Birthday banner taped over the door. Wills rode on my back with his head buried in my hair, and Michael, thankfully home from Chicago on one of his quickie weekend visits, carried the gift.

"We'll stay fifteen minutes, okay?" I said, per Katherine's advice. "After fifteen minutes, if you aren't having a good time, we'll blow out of here. Does that sound good?" I asked.

No response from Wills. His hands were balled up into little fists under my chin.

I gave his legs a squeeze.

"I'm sorry this is hard, Wills, but maybe you'll end up having

fun," Michael said, and I knew that deep down, Michael believed
it was possible. He'd missed the last birthday gig, where a balloon
had accidentally become untied and, as it floated up and away from
where we were standing, Wills began screaming and slapping his
face.

After ringing the doorbell, I turned to see an unusually tall man
unfolding out of a Honda hatchback. He threw a backpack over his
shoulder, and sticking out of the top flap I saw black plastic Batman
ears. Holy crap, he was the entertainment. Wills was going to lose it.
I set my son down on the sidewalk, holding onto his hand.

"Batman just walked in," I whispered to Michael.

"You're shitting me," he said.

"I saw bat ears."

"Okay," Michael said, "we'll ask Jackson's mom to give us a
heads-up before Batman makes his entrance, and then I'll carry Wills
to the front yard."

That sounded incredibly rational. Michael really needed to quit
Chicago and normalize the insanity on the home front. Wills had
broken free and tucked himself behind Jackson's front bushes. I
could see his sneakers.

"Come out, Mr. Wills," I said. "The quicker we go in, the quicker
we come out."

Nothing. Michael and I didn't want him tearing off down the
street, so each of us picked a side, and moved toward him slowly.

"You know, Wills, nothing would make Jackson happier than
seeing you at his party," I said, taking his arm, and gently pulling
him toward me. "He's crazy about you." Which was true. Jackson
had invited Wills on about six playdates and never took his refusals
personally.

"Let's go see where the fun is," Michael said, scooping Wills up
in his arms and carrying him in. Wills's spongy blue earplugs stuck
out from the sides of his head like stubby antennae. The earplugs,
a suggestion from Dr. Todd, had been helping quite a bit. We took
Wills to a hearing specialist to be tested and he was diagnosed with

hypersensitive hearing. If we could lower the volume in Wills's world, maybe he wouldn't be so distracted and panicked.

Jackson's house was a beautifully renovated Craftsman and in the sunny, cherry wood kitchen, a catering company was laying out gorgeous food that I knew I would not be consuming. Not only would we not be there long enough but my stomach was in knots.

I was talking to one of the other moms on the back patio, when, out of the blue—and way too early in the party—Jackson's dad strode out of the kitchen holding a blazing birthday cake and singing "Happy Birthday to you. . . ."

Oh my God, DEFCON 2.

I looked for Wills, and saw him bolting toward the front gate. He was so panic-stricken that I knew if he got past me, he'd be in the street in a nanosecond. I knocked over my chair, trying to catch him.

My mind was racing: What if I wasn't fast enough? What if he disappeared into the neighborhood and I couldn't find him? *I would be fast enough,* I thought, *even in my eighties.*

I grabbed Wills around the waist and turned back toward the yard in time to see Batman walk onto the balloon-infested patio with his hands on his hips and his cape billowing out behind him, calling out, "Someone here is having a Bat-Birthday."

"NOOOOOOOOOOOO!" Wills screamed. I sat us down on the grass and wrapped my legs around him. The kids, the parents, and Batman were all staring at us.

"I think Wills is overwhelmed," I said, handing him to Michael, who spirited him away. "Jackson, I'm really sorry Wills got scared," I said, "but happy birthday, buddy!" I gave him a hug.

As I climbed into the backseat with Wills (preparing my "Batman was just this guy in a costume" speech), Wills looked over at me and said, "That was a fun party!"

"Really?" I asked, wondering why I'd felt like throwing myself under a bus.

"What was your favorite part?" Michael asked, saving the moment.

"Goodie bags," he said, holding up a plastic sack with a cartoon Batman and Robin driving around the outside of it in the Batmobile. Jackson's mom had run it out to the car for him.

"What's in there?" Michael asked, and Wills began pulling out candy and small rubber Cape Crusaders, describing each one.

"We're proud of you, honey," I said.

"Can I eat this?" Wills was holding a Tootsie Roll.

"Sure," I said.

Wills now knew that "goodie bags" were a result of "party going," and that was a good incentive. We'd never stayed at a party long enough to pick up a goodie bag before.

Even so, Michael and I were exhausted and shaky. What in the world were we going to do to help this boy? Surely this wouldn't be his life—surely there'd be more than this.

"He's proud of himself," Michael said, as we got ready for bed. "Today was a huge accomplishment."

"He did the best he could," I admitted.

That night, my heart softened around Wills's autism. Clearly, Katherine had been right. I couldn't isolate him. As painful as it was to watch him paralyzed with fright, I knew that he was happier when he tried. Not showing up was admitting defeat. Admitting that he couldn't do it. Admitting that the autism was bigger than him.

For all of Wills's accomplishments, there were still enormous hurdles for him to clear on a daily basis. At the top of that list was taking a bath.

Wills hated baths, and showers were even worse, where his sensory overload was amplified. He couldn't tolerate bubbles, because they still "hurt" his skin, and even warm water bothered him. Once Wills was in the tub, bathwater mixed with tears as he anticipated my shampooing his hair. I told my shivering, jittery boy the same thing every time he took a bath, "I'll go really fast. You'll be done in just a minute, honey." But that didn't really help. I tried putting goggles on him and letting him pour the water over his hair himself. I let him hold a washcloth over his eyes and announced each time the water was coming. I even played his favorite Parachute Express song, "Happy to Be Here," on his boom box, but nothing made him more comfortable or less afraid.

The worst part for him was at the end when he'd sit on his knees, watching the water disappearing down the drain. He'd hold his hand over the holes, trying to stop it, but it slipped between his fingers anyway.

"Let's get you out of the tub before the water drains," I told him.

"I have to be here," he'd say, sobbing.

I tried leaving the water in the tub all day and draining it once he went to bed, but he obsessively checked throughout the day. "Better to let him grieve it than to prolong the loss," Katherine said.

Over the next year, as Wills slowly navigated the preschool mine field of noises and messes and crowded hallways, my animal fixation persisted. With every new problem Wills encountered, I bought a new pet. We now had six more hermit crabs and two more hamsters. I cruised Petcos the way drunks frequent bars.

But Wills was beginning to realize the potential that Katherine had hoped for—through her therapeutic skill, the help of his preschool teachers, and my work with him every day, Wills was beginning to separate from me.

We were still narrating his activities and feelings: "You look really mad right now," or "You seem worried to me." And, just as Katherine had predicted, he was beginning to articulate his feelings on his own. "I don't like this," he would tell me, or "It's too loud in here."

He made his first friend, Brandon, who drew pictures of himself and Wills playing on a Santa Monica beach, two stick figures, one with yellow hair (Wills) and one with brown hair (Brandon), holding hands. And whenever Wills ran up against something he couldn't handle, I knew the answer . . . and it was usually something with paws.

One day while I was picking up Wills from school, I noticed a hefty black-and-white flop-eared rabbit busting ass around the corner of the classroom.

She lost her footing on the turn and slid into my foot. Several rabbit droppings rolled in the opposite direction from sheer velocity. All of a sudden, she flopped onto her side and fell asleep on the spot. Needless to say, she was charming, and had attitude to spare.

"Who's that?" I asked Wills's teacher, Kim, pointing to the rabbit.

"Ruby," she said. "She lives in the front classroom."

"She's so bushy," I gushed. I'd never seen such an enormous rabbit, with so many double chins! (That was her "dewlap," as we would soon discover—not "chins.") "Wills, look at Ruby." He turned his head and laughed. You just had to. "Isn't she great?" I asked. He kept laughing.

"We're looking for someone to give her a good home," Kim said. "She's getting too big to keep here at school. Would you be interested?" Wills and I looked at each other.

Oh no! I couldn't take on any more animals. Still, I hadn't gone looking for this one; it wasn't as if I'd shop-lifted a parakeet from PetSmart. No, this opportunity had fallen into my lap—from God probably.

And Kim, being so sweet, with the naïveté that only comes from being in your early twenties, had no idea she was feeding my animal addiction.

Michael was now in his second season writing in Chicago, his housing stipend had been increased and he was able to move from a small studio apartment to a truly beautiful (and roomy) place on Ohio Street with a wall made entirely of glass overlooking downtown Chicago. The bigger apartment was a welcoming gesture from Michael, and even though we were maintaining two households now, it was worth it. Wills and I could visit more often and stay for longer periods of time. With drawers for our pajamas and plenty of beds for everyone, Wills and I felt like we were a part of his Chicago life, and that he wasn't in some abstract place where we didn't belong.

After preschool the day we met Ruby, Wills and I stopped by the Pet Exchange and bought a double-wide hutch for her, a wire hay holder, a water bottle, a food bowl, four bags of timothy hay, rabbit food, salt licks, and two wooden chew sticks. It cost $385.00; not surprisingly the Visa was denied. I used my emergency American Express.

When we got home, it took me two hours to put the hutch together. My genetic handicap in terms of following directions hadn't improved. Wills, in his striped cotton pajamas, filled the hutch with hay, one handful at a time, laying it carefully across the bottom. This also took two hours.

The next day, Ruby rode home on my lap, wrapped in a red polka-dot beach towel. She was a nervous wreck, her nose twitching wildly. Once home, she made that double-wide her own, shoving the hay into a birds' nest formation and then hunkering down for a nap. After an hour or so, I let her check out the perimeter of the backyard, where she tore a path through Wills's garden and sniffed along the bottom of our old tin shed behind the garage. The next thing we knew, her head was down, her ears were back, and dirt was flying out between her sturdy back legs. She'd found a place to burrow. Wills and I sat on top of the picnic table, in stitches. That bunny knew how to excavate.

By the time Michael came home the following weekend, Ruby's tunnel under the shed was progressing nicely. He stood in the yard staring at the new addition. "What's in the hutch?"

"Ruby the Rabbit," I confessed. "She's from The Early Years."

"Is she going back to The Early Years?" he asked.

"Probably not." I was standing at the back door with a dish towel in my hand, trying to be nonchalant.

"Did they give her to you?"

"She didn't have a home."

He shook his head in disbelief and walked into the kitchen. "When are you going to stop bringing home animals?"

"I don't know, Michael, when the world finally feels like it's right side up again."

"I really think Wills is doing better," he said, "so maybe you guys can come to Chicago and stay for the rest of the season. What do you think?"

"Were you at Jackson's party?" He just stared at me. "He's not ready to leave Katherine or The Early Years. If we knew that the show was going to last a long time, we'd move there in a second, but it doesn't look like it's going to go."

"Why are you so mad at me?"

"Because you're 'Happy Days Are Here Again' every time you come home and when you leave, it's just me. I'm standing in mud up to my waist."

"What do you want me to do?"

"You can initiate phone conversations with Katherine, read the books on autism I sent you, and start paying attention to the fact that he and I aren't out here skipping along. He really needs our help."

"I think I've been helpful."

"You are helpful in so many ways, but when I bring up autism, I see you starting to check out. It's like you don't want to admit it or something."

"What am I supposed to do? I'm working my butt off out there."

"Don't leave me alone with this," I said. That's where the panic was coming from. I pulled my hair back into a ponytail, snapping the elastic band in place.

"I love you both," he stammered.

"It's not about love." I started crying, which pissed me off even more. "I *know* you love us. I'm really scared, Michael. Sometimes I just walk around the house too terrified to do anything. I'm reading everything I can get my hands on, and searching the web for information. I'm afraid I'll look back and see that there was something more I could have done, but I missed it. And then it will be too late."

"I shouldn't have taken a job so far away," Michael admitted. "It was a big mistake."

"We need the job," I said. "It's just been such a long time."

"I'm sorry," he said.

"*I'm* sorry."

We held each other on the couch and I cried all over his oxford cloth shirt, which was exactly what I needed.

The next day, in an effort to join ranks, Michael took Wills and me to Petco, where we bought some African dwarf frogs. They were tiny, acrobatic, and slept in piles—a Ringling Brothers and Barnum & Bailey aquatic circus. Funny as they were, they had no effect once Michael climbed back on the plane. The laughter went with him.

* * *

Three months later, as Wills struggled his way through his second year of preschool, out of the blue Michael's show in Chicago was mercifully canceled.

Michael was home now for good, in the same town! The house was filled with his contagious laughter (albeit quieted down for Wills's sake) and his shoes were sitting in the closet right next to mine. Wills climbed all over him in the mornings, and on the weekends I followed him around like a shadow, watching him brush his teeth or complete the *New York Times* crossword puzzle.

In another miracle, Michael immediately landed a more stable sitcom job twenty minutes away.

Things were definitely going our way, and still our menagerie continued to grow: a new hamster, Bennett, to replace Madeleine, the hamster who ate her own babies and had to be returned to the store; Underwater Hank the sea turtle; and two fiddler crabs, named Fiddlin' Joe and Fiddlin' Joe A, who marched across the floor of the aquarium waving their gigantic claws over their heads like Run-DMC.

Ruby watched these animals come and go with stoic bemusement.

As it turned out, Michael wound up loving the animals as much as Wills and I did—except for Ruby. It was difficult to love Ruby.

She was sweet with me, but every time Michael opened her hutch to feed her or lift her out, she slowly backed up, and with awesome speed launched herself through the air, thumped him in the center of his chest with her strong back legs, and then bounded around the side of the garage like an escaped con on a prison break. Michael became more of a hamster/frog man.

It was a good thing that Michael had become an animal lover because on a sunny Saturday afternoon Wills mentioned the one thing I hadn't thought about for two years: "Mommy, we should get a puppy!"

"A puppy?" I asked.

"Like the ones at Pets of Wilshire," he said.

Worried about falling off the wagon, I did what any responsible addict would do. I turned the decision over to someone else. "Michael, Wills has a question," I called out to him in the backyard where he was putting together his first (and last) hammock.

"Can we get a brand-new puppy?" Wills asked. Michael smiled and lifted his son onto his shoulders.

"You've been wanting one of those for a while," he said, walking over so Wills could touch the big limb of the pear tree.

"Can we get one?" Wills asked.

"Someday soon," Michael said.

I relaxed into a deck chair, the weight of the world lifting. Michael could oversee the farm for a while.

CHAPTER THREE

Wills grew to tolerate, if not actually enjoy, his time in preschool, and as he neared his sixth birthday in the winter of 2003, we knew his biggest challenge yet would come the following fall: kindergarten. There was no way I'd be able to rush in and rescue him once he started "real" school. Preschool was a shaky trial run, but at least I could pick him up early if he really needed it or take a few days off here and there. Also, it was only three hours a day. In kindergarten, he'd be away from me all day long. I couldn't imagine it.

The first thing we had to do was find the right school for him. We wanted him in a small private school. Michael and I were both products of the public school system, but Wills was barely capable of handling a tiny three-room preschool. The thought of him trying to negotiate his way around a much larger school was paralyzing to me. Maybe down the line, but not in kindergarten.

We toured twelve private schools, spent hours filling out applications, sent neatly printed thank-you notes to school administrators, and called friends who were friends with other friends who could put in a good word for us.

Not surprising, but equally devastating, was that very few private school directors were willing to take a chance on a child with high-functioning autism. "He needs a 'special school,' " they'd say. So we toured the "special" schools but didn't see one that fit Wills's needs.

It seemed to us that he needed to be with mainstream children, so he could have a strong model for social interaction in the real world, but this was going to be a challenge for him. At the schools for children with learning differences, we felt that Wills was going to be too protected, and not challenged enough academically. The truth was, Wills fell somewhere on the spectrum between a mainstream school and schools for children with learning differences.

Katherine also felt strongly that Wills needed to be mainstreamed. "He needs to be in a social environment where he can watch how other children interact and converse," she emphasized. "At least right now, I don't want to see him isolated from a typical classroom situation. I think he can handle it."

The first of March came—the day all the families received letters from schools letting them know if their child made it in or not—and we received twelve rejections—0 for 12. We were the Detroit Lions of school applicants.

Tama and Joy, the ingenious directors of The Early Years, had one more suggestion. There was a small progressive school called Children's Community School in Van Nuys that might be open to admitting a child with high-functioning autism. Better yet, Tama and Joy were personal friends of the director because he'd taught their children years earlier.

I called right away. Two days later Michael and I took a tour and met the director, Neal Wrightson, who looked like central casting's version of Tevye in *Fiddler on the Roof.* He was sweet-faced, roundish, and hairy. But the best part was the speech he gave in the library after the tour.

He talked about how important it was to trust our children, to believe they know where they are going and where they need to be. And that our job as parents, and the school staff as educators, was to step back and lend a hand, but not direct or peek over their shoulders, constantly making suggestions. We were there to offer support and encouragement. I was in love—educationally speaking—with Neal. He wasn't just an educator, he was an innovator. This was the school. We'd found it.

He gave us a packet with handouts outlining fees, class size, and criteria. We were further heartened that all families were considered for admission, regardless of ethnicity or financial ability. The population at CCS was as diverse as Los Angeles itself.

The packet also contained an article Neal had written entitled "The Emotionally Safe Classroom." Was there anything more comforting than that? Didn't we all want to be emotionally safe?

After Neal observed Wills at preschool, we felt hopeful that Wills would get in. Even though there were no guarantees, we knew we belonged there, and, because of Neal's connection to Tama and Joy, we felt we just might make it. Two weeks later, we got a letter from their admissions office telling us Wills was wait-listed.

I cried for an hour straight, as our last shot vaporized—and not just a "shot"— the most loving, creative school I'd ever encountered. When Michael got home, I detonated—an hour-and-a-half rant. "We have emotionally safe classrooms—but not for you! Didn't Neal say he accepted an array of children? When we told him Wills's diagnosis, didn't he say it didn't rule him out?" I unloaded the dishwasher in under two minutes and was heading for the cleaning supplies. We were completely screwed now.

"I'm going to home-school Wills in a trailer right outside of that place and every time Neal walks by I'll wave and say, 'Just teaching Wills out here. No problem, as you can see.' "

I was in a rage that had little to do with the school and a lot to do with not being wanted. We were outsiders, abnormal, the wrong ones.

Michael suggested I call Neal to clarify what the situation was. I stared at him with red, bulging eyeballs in complete disbelief. "The situation is—we didn't get in. *That's* the situation."

Michael retreated into the kitchen while I obsessively sorted toy trains and pieces of wooden tracks into plastic drawers.

The next morning, I called Neal.

"What are our chances of getting in from the wait list?" I asked.

"You're first on the list," Neal said. I seriously doubted it, but it was kind of him to attempt to soften the blow.

Then I did something that seemed crazy, even to me who *felt* crazy. With all the private schools full, with not one possibility left, I dipped into Wills's college fund and hired Lana Brody, a professional headhunter for kindergarteners. My six-year-old had an agent. It was absurd that such a profession existed, but Lana assured me that she hadn't "let a family down yet."

"Consider me your fairy godmother," she'd said. I'd needed one for so long.

Lana called two days later with a lead. There was a school in Pacific Palisades called Seven Arrows that still had two spots left for boys. They were more than happy to see Wills, but the visit needed to happen right away since spaces were being filled so rapidly. "Wills's preschool is on vacation this week," I told her. "They can't observe him."

"Let me see what I can do," she said cheerfully. An hour later she called back. "They can send someone to your home the day after tomorrow to meet Wills. This is very lucky, they hardly ever do this."

It should have been the best news of my life. We had a perfectly wonderful home, and God knows it was clean. But I was sure, in an I-need-to-be-institutionalized way, that my unworthiness, that Wills's diagnosis, would be draped on every lamp, bookcase, and table.

In a frenzy, I cleaned some more and bought new rugs and guest towels for the bathrooms, dressy-yet-casual outfits for Wills and myself, and ordered beautiful food prepared by a local Thai restaurant.

It was time for Becky, our only hope, the admissions director of Seven Arrows, to arrive. I was on edge and panicked, knowing that we'd be judged for the fourteenth time, only now our home would be included. I worried the visit would be a disaster, and Wills would end up lost in a huge public school where he'd be invisible—unable to ask for help. Or worse, *actually* home-schooled by me—who sucked at historical dates and long division.

I was uneasy about how Wills would do. His hamster Booner Schooner was at the vet with an affliction identified as "wet tail"—

which was pretty much what I had at that point. He was also grieving his other hamster, False Alarm, who had disappeared three days earlier. In the past, bringing out his hamsters usually helped break the ice and put Wills at ease. But there was no hamster for either of us that day.

I decided to do everything I could to help Wills ace this interview, so I laid out, in what I hoped was a casual fashion, his favorite science books, his complicated marble maze, his homemade and sophisticated maps, even his purple L.A. Lakers basketball that he'd never touched. I hoped Becky would see he was well-rounded, which was so horribly shitty of me, because he was smart and curious and sweet all on his own.

Becky arrived at one o'clock, right on time. Wills was sitting on the back of the couch waiting with his new babysitter Evelyn, whom I had recruited for support. I greeted her at the front gate with sweaty hands and a nervous smile. "Hi, Becky, I'm so glad you here now and you drive okay?"

What the hell? I tried again. "Was there trouble here finding?" I couldn't speak to save my soul. To make matters worse, my bowels began roiling with a threatening fierceness.

I turned to walk into the house wincing and cursing myself. I was going to doom us before Becky had even met Wills. I pictured the roof collapsing around us as I tried to show her how worthy we were, how well we would fit in at her expensive school.

When Becky met Wills, he was completely and unexpectedly at ease; my shy, tense boy who was petrified of strangers was not anxious in the least, and I was ready to jab a steak knife into my eye. Wills wanted to show Becky his wooden fort behind the house. I wanted to show her back to her car.

We walked through the house and into the backyard, where I promptly stepped backward onto Wills's purple basketball and, somehow flipping forward, landed on my stomach. It happened so fast, I wasn't even sure it *had* happened except I was on the ground looking up at Becky with the wet grass soaking through my linen pants. I knew I deserved this for being such an asshole mother, but it was still mortifying.

Standing up, my ankle twitched in pain. "Well, my worst night-mare has occurred, so now I can relax," I quipped, following Becky's eyes to the green stains covering each of my breasts. "I'm going to go in and change. Wills, why don't you show Becky your garden?"

I walked calmly into the house, trying to ignore my throbbing ankle. I had never felt so stupid. If I could get Wills into just one school, if he had just one place to go, I wouldn't care whether I walked or limped across the finish line.

As I was changing clothes, Wills came running through the family room yelling, "Mommy, it's a total hose-down. I'm not kidding, it's a hose-down."

I met him in the hallway, half-dressed. "What's going on, honey?" I said, pleasantly, because Becky was right behind him. "Louie did a big diarrhea poop out by the garden. It's huge."

Louie was our neighbor's chocolate Lab who loved to wander into our yard to do his business. I didn't want Becky to think I was the type of mother who couldn't talk poop, so I said, "Wow, as soon as I get dressed, I'll pick that right up."

"It's three different colors," Wills said enthusiastically and began describing the shape. I knew the only way to stop him was to say, "I'll go pick that up right now so you can concentrate on your visit with Becky. I'll be right back." I grabbed a plastic grocery bag and walked out to the garden.

Sure enough, there was a huge diarrhea poop, and it *was* three different colors—four if you looked at it closely, which is what I was forced to do. I picked up what I could and threw a big rock on top of the rest.

"Becky, help yourself to some lunch," I offered as I walked back in the door.

"Thank you, I would love a little something," she smiled, look-ing at the spread on the kitchen table.

Sitting in the family room, Becky had lunch at the coffee table and Wills ate a cookie. He'd brought out some books and a word game to show her. Wills was brilliant, and it seemed as if it just might work out after all. I was thinking how proud I was of him, when he yelled to me, "Mommy, can you get me that fart tape?"

"I'm not sure what that is," I lied.

"The one you bought for Daddy." He stared at me. "You know, the one with all the fart sounds on it."

Becky saved the moment, turning to me and saying, "Why don't you and I talk over coffee."

"That sounds great," I lied again, and led her out to the patio. By now my right ankle had swelled up around my loafer like a muffin top. I hoped she couldn't see it.

Wills stayed in the house with Evelyn while we walked outside to talk. Becky began describing Seven Arrows Elementary School and their philosophy of "every child's right to be a part of a democratic society" when over her right shoulder, I saw Wills pull open the curtains on our back sliding doors, do a crazy dance, then whip them shut. Again, very uncharacteristic of him. I was trying to pay attention to Becky as the curtains reopened with Wills wearing three hats, turning around in circles. I finally excused myself and asked Evelyn to please play with Wills in the front yard. Who was this child? Clearly he had no idea I was negotiating his future.

I sat back down and we finally had a successful conversation until a squirrel caught my eye as it ran along the top of the back fence. It was carrying something gray and furry in its mouth. "What is that squirrel carrying?" I asked. Becky turned to look just as I realized that it was Wills's lost hamster. And just to confirm it, the squirrel dropped its lifeless body long enough for me to see that it was indeed False Alarm. The squirrel picked it up by the neck and ran onto the roof of the house, hopped onto the branch of the oak tree in the side yard and disappeared up into the leaves.

"That's so cute, it was carrying its baby." Becky smiled.

"Adorable," I said, and left it at that.

* * *

At last the visit was over. We walked to the gate and Becky shook Wills's hand; he had done a wonderful job. Then she turned to me and said, "I had the most delightful afternoon and you are such a generous host. We would love to have your family at our school." At which point she pulled a contract from her briefcase and handed it to me over the gate.

"Wow, I'm so surprised. Thank you so much for offering us a place," I said, clutching the Golden Ticket.

She smiled. "Take a week to decide."

And just like that, Wills was in.

Becky waved and got in her car. I hobbled into the house; the pain in my ankle was suddenly excruciating. I kissed Wills, grabbed my purse, and told Evelyn I was going to the hospital.

At St. John's emergency room, I barely noticed as the doctor treated my throbbing ankle. I felt as though Wills had just saved *Apollo 13*. That was worth a dozen broken bones.

Then my cell phone rang. It was Neal calling from Children's Community School. The family ahead of us had dropped out, and Wills was in. He offered him a spot in their kindergarten. Neal had told the truth; we *were* first on the waiting list. That was the last time I would ever doubt him.

I called Becky at Seven Arrows and explained that CCS was closer to home and thanked her profusely for offering Wills a spot. She couldn't have been more gracious. She even asked how my ankle was doing, which surprised me. I thought I'd hidden it well.

"Broken," I said, and we both burst out laughing. "I swear this was the most surreal afternoon of my life."

The visit wasn't a total wash for Becky—at least now she had a good story to tell nervous parents on her school tours.

I clanked through the hospital waiting room in my new metal walking boot, and drove like hell to drop off a check at CCS, Wills's new school.

CHAPTER FOUR

Wills had a kindergarten to attend. Now we had to get him ready for it.

In July we received the Children's Community School class roster with phone numbers and addresses. Katherine encouraged me to begin setting up playdates with the children in Wills's class so he'd know a few of the children before school began. And meeting them in his own home was crucial. His visit with Becky had proven that. As I ran my finger down the roster, the thrill of victory quickly dissolved with my realization that Wills would not only be in a new school, he wouldn't know anyone there. The enormity of the adjustment was going to be unmatched, but I hoped to soften it as best I could.

Our first baby step was to do a quick drive-by of Children's Community School. We circled the block twice, so that Wills could see the outside. Eventually, he was brave enough to peek in the gate at the pyramid-shaped climbing structure in the play yard. Wills remained extremely quiet, his face pale with dread, and I was talking like I'd just had five espressos, highlighting all the wonders of CCS. Shockingly, on the way home we went to Petco on Sepulveda Boulevard and bought a land turtle. Wills named him Richard.

Richard clunked around his glass cage with the heat lamp on

until we let him lope along in a wire pen we'd set up in the backyard. Richard was happiest there, which did not please Ruby the Rabbit one bit. She was terrible—bounding by his pen, and throwing her hind end into the air, shooting little black pellets out of her ass. Luckily for Richard, she was no Annie Oakley and, for the most part, he escaped the assault.

In anticipation of the long summer days ahead, Michael and I drove to Sears and bought a trampoline for Wills. We hoped that providing him with something not only fun but highly physical might relieve some of the anxiety about kindergarten. It turned out to be a great idea.

Wills dragged two large basketfuls of stuffed animals out to the trampoline and shoved them through the slit in the black netting that surrounded it. Then he tumbled in as well, bouncing ever so gently so that the plushy snakes, orcas, the Grinch, and a three-foot-long hammerhead shark flipped around like bacon on a skillet.

Once he really got going, he'd launch the animals over the top and I'd try to catch them. Wills's aim, which wasn't the best when he was standing still, was far worse when he was tossing midair, so I was all over that yard—often climbing over our front fence to retrieve a fuzzy kangaroo or a striped-tail lemur.

Once all of the animals were on the outside of the trampoline, I'd throw them back in, encouraging Wills to jump up and catch them. It was great practice for his coordination and a pretty good workout for me.

The thick netting allowed Wills to bounce as high as he wanted without any worries about falling off the side. He let himself flop around, losing control a little bit. It must have been so freeing, letting loose like that, since Wills was usually very cautious. When he bounced, he sometimes closed his eyes, smiling—no fear.

When I finally got up the nerve to call and set up a playdate with one of his future classmates, I was surprised to find that the other mom was as nervous as I was. I'd arranged sandwiches on a Spode Blue Italian platter from our wedding, for two five-year-olds and a couple of mothers.

"I overdo it when I'm nervous," I explained to Nicholas's mother, Chelsea, a blond version of Eva Longoria.

"I know, it's hard to just relax," she agreed.

"Wasn't it crazy trying to get into a school?" I asked, letting my guard down.

"CCS was the only school we applied to, and we got right in." She shrugged, looking out at the two boys, who were jumping up and down in the trampoline.

"We applied everywhere," I said, squeezing my sandwich into an unrecognizable ball of dough. "But Children's Community School was our first choice."

"Well, that worked out." She smiled with unbelievably perfect teeth. "Nicholas was kicked out of every preschool I enrolled him in, but now he's doing so well that CCS let him in without my saying a word about it. They observed him and he was accepted." Her left leg, which was crossed over her right, bounced up and down, her flip-flops and manicured toenails distractingly adorable.

"What was 'it'?" I asked. "If you don't mind my asking."

"Nicholas used to have autism," she said, nonchalantly. My head jerked up and my crystal cut glass of lemonade hit the kitchen table with a thud.

"But I cured him."

What were the odds that the first family we met at CCS had dealt with autism? And she *cured* him? How does a person cure autism? Had my head been up my ass all these years? Had I missed the "Big Cure" segment on *NBC Nightly News with Tom Brokaw*?

"Yeah, he *used* to be autistic but not anymore." She shrugged her shoulders.

Did she actually have the audacity to repeat it? She REPEATED IT? I didn't know what to say.

"Wills is autistic," I said, hoping it would help rein in her bravado or, at the very least, implore her to enlighten me. Any of us who'd been through it knew that you couldn't cure autism.

But here she was right in front of me, adorable, chesty, and confident.

"Oh, you can cure him. You just need to change his diet." Her right eyebrow arched and her brown eyes popped with enthusiasm, realizing that a possible recruit was sitting across from her in denim cropped pants.

She meant well, she must have meant well, so why did I feel like kicking her teeth in?

"What you need to do is get all of the metals out of his system," she began. And fifty minutes later, she was writing down websites and telephone numbers of places where I could order gluten-free meats and flourless cookies.

What really pissed me off was that Nicholas *looked* cured. He seemed perfectly fine—sporty and talkative. I knew, looking at this child who was making me feel so insecure for not helping Wills by taking away his flour, that it would be irresponsible of me not to explore Chelsea's miracle diet.

Wills had early-onset autism, which meant that he was "Wills" as we knew him pretty much from birth—unlike Nicholas, who, as Chelsea put it, "was developing normally until he received his MMR [Measles, Mumps, and Rubella] vaccination. Then he stopped talking, wasn't capable of focusing on me at all, and began acting out. I couldn't control his behavior. It was like someone took Nicholas, and left me with a completely different boy."

I'd read in several books that the large amounts of mercury in these vaccinations could trigger autism in children who might be genetically prone to the condition. There hadn't been enough scientific research to prove this, but parents all over the country were beginning to question the safety of those vaccinations.

As I processed Chelsea's story, Wills and Nicholas asked for help filling up water balloons. She and I took a break from our conversation and sat on the back step, stretching the lip of the "water bombs," as the plastic cover read, over the outside spigot. The next thing I knew, Nicholas slammed a balloon into Wills's chest.

"NICHOLAS!!!" Chelsea scolded. She was running to help Wills. I was on my feet, too.

Kids throw water balloons at each other, that's what they do, I reasoned. I'd done it as a kid; we'd all done it. Nicholas wasn't trying to hurt Wills. So why was the bright red bruise the size of a silver dollar in the center of Wills's chest making me want to throw a balloon at Nicholas's head? Wills stood stock still—shell-shocked.

Chelsea turned to me and explained, "Sometimes Nicholas is too rough."

"Wills is really gentle. He doesn't play rough. I know a lot of boys do, but not him." I looked at Nicholas, who was now tossing water bombs against our flowering pear tree with the velocity of Randy Johnson. "That's a great idea," I told him. "If you want, you can climb that wooden ladder against the tree and toss them out onto the sidewalk." The boys loved that idea. Nicholas climbed into the tree and Wills handed up water bombs for Nicholas to splatter on the driveway.

Wills recovered quickly, but I worried that maybe I should have told him years ago about water balloon fights. Again, the packaging did say "water *bombs.*" But it never occurred to me.

"Thank you for telling me about Nicholas," I told Chelsea.

"I just had to." She smiled.

"Why?"

"I thought maybe Wills was on the spectrum." She nodded. "I've been around enough autistic kids to spot it."

When they left a few minutes later, I was still stinging from her last comment. I had hoped that since some of Wills's anxieties and fears had simmered down, his autism might not be so easy to detect.

In a mainstream kindergarten, it was going to matter, no question about it.

Next on my list of to-dos to prepare Wills for school was to buy him children's books that we hoped would help him with the transition.

His favorite was *Miss Bindergarten Gets Ready for Kindergarten,* a story about a warm, creative teacher who was a little unusual.

"She's a dog," Wills said, running the tips of his fingers across Miss Bindergarten's black-and-white face.

"She's a border collie," I told Wills, "with pearls and a dress."

"What do they do?" he asked.

"Border collies like to herd other animals. Maybe Miss Bindergarten likes to herd her class—take care of them."

"She's tall," he said.

"In this story she's standing on her two back legs," I explained. "Most doggies look smaller because they walk on all four of their legs."

"Can we get a puppy?" Wills asked, turning the page.

"Sure, we could get a pup sometime," I said, wondering how many times this would come up before I would actually have to *do* something about it.

"Tomorrow?" he asked, excitedly.

"Not tomorrow," I told him. "Getting a dog is a big decision, and it takes a long time."

"A week?"

"Sometimes a year," I said.

"Daddy said it was okay," he said, looking at the pictures.

"He's probably the best one to talk to about this. Let's give him a call."

Wills shook his head. He refused to talk on the phone.

"We'll figure out a good time to get a puppy, okay?" I reassured him.

"Let's read," he said.

A week later Michael, Wills, and I were at Barnes & Noble when Wills headed straight to the animal section. We'd been there many times before, and he sat in his usual spot on the carpet in front of the bookshelves.

"What animals are we looking for today?" Michael asked him.

"Dogs," he said.

"Mommy said you want to get a new dog," Michael said.

"We *are,*" Wills told him, pulling out an oversize book of photography with a fluffy, doe-eyed golden retriever puppy on the front. We were going to be here a while.

"When are we getting it?" Michael asked Wills.

"It takes a long time," Wills said.

The three of us settled in.

"I like golden retrievers," I said. "They're adorable."

"We had black, short-haired dogs when I was little," Michael said.

"Maybe we could get a mutt," I offered. "Like when Daddy and I adopted our dog Hallie."

"Hallie wasn't a puppy," Wills said.

"We should find pictures of puppies we like," Michael said, "and cut them out."

"They have doggie magazines," I told them.

And that's how the dog journal began.

Within a week it was bursting with pictures of poodles, bulldogs, mutts, and, of course, golden retrievers. Putting Wills to bed one night, I noticed a picture of a golden retriever puppy that had been ripped out of the Petco mailer, sitting on the nightstand beside the pink bed in the master bedroom—which wasn't actually pink, but was in a pink room, so Wills called it the "pink bed." I taped the picture of the puppy to the closet door, so we could admire it. I kissed Wills good night, he kissed me back and then got up and kissed the picture of the puppy.

"I love you, Wills," I told him, as I turned out the light. Wills hadn't told Michael or me that he loved us yet. Whenever I'd ask, "Who do you love?" he'd begin to cry, as if it were too intimate to say. But he showered us with affection. Wills was the "great snuggler," often climbing onto my lap and smushing his face into my cheek—a Wills kiss—followed by a big squeeze.

As July turned to August, the staggering prospect of Wills attending a mainstream kindergarten loomed larger. I redoubled my efforts to get him ready, turning almost every activity with him into a kinder-garten training session. Late one afternoon I was swimming in the pool. Wills was sitting near the top step. He didn't like to be in the water. I pushed a green mesh float toward Wills.

"It's a floating kindergarten," I explained. "The kids have to sail in a boat to get out here."

"Where are the kids?" he wondered.

"I'll get them—just wait on the patio and I'll be right back." Wills looked skeptical. "It'll only take a minute."

I ran, dripping, to the toy room, which had once been our dining room, and grabbed the basket that held his Playmobil people with painted-on pants and the small rubber animals we'd accumulated from the L.A. zoo gift shop.

"Here they are," I announced, running back outside, "these are the students."

Wills picked up his plastic sailboat. I clasped my hands in front of me. He was going to play along! He sat down near the top step of the pool and placed three plastic figurines and two rubber whales inside the boat.

"The school bus is coming," he announced, shoving them out to where I was waiting in the deep end.

Once they arrived, I'd greet them with happy hellos and "My, you look ready for kindergarten," and then I'd drop each one into the water, where they'd sink down below to the classroom. When the bus was empty, I floated it back to Wills. He sat there a few min-utes and then yelled, "TIME TO GO HOME!" and sailed the boat back out.

I'd dive down and gather up the kindergarteners to send back on the bus that was waiting above me. Then we'd start the whole thing over again. We must have played that six or seven times a day as the summer came to an end.

Labor Day signaled that we'd done everything we could to pre-pare him for school. It was, despite my worried heart, showtime.

CHAPTER FIVE

The photograph Michael took of Wills on his first day of kindergarten said it all. He was standing beside his new classmate, Benjamin, and his mom, wearing a tie-dye T-shirt, lime green sweatpants that sagged at the knees, and brand-new leather Nikes. He was clutching a dark purple blanket in his left hand, its bottom swirling around his feet. But it was the tears that were about to flood Wills's cheeks, the devastation in his eyes as he looked up at the camera, that are forever seared into my memory.

Regardless of our preparations—playing school, going to Katherine's, playdates with classmates—nothing could have braced either of us for the shock of just how difficult and gut-wrenching this separation was going to be.

I put on my best cheerleader persona. "I'm so proud of you," I gushed. "What a big boy you are, going to kindergarten!"

"It's going to be great, buddy," Michael said, leaning down to kiss Wills's anguished face. And then Daddy was gone, off to work, and I was alone with Wills. Again.

Michael was finally home, but he was still checking out of dif-ficult situations, leaving me to plug up the leaks in the boat.

"Mommy will be right here when you are done," I assured him. "I'm going to meet you in your classroom the minute school is over."

Jumbo tears rolled down his cheeks. "I want to go home," he told me, as if it should have been obvious.

"We'll go home right after school, pumpkin," I said.

"Now," he said, barely audible.

"I know you're scared, Wills," I told him in my best Katherine voice. "I know you don't want to go to school, but all boys and girls go to school, and you'll get used to it. Maybe not today, but soon." I had literally memorized this speech from an earlier conversation I'd had with her. She'd gotten us through preschool by advising me to "keep taking him back," which was against every instinct I had at the time. Kindergarten would be no exception.

He stared at me without blinking or wiping the tears off his chin. They dripped small wet circles onto his colorful, happier-than-we-were shirt.

Meanwhile, a gaggle of parents began swarming the archway behind us, where an older student was holding the gate open. Some of the other kindergartners were clingy, but none seemed even remotely as shaken as Wills. I'd expected this, but it still pinched.

I found myself pushing back the feeling I'd often had—the over-whelming desperation to flee with Wills, his hand in mine. Instead, I gently guided him toward the classroom.

His new classmate, Benjamin, walked into the room ready for anything, as if he were at his grandmother's house, all comfortable and loose.

Once inside, Wills became inconsolable: "No, Mommy, don't go. Please, Mommy. Mommy, please stay. Don't go." His teacher, Terri, knelt down to calm him. The assistant teacher, Daniel, greeted the other parents, as Wills's screaming escalated. Terri politely asked me to leave the classroom, but I could still hear Wills as I unlocked my Jeep, which was parked near the gate.

By now tears were pouring down my face, and although we'd

been through it in preschool, this was actually worse. He *had* to attend kindergarten. I couldn't stop it from happening.

There was a rap on the passenger-side window. It was Benjamin's mom, Susan.

"Oh, he didn't take that well at all, did he?" She was laughing.

I wiped my face. "No, he didn't."

"He'll be fine," she said in a singsong tone of voice, waving my distress away with her hand. "Give him a couple of days." As she walked down the sidewalk, I could have sworn she was skipping, but that was probably just my jealousy. Benjamin had done so well.

As I started the car, my thoughts shifted to an entirely different concern. *What will Susan think when she discovers Wills is autistic? What will the other parents do? Will they worry that Wills's diagnosis might take away from their own child's experience? Will we be welcomed into the circle or shunned?*

I pulled out of the parking lot and into the day ahead—the one without Wills, who I knew needed me—my cell phone practically Superglued to my hand. The only thing I'd left behind to comfort him was an oversized stuffed ladybug that he'd slept with since he was two.

I sat at home for the next six hours simultaneously sobbing and sucking down Imodium. I couldn't imagine what horror was taking place inside that leafy, brightly colored elementary school. I prayed that Neal's philosophy would rub off on Wills instantaneously and that he would feel emotionally safe by lunchtime.

No such luck. When I picked him up, I knew things had gone badly. Wills was lying on his side, face blotchy and red, his head resting on his outstretched arm. The other children were running toward their parents, most of them smiling and chatty about their first day of school.

"Wills," I said gently. It took a few seconds for him to focus on me. He was spaced out big-time.

I knelt down on one knee. "We can go home now, honey."

He looked up sleepily, but didn't speak. His head was resting on his plushy ladybug.

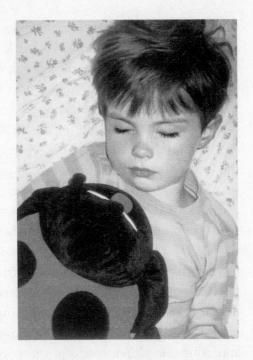

Terri walked over. "Wills had a rough day," she said, patting his back. "This is going to be an enormous adjustment for him, but we're going to help him in every way we can. Right, Wills?" No reaction.

"Thank you so much, Terri," I said. "Michael and I will help. Whatever you need. I can volunteer in the classroom or sit outside in the playground where he can see me." Even though Neal had pledged his forbearance, I would have done anything to make sure Wills could stay at CCS.

The rest of the week went exactly the same for Wills—sobbing at drop-off, withdrawn and sleepy at pickup. On Friday, Terri asked, "Can I call you tonight?" She was gentle and soft-spoken, but I knew Wills had not passed the first-week test.

"Sure," I responded, dread knocking at that sensitive spot right behind both of my eyes.

I lifted Wills onto my hip. His body folded into mine and he buried his head deep into my neck. Suddenly, he was sleeping j-u-s-t l-i-k-e t-h-a-t. Oh, this was bad, this was very, very bad.

The call I didn't want to receive came at 8:00 p.m., right on time. I was sitting at the kitchen table.

"Hi, Monica. Is this a good time?" Terri said, sweetly.

"Yes," I told her, resisting the urge to drop the phone, run into the street, and dive under a UPS truck.

"I know this is extremely difficult for you, but we've got to do something here." I was trembling as if I were detoxing. "Even if it's hard to hear, we need to acknowledge that something needs to be done—for Wills's sake and for the sake of the classroom."

"Of course," I said, popping every knuckle in my right hand and then switching to the left in an anxious musical pattern.

"When everyone is outside playing, Wills leans against the fence and rocks back and forth." I knew what she was talking about—I'd seen it in preschool. "He isn't eating his lunch or going to the bathroom. I can't keep him a whole day if he isn't eating or peeing."

I wasn't surprised about the bathroom. Wills refused to use *any* public restroom—a bush, an ivy-covered hill, or the bathroom floor trumped a toilet every time. The jarring echo of the flushing combined with the fact that his pee, an intimate part of himself, was disappearing into oblivion, was just too overwhelming. Even at home, Michael or I flushed Wills's toilet while he waited nervously on the back patio. He'd recently peed his pants at Burbank Airport when he walked into the restroom and saw toilets that flushed automatically. It was instant, the way a gecko drops his tail.

"I talked to Neal about the bathroom," I explained, "but he thought it would be best to wait—that maybe Wills would be capable of entering the bathroom if he saw other children doing it."

"I'm sorry, Monica," Terri said.

"I didn't realize he wasn't eating." I visualized just how much fear it would take for my son to sit there, watching other children enjoying their food, his stomach clenched and empty. It was crushing.

"He sits apart from the other children—"

"He's bringing home an empty lunch box," I interrupted.

"He dumps the entire contents into the trash before putting it back in his cubby," she said.

I yanked the dishtowel off the drying rack to wipe my face.

"Wills lies on his side most of the day with his shoes off, sometimes with his eyes closed." He was clearly so overwhelmed; his only alternative was to sleep.

I threw my head back, resting it against the ladder-back chair. "I don't know what to say." I was looking up at our pristine, beige ceiling with no cracks or smudges, unlike my life. "I can talk to Katherine first thing in the morning."

"That would be great," she said. "Meanwhile, I think you, Michael, Neal, and I should schedule a meeting as soon as possible to discuss ways we can help Wills."

"Help him?" I asked.

"Of course," she said.

"Do you think he'll be able to stay?" I asked.

"Children are exceptionally resilient," Terri said. "We have to leave a little room for trust, Monica."

Trust was exactly what I was running short on.

We scheduled the meeting for Monday, two days away. It felt like a year.

Neal's office was the most comfortable, sunny place, but Michael and I had passed comfort days ago. We timidly tucked ourselves into the plaid couch. Neal rolled toward us in his desk chair while Terri sat to our right, hands cupped in her lap. Her assistant, Daniel, was running the classroom.

"We all know why we're here," Neal began, "so we should just get right to the meat of it." Michael and I nodded. "Wills is having a particularly difficult time adjusting to school." We nodded again, stiff as statues, waiting for "he's not going to make it at a mainstream school" to cross his lips.

"I have a suggestion that might or might not be helpful, but I think we all agree, we can't continue—for Wills's sake—the way it's been going."

"Yes," I managed to squeak out. "Of course, we're worried about Wills, but we also don't want Wills's issues taking up too much of Terri's time. We don't want this to affect the rest of his class."

"Let *us* worry about that," Neal said, smiling. "Look, these things happen. We've dealt with difficult situations in the past. We're not going to let the quality in the classroom suffer. And I don't think it is suffering, do you, Terri?"

"No," she said, rolling up the sleeves of her embroidered jacket and leaning forward. "Several of the children have asked why Wills is crying, and I explain that every child is different and that it's going to take Wills a little longer to get used to kindergarten." I wanted to hug her—tightly. "Children accept these things. They just need their questions answered and then on they go."

Maybe we'd found a place where we belonged. I broke down into embarrassing sobs.

Neal was sympathetic. "I know this is difficult, Monica."

I shook my head, rifling through my purse for a Kleenex or a Starbucks napkin. "I'm not crying because it's difficult, it's *always* been difficult. I'm crying because you care so much. I'm crying because you aren't giving up on Wills."

"CCS is a community," Neal explained. "It's good for other students to see that someone can struggle and still be accepted."

Michael hadn't said a word. Taking his hand, I scooted a little closer. The feel of his long slender fingers wrapped around mine had always buoyed me. Maybe I could do the same for him. Michael had come through on his promise to step up—attending Wills's after-school therapy sessions, reading Wendy Lawson's *Life Behind Glass: A Personal Account of Autism Spectrum Disorder,* one of the many books I'd been shoving at him, and most important, spending huge amounts of time with Wills, making every Saturday "Wills and Daddy Day." But he was still struggling to accept Wills's diagnosis and the blunt reality of where we were with it. He was getting a full dose today.

"As you both know, we're not a 'special needs' school and there's only so much we can offer you," Neal said. "But I do think it would lend tremendous support to Wills for him to be shadowed by an aide in the classroom."

"That's PERFECT," I practically shouted. Wills's preschool had resisted an aide, worried that it might disrupt the classroom. I shifted forward in my seat. "That would help him so much." Someone's eyes on Wills all day long? A dedicated person to gently nudge him through his day and help shoulder some of his anxiety? It would be an enormous relief.

"Also, I think it would be wise to get some testing done. Let's get a clearer picture of what's going on here—his strengths and his weaknesses. That way, we can see where he needs extra support." Just like that, Neal managed to assuage some of my fears. It was going to be tough, but CCS was game.

Outside the front gate, I celebrated our extraordinary good fortune. My faith that there were educators who wouldn't automatically exclude a struggling child but who, instead, would give him the best shot possible, was restored. But Michael's forehead was crunched into thin lines of worry. "Wow, it's sobering to think that Wills needs a full-time aide."

"Believe me, he needs it."

"I wonder how expensive it will be," he said.

This was an excellent question—and I had no idea. My newly established writing career was yielding very little income, and as far as getting a part-time job, I didn't know if there'd come a time when Wills wouldn't need me off and on during the day. Certainly he needed me after school and at night. "He needs someone in the classroom, I'm telling you. This is something we *have* to do."

"This is really bad."

"Bad?" I said in disbelief. "This is *good*. This is the *best*! We've found a school that understands and is willing to help us."

"But a full-time aide," he repeated, and I knew what he was feeling. Grief. Sometimes it hit me out of the blue and sometimes it just sat around the house for days at a time—like an uninvited relative.

"I can understand that Wills needing an aide is shocking," I agreed, constantly surprised by how far apart Michael and I were in terms of dealing with the autism, "but think of it this way. It would be more devastating if we had to search for a new school rather than a helpful, caring companion."

He nodded. "I should get back to the office."

"Can you take an hour or so to get coffee?" I asked.

"We have a table read," he said. "I can't miss it."

As he turned to go, I watched him walk down the sidewalk. I missed him more right then than the whole time he was in Chicago.

Two days later, I was sitting at Starbucks on Victory Boulevard, twirling my chai latte around on the table and waiting to meet Lynn, whose son was a sixth-grader at CCS and whom Neal had suggested as a possible aide for Wills. The idea that Wills would have one person helping him all day even if it wasn't me (I still had major separation anxieties)—was still too brilliant to believe.

Lynn bounded into Starbucks with the energy I used to have.

"Hey, there," she said, as she skooched her tiny body across the bench in front of me.

"Are you Lynn?" I asked.

"I am," she said, patting the table with both of her palms. "How did you know I was Monica?"

"You're not Hispanic," she said, laughing.

I looked around and, it was true, I was the only Caucasian person in the place. Lynn herself was Japanese with jet-black hair and a few gray streaks that gave it a sophisticated yet hip look. She wore no makeup, and I was dressed for the prom in my long flowered dress and pink lipstick.

"Let me grab a coffee," she said, sliding back out, and three minutes later, she was back.

I explained what we had discussed in Neal's office as she sipped her black coffee, unruffled. "You know I've never done anything like this before, right?" she asked. "This would all be new for me."

"Neal thought you might be suited for it," I said.

"I'm good with coming up with ideas, and I like being in the classroom," she said.

"Have you ever worked in the classroom?" I asked.

"I worked part-time as a preschool teacher," she told me, "and

I've been a room parent several times at CCS, working in the class-room with my son, who's now a sixth-grader there." She looked out the window, thinking. "There must be people who train professional aides, right?"

"I'm sure there are, but we'd need someone right away. You wouldn't have time to train before starting the job, but you could do it as we go along." I was no longer drinking my chai. I had a feeling—out of desperation or strong intuition—that this earthy, energetic woman would be the perfect match, even though she didn't have the credentials and Wills's disabilities were a formidable challenge. I glanced at my watch. I had two other interviews lined up, but sitting here with Lynn, I couldn't imagine anyone else being with Wills.

"Does he have any behavioral problems?" she asked, a little shyly. "Acting out or hitting?"

"Oh no," I said, "he's never hit anyone in his life. If anything, he's too gentle, too timid. He'd rather blend into the wallpaper."

"I see."

"We want him to take up more space in the world," I told her, "to relax and enjoy himself—especially with his peers."

"He sounds really great," she said.

"He's an angel, I'm telling you. But trying to settle into a new environment where he doesn't know anyone has completely undone him. He's so terrified at school that he's rocking back and forth instead of playing."

"I've felt that way about a million times in my life," Lynn said, not the least bit alarmed. "When I teach yoga, I encourage people to wrap their arms around their knees and rock. It's soothing."

We talked about money and that was a deciding factor for sure. Besides Lynn being simply amazing, we'd be paying her half of what a professional aide would cost. If she was able to train while working with Wills, and it worked out, we could afford her—at least as long as Michael's job lasted.

"What do you think about trying this?" I asked. "Is it something you'd be interested in doing?"

She pursed her lips together. "Sure," she said. "You know, I could try it, and if it turns out that he needs someone with more expertise, no problem."

Done.

She'd need to give notice at her current job and wouldn't be able to start for two weeks. It felt like an eternity, but I knew she'd be worth the wait.

Even before Lynn arrived at CCS, mini-breakthroughs had miraculously begun. Wills was lying on the classroom floor near the kitchen play area when a young Sally Lou Who type named Abigail scooted toward him on her tummy. She had an animal puppet on each finger. Wills stared at her. Abigail smiled, undaunted.

"I like you," she said in a high-pitched animal voice. Wills didn't move. "I wish you would play with us." Abigail wiggled all ten fingers.

She rolled a little to the left, out of his range of vision. He shifted his position so he could see her better. "Let's play." She smiled. Wills sat up.

Abigail held out her index finger with a knitted doggie on it. Wills took it. She used a zebra puppet to kiss the dog.

Katherine and Wills had been working with finger puppets since he was eighteen months old. Puppets were not intimidating to him. They didn't require a response. Out of kindness and curiosity, Abigail had reached inside the abyss and located the boy who was aching to be rescued. She was barely five years old.

Terri called me that night to relay the puppet story, and to say that Wills walked outside with the rest of his class to continue playing puppets with Abigail and then shortly after, a darling brunette named Sacha joined them. Terri summed it up perfectly: "We can never underestimate the goodness of children."

A week later, I was picking up Wills from the classroom when Terri pulled me aside to say that Wills had ventured into the sandbox by himself to play with the hose. He'd created craggy rivers that snaked through the sand and eventually pooled into a round metal bowl he'd found in the arts and crafts area. He was finding the familiar in his new environment, engaging in activities at school that he loved doing at home.

When Lynn finally started the following week, Terri enthusiastically filled her in on Wills's recent breakthrough. "The first month of school was hard on Wills," Terri explained. "But he's doing better now. His anxiety is really settling down." Lynn could see there was still plenty of work to do, but she was up for it.

It was brilliant of Neal to introduce Lynn, not as Wills's aide but as a third teacher. None of the children, including Wills, knew that Lynn was there specifically for him. Whomever Lynn could assist, she did, and Terri or Daniel could jump in for Wills if he needed it. It was seamless. Wills was not set apart from the rest of the group nor perceived by the other children as acting "strange" or being "disabled." He was just a kid making his way through kindergarten—just like everyone else.

Wills, and the other children, took to Lynn immediately and she quickly became irreplaceable, coming up with creative ways to coax Wills out of himself and into the fun and excitement of the classroom. Lynn would call Katherine with questions and the two of them would figure out a plan to help him. Katherine also suggested a support group for Lynn, facilitated by a woman who trained therapeutic companions. Lynn was at the meeting the following week.

She even made the dreaded morning drop-off at school go smoother for Wills. In one of Lynn's talks with Katherine, they'd determined that if Wills was the first one in the classroom, he wouldn't be so overwhelmed when it filled up with children. If he entered the room after it was crowded and noisy, it overwhelmed him and he would be shut down for most of the morning. So Lynn met us at the gate twenty minutes early every morning and Wills would settle into the classroom like a fish adapting to a new aquarium.

His assistant teacher, Daniel, was in his mid-twenties and was a smart, creative person who loved to sail. He built his own boat in

Bangladesh and was attempting to sail to Australia when he had to be rescued in the Indian Ocean and taken to Malaysia by a Ukrainian tanker transporting palm oil. Wills was intrigued by Daniel's story and all the pictures he'd shown the class of his adventure. Using scrap wood and an old washcloth, Wills tried to re-create a miniature of Daniel's boat.

We called on Daniel to help soothe Wills's bathroom anxieties. He offered to go in with him, took Wills when all of the other children were still in class, or tried guarding the door so Wills would have privacy, but he still refused to use the boys' bathroom. After a brief conversation with Neal, Terri, and Lynn, which included a conference call with Katherine, it was decided that he was too traumatized to force into a public bathroom at the moment.

We were working on it at home. Wills collected small toy potties. They were usually sold as furnishings for a dollhouse. I sometimes found them lined up in a row against the bathtub—a Playmobil person sitting on each one. Or he'd put his hamster Booner into the bathroom and encouraged him to go in the plastic toilet that was "just his size." But whenever Michael or I took him to a public

restroom, he resisted. Whatever was causing the anxiety refused to budge.

Wills was doing so well in so many other areas, we didn't want his phobia with the bathroom to stop his progress. Neal suggested that Wills use the faculty bathroom in the main office. It was a private, one-person facility ideal for him.

Using that bathroom led Wills to another very special friend. Helen was Neal's assistant, and two times a day, he stood beside her desk in the office waiting for his turn to use the bathroom.

"Hi, Wills," she'd say, and he would do a little wave without actually acknowledging her.

"Ruth's in there," she'd say, without looking up from her computer. It was clear to her she needed to keep her distance, but she also sensed that Wills, however anxious, needed to be noticed. "She'll be out soon." Wills didn't respond, his hands shoved deep into his pockets.

Ruth, the music teacher, came out and as Wills stepped forward, Helen said, "See you in a minute."

When he left the office, Helen called out, "See you soon, Wills." He pulled open the heavy door and walked back to class, his eyes on the cement floor.

One afternoon after picking up Wills, we took a detour to Baskin-Robbins for a scoop of Quarterback Crunch ice cream, his favorite. Driving home, I asked Wills, "How was school?"

"Olivia has a rabbit," he said, spooning ice cream into his mouth, his hand curled into a fist around the tiny pink spoon.

"Just like Ruby?" I asked.

"It's not alive," he said.

"Would you like a bigger spoon?" I asked.

"I need to use the pink one," he said, probing his ice cream for the chocolate vein.

"Is it okay if I use the big one?" I asked.

"Use the spoon he gave you," Wills insisted.

"He gave me the big one."

"Then it's okay."

Wills followed rules. That was part of who he was—the autistic, the boy, my son.

On the way home, we stopped by the Van Nuys train station to watch the Metrolink commuter trains go by. Wills's obsession with airplanes had transferred to trains over the past year or so, and his interest had reached a fever pitch. Wills wanted to know *everything*. He and Michael spread out Surfliner schedules on his bedroom floor and created a train-watching timetable for "Saturdays with Daddy." They now spent weekends riding up and down the West Coast on Amtrak, going from L.A. to Santa Barbara or San Luis Obispo or San Diego.

We accumulated thick, fact-intensive books filled with diagrams of how coal-run engines are constructed, the mechanics of the turning wheels, and the history of the U.S. passenger rail industry.

Wills's fascination with trains gave Michael something concrete to latch on to. Watching his son develop a passion for something new endowed Michael with a better understanding of what made Wills tick. They'd found common ground and Michael seized the "train" opportunity to give himself over to every aspect of Wills— the genius, the scientist, the anxiety-ridden six-year-old. He was finally accepting the whole package.

One afternoon in late September, I attended my first all-school meeting, which included parents and students. As I got out of my car, I ran into Amanda, whose son, Patrick, was in Wills's class. She approached quickly, ambushing me.

"Monica, what's going on with Wills?" she demanded.

I was thrown by her question. With Lynn in the classroom, things were much better. "He's still trying to adjust to school," I said, hoping that would end the conversation.

"Well, I'm one of the class parents, and I was volunteering in the classroom yesterday." She took a deep breath. "Wills seems like a tiny frightened bird." She stared at me, expecting an explanation.

"He gets worried," I told her. "Like I said, he's having trouble transitioning."

"Maybe he's not getting enough love at home." She crossed her arms. I thought I'd been stunned and hurt so many times by people who didn't understand my struggling son that I was immune by now, but I was wrong. "You need to get him some help!" she continued, as if scolding a child. I actually started to laugh.

"Hey, good idea," I said. "Maybe he needs caring professionals who can love and support him. Boy, you have all the answers." I turned to leave but she grabbed my arm.

"If there's any way I can help, I will." I pried her bony, self-righteous fingers off my arm.

Did other people think we were neglectful parents? Unloving?

Bolting from Amanda, I hurried into the auditorium. Wills was sitting with Lynn on the other side of the room, wiping away tears with the back of his hand. He looked so vulnerable and young—not big enough to be here.

My instinct was to race over and pull him onto my lap, where I could beam encouragement into the top of his worried head, but, as Katherine was constantly reminding me, he needed to trust that Lynn could handle his feelings. With uncharacteristic restraint, I willed myself to stay put.

Next to me, a five-year-old, brown-eyed beauty in a retro sweater that could have come straight from Anthropologie was sniffing a long, scraggly piece of gray-brown fabric. I knew—I don't exactly know how—that this was Olivia.

"Is that your rabbit?" I asked.

She nodded, solemnly.

"He's pretty great," I said, marveling at how "normal" it was to need something to cling to: to do something "out of the ordinary" when you're stressed, like sniff a piece of filthy fabric or rock back and forth or pick up leaves in the backyard.

Olivia began sliding the moist, strung-out piece of cotton under her nose, like a shoeshine boy. It was only one jowl with three scraggly whiskers. That was all she had left of him. But that scrap of stringy fabric was enough to keep her centered for the moment. Throughout the meeting, she pressed it against her nostrils. She made me so happy.

Ruth, the music teacher, stepped onto the auditorium floor with her guitar strapped comfortably around her neck—as if it were a part of her pant suit. She was born in South Africa and spoke with a calming, slightly British accent. Ruth invested herself wholeheartedly in the philosophy of CCS, driving three hours round-trip to be there. With her students she stressed the importance of music throughout history, and its ineffable power to unify people and nations. Heady for kindergarteners, but a concept we believed in and hoped to instill in Wills.

When Wills first started music class, he couldn't get through it. "He can barely bring himself to come into the auditorium," Ruth had told me. "And once he sits down, he's in tears immediately— hands pressed over his ears. He's absolutely miserable."

I understood why Wills was distressed. With all of the instruments onstage, the piano sitting within three feet of him and, of course, Ruth's guitar, Wills panicked in anticipation of loud music and unpredictable new songs belted out at top volume with little warning. But Lynn had changed all of that. She'd talk to Ruth in advance so she could tell Wills exactly what was going to happen in class that day. The most important component in keeping Wills calm was avoiding surprises, and knowing the schedule allowed him to make it through the entire class without being excused to spend the rest of the period with Helen in the office. He sat in class distressed, with his hands covering his ears, but at least he was there.

Now, with Ruth standing in front of the CCS community strumming her guitar, the musical portion of the all-school meeting started. I wondered what songs the kids would sing. "This Old Man"? "Zippity Doo Da"? "Row, Row, Row Your Boat"? Instead, Ruth launched the kids into a rousing gospel-tinged polemic about Martin Luther King. Martin Luther King Day was months away, but as Ruth pointed out, "Every day is a good time to remember Dr. King."

Then I heard the lyrics, "On a balcony in Memphis, some sick man shot him down." I wasn't sure I'd heard correctly, and to add to my confusion, Ruth was waltzing around politely and smiling. No one seemed taken aback but me. Even Olivia was singing loudly underneath her stringy rabbit jowl, unaffected ". . . some sick man shot him down."

I'm not sure why I expected something different. This was Ruth's philosophy, teaching songs that mattered about people who'd changed the world. Still, it was a sunny Friday afternoon, and murder was so sobering.

Wills was crying harder now, and it had nothing to do with the assassination of Dr. King. His hands were smacked over his ears and he was slumped forward. I had to help him—how could I not? But the echo of Katherine's voice in my head, the words she repeated to me on more than one occasion, kept me bolted to my seat. "He has to trust Lynn. That's the only way she'll really be able to help him. If Mommy's right there to rescue him, it'll be more crippling than helpful."

After the meeting, I buckled a weepy Wills into his car seat, and stole looks in the rearview mirror at my darling, while he swiped his nose on the sleeve of his blue-and-white–striped T-shirt. Had I pushed too hard for Wills to be mainstreamed? I wondered. Maybe *I* was the problem, shoving him beyond what he was capable of doing because of my own selfish expectations. And yet so many things had helped—putting Lynn in the classroom, Abigail's puppets, Helen's magic bathroom. Everyone was doing their very best, throwing all of their support behind us, but Wills still wasn't adjusting.

We were sitting in the drive-through at In-N-Out Burger when I was seized by an uncontrollable urge to make everything better— for Wills and for myself.

"I think it's about time to get you a puppy!" I said.

Wills's eyes lit up as soon as the word "puppy" escaped my lips.

"Really?" He pushed both feet against the back of the passenger seat.

"Don't you think?" I asked, nodding.

"A golden retriever?" Wills asked.

"That's right," I said. "How about for Christmas?"

"Christmas!!!?" His bottom lip curled forward. "Not today?"

I should have known that "let's get a puppy" meant this afternoon according to Wills, who was so concrete.

"I'm sorry, honey, I didn't mean today. We can't get her until she's born, and then she has to stay with her mommy for eight weeks."

He looked out the window, touching the cool glass with the tip of his tongue.

"A girl?" he asked, expelling a big puff of air.

"I think so, but we'll check with Daddy."

"My puppy?" he asked again.

"*Your* dog, warm and soft. Maybe she'll even sleep with you in your bed! Should we stop by Barnes and Noble to get some books on goldens?" I asked.

"Yes!" he said, emphatically. "We need to know *everything*."

The two of us came home with *Golden Retrievers: The Complete Owner's Manual.* This was a good start. Wills laid on his tummy, with me beside him, and a bowl of Rold Gold pretzels between us.

We were still on the carpet an hour later when Michael walked through the back door. As soon as he saw the book, he said, "It looks like somebody's doing research!"

"It's for our new puppy," Wills said, not looking up.

"Wills had a rotten day," I told him.

Michael leaned down to give me a kiss and shot me a wry "I know what you're up to" look.

"What happened, Wills?" Michael asked.

"We're getting a puppy for Christmas," Wills replied, "that's one thing."

Michael hugged Wills and said, *"WHHHAAAATTTT,"* the pitch of his voice rising all the way up until the final "T."

"I thought that Christmas might be a good time," I said, feeling appropriately crappy about not checking with him first.

"Christmas it is!" Michael declared.

"I'm sorry I didn't call you first," I said. "It's just . . ."

"Let's not ruin tonight," he said, kissing my cheek. Turning to Wills, he said, "We're going to get a puppy!"

"I know," Wills said. "This is her picture." He held up the books to show Michael the golden retriever puppy on the cover. "That's probably her."

"She's great," Michael said. "We're going to have so much fun!"

"I know," Wills said with the self-assured ease of a White House press secretary. Seeing his baby blue eyes flicker with confidence, I wondered why we'd waited so long.

A puppy.

That's exactly what Wills needed—he needed a puppy that needed him right back.

CHAPTER SIX

The next morning, after I dropped Wills off at school, I surfed the Internet for local golden retriever breeders. On almost every website I read a somber warning, *NEVER BUY A DOG FROM A PET STORE*. I pulled up information on "pet store puppies." Article after article detailed the horrors of puppy mills and how dogs were heinously mistreated, arriving ill and malnourished. "You're setting your family up for heartbreak," one of the articles read. *Great,* I thought, *and our hearts haven't been broken enough already.*

I knew that rescuing a dog would be the right thing to do. Rescuing our dog Hallie had been one of the greatest joys of my life, but it was just Michael and me then. We didn't have a child to consider and, as it turned out, Hallie was skittish and anxious around children. This wasn't her fault, of course, it was a combination of her temperament and also what she'd been through in the six months before we'd found her, which we couldn't have ever known. But now I needed a kid-friendly dog—a sure thing. I'd read that golden retrievers were known for their gentle nature, especially with children, and that they were often used as companion dogs for children with disabilities. That was what I needed.

By the time I picked Wills up from school, I'd struck out with every breeder in Los Angeles County and had begun searching all of southern then northern California. The pressure was mounting.

I still had two months, but if they didn't have dogs available now, it would only get worse closer to Christmas. Some of them said they might have puppies by then, but could not guarantee it. I needed a guarantee.

Meanwhile, Wills had propelled himself into full doggie mode. After reading *Ten Minutes Till Bedtime,* a literary hamsterfest (filled with hundreds of tiny, fully clothed hamsters having little parties and preparing themselves for bed), Wills and I would lie in the pink bed thinking up puppy names. I wrote each one down on a three-by-five index card and taped it to the closet door, where we could move them around according to rank, from least favorite to wowza, the hierarchy changing daily.

Wills loved index cards. He used them to keep track of facts and dates we'd read about—he'd dictate the coveted information and I'd print it neatly onto the cards, such as the day Mount Vesuvius buried Pompeii (August 24th) or the names of all the South American countries. He sometimes used the cards to draw hermit crabs sitting on rocks or three faceless people—Michael, Wills, and me—with arms coming out of our hips. There were at least fifteen cards taped up there, with names ranging from Princess to Jonathan the Third, but we still hadn't found *the* one.

Wills was a pro at naming just about anything—God knows he'd

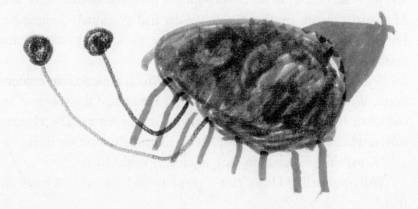

had practice. Aside from our many animals, he named a rubber baby doll Baby Wertheimer after NPR's Linda Wertheimer. (Clearly we'd sat in L.A. traffic way too long, trying to get him to and from therapy, with the radio blaring.) Husky Black Eyes was one of his hamsters, and he'd named the preschool rodent Red Rat Dirt. His black rubber corn snake was Princeton Spider.

Choosing his puppy's name, however, was altogether different, and he wasn't about to do it willy-nilly. This name needed heft, like Abraham Lincoln or the *Titanic*. (Wills had National Geographic DVDs about both.) Those names were substantial—significant enough to last throughout history.

Sitting at the kitchen table making vanilla cupcakes one afternoon, Wills said, "Kona's a good name." He turned the crank of an old silver hand mixer to whip up white, foamy batter. The electric mixer, which took half the time, made too much noise for him.

"Kona's fun," I said, dipping my finger in the batter.

Wills pointed. "That's not a good thing," he said. "Don't do that."

"Tastes good, though," I said. "Don't you want to try some?"

"Your finger will come off if it gets in between these things," he said, indicating the silver blades that were turning about as slowly as Michael's bicycle wheels whenever he headed uphill.

"My finger won't come off," I said, "but it wouldn't feel very good."

"It *would* come off, Mommy." Wills was holding up the hand mixer and watching the batter drip in thick, gooey blobs into the bowl.

"What about calling her Harley?" I asked.

"Vincent," he suggested. I was wetting my fingers on a damp sponge, attempting to separate the paper cupcake liners.

"Vincent! Where did you hear that one?" I asked.

"At the library." He was now spooning lumpy white batter into the paper cups, stringing goop from one to the next.

"Vincent is good," I said, hoping we'd come up with something more upbeat and less like the conniving killer with the bone-chilling laugh in *The House of Wax.*

"Ringo?" I suggested, which was about as feminine as Vincent. After all, we'd decided to get a girl. It wasn't that girls were so much gentler, although sometimes they were smaller in size, it was that I had had a female dog when I was little—Sugar. She loved us so much that she would run down the middle of the street right behind our car trying to catch up with us. Luckily, we lived in the rural Midwest, where there was hardly any traffic. She followed us everywhere, across the fields or down to the post office to grab our mail. We got her the year I was born, 1962.

"Cowboy," said Wills.

"I *LOVE* Cowboy," I told him. "What made you think of that?"

"The bedtime song," he said.

" 'Cowboys Sing Good Night'?" I asked.

He nodded. "Cowboys Sing."

"Perfect." I smiled. "And it's okay that Cow*boy*'s a girl?"

"Who cares?" he said in a singsong voice. I had to laugh. The cupcakes were ready for the oven, and the name had been chosen.

"Let's write it down on a really big piece of paper this time and tape it to the back gate so Daddy will see it when he comes home," I said.

Seeing the big bold letters made it a reality for Wills. The idea of a name didn't make as much of an impression as the black-and-white of a name. Something solid you could look at and hold onto.

Cowboy was coming.

And I still wasn't any closer to finding her.

While we prepared for the arrival of our mystery puppy, I heeded the school's advice and began taking Wills to a pediatric neuropsychologist, Dr. Bauman, whom Katherine had recommended for testing. Dr. Bauman was a dead ringer for Steve Martin in *Looney Tunes: Back in Action,* with his bow tie and pageboy haircut, parted down the middle. But his weekly bill was no joke. I pictured the Writers Guild Health Insurance kicking us to the curb—more claims were coming their way.

Every Wednesday I'd pick Wills up from school an hour early and drive him to Pasadena, forty minutes away. The weekly appointment—adjusting to a new environment, the questions and tasks he was being asked to execute, and not knowing Dr. Bauman—triggered Wills's acute angst, leaving him nearly incapacitated. Right away, Bauman picked up on his avoidance of eye contact, his difficulty separating from me, his inability to sit for more than an hour, and his tendencies toward self-soothing (in Wills's case, taking off his shoes and socks). As Dr. Bauman noted, *Throughout the testing, Wills moved his chair further and further from the testing table, turning his body away from the evaluator, and getting up and walking about the room. These behaviors occurred even though he was allowed to take a break to seek calming from his mother.*

Wills was not being oppositional. His distress seemed very genuine, and he seemed to be a kind and intelligent boy who actually wanted to connect with, communicate with, and please the evaluator.

After a few sessions, Wills made it into Dr. Bauman's office without my being with him, but asked that I sit where he could see me. The only window in Bauman's office faced the woods, so I sat on a stump near the tree line. I'd spend the hour reading a book, and avoiding looking through the window for fear of throwing Wills off his already very shaky game. Ultimately, it didn't matter if I peeked or not because by the end of the hour, Wills would be lying on his back under Bauman's large, hickory worktable—supine, no gestures, just the toes of his shoes banging back and forth. And despite his substantial stomach, Dr. Bauman would make a brave effort to bend down to ask his questions.

The same scene played itself out every week for the next month. Will's testing was going slowly and, according to an unflappable Dr. Bauman, not well. He was observing Wills and also administering neurocognitive and also psychological tests. In his time with Dr. Bauman, Wills was expected to answer multiple-choice questions, complete sentences, re-create geometric shapes that he saw on a page, look at several objects in a grouping and pick out the two that were related, create scenarios from a series of pictures, respond to sounds through earphones, and answer questions regarding logic and inference. And this was just the tip of the iceberg. It sounded exhausting to *me*.

Normally we'd swing by a pet store after a particularly grueling day, but we were out of hermit crab territory. I *had* to find Wills a golden retriever puppy by Christmas.

Despite widening my search for breeders to the entire Northern Hemisphere, I couldn't find a single available puppy. Not one. Why had I promised him a puppy by Christmas? Who would have thought it would be so difficult? Everything hinged on this.

Finally, after six weeks of futile searching, I decided to throw a Hail Mary pass and go to a pet store. *What other alternative did I have?* At least, I reasoned, I'd go to a fancy store in Bel Air. Surely the Pet Chalet wouldn't have the audacity to sell puppy-mill puppies to millionaires.

Despondent yet optimistic, I changed out of my UCSD sweatshirt and into a sweater set from Nordstrom's in a lame effort to fit in, and drove up curvy Beverly Glen Boulevard to the Pet Chalet. A woman named Amy greeted me from behind the counter.

"I'm in big trouble," I said. "I promised my six-year-old a female, blond golden retriever puppy before Christmas, and there aren't any." I had a sweat mustache.

Instead of laughing me out of the 310 area code, she smiled. "Our Christmas orders are already in, but I could probably do a search and find one."

"Oh, please, that would be unbelievable!" I told her, unconsciously drumming my fingers on the counter. Amy looked up. I was beaming. It was going to be a Cowboy Christmas after all.

"Let me get your information." She pulled out a drawer to find a pen. "We'll just need a deposit before we place the order."

"No problem," I said, slapping my checkbook onto the counter. Even though I'd been anticipating it, the cost would still leave us stretching it until the end of the month. But I would have put my car up for collateral if need be.

Three weeks later, there was a picture of baby Cowboy sitting on a horse blanket staring back at me from my computer. She'd been born to a breeder in Missouri. Amy had come through. I spun around in my chair. The puppy was so adorable, I could have eaten her up.

Michael and I didn't show Wills the photograph in case something happened between then and Christmas, and this puppy didn't end up being our girl. Still, preparations accelerated. With the gusto of parents preparing for a newborn, Wills and I began collecting puppy booty: a purple collar from Pet Headquarters, gnarled chew sticks from our Santa Monica mountain hikes, Michael's thick, holey socks rescued from the garbage ("excellent for playing" we'd read in *Dog Fancy* magazine, which we now subscribed to) and, at the market, instead of asking for paper grocery bags which we could recycle, we asked for plastic, anticipating the thousands of poops we'd soon be picking up.

Lynn helped Wills prepare for Cowboy's arrival by suggesting he write a journal at school. He drew the pictures himself, but since he couldn't write yet, he dictated the words and Lynn wrote them down:

THE COWBOY AND WILLS SERIES

by Wills Price

This is Wills. He wants a puppy. He asks his parents,
"Can I have a Golden Retriever puppy and name it Cowboy?"
They say, "Yes." The puppy is being born.

End of CHAPTER ONE.

Wills was ecstatic. Even his classmates were looking forward to meeting Cowboy as Wills regaled them with stories of our preparations.

"We just bought gray steps," he told them. "They don't go anywhere. We can push them up against things so she can climb onto the bed or the counter."

Wills began constructing a doghouse out of an eighteen-by-twenty-four-inch cardboard box he'd saved from our recently delivered Kenmore dishwasher. All of his spare time was spent inside that box, hot-glueing carpet scraps we'd picked up from Carpet One onto the floor, taping silk sunflowers and roses above the entrance, and adhering fuzzy multicolored pompoms all over the outside. After I helped him cut out the windows, complete with panes, and paste on cardboard shutters (just like our house), Wills drew a picture of what Cowboy might look like on an index card and asked me to write "Cowboy's Place" above it. He glued it over the doorway.

"That's Cowboy's house," Wills said. Every time I heard her name used in a sentence, it *did* sound significant—in a John Wayne, Abraham Lincoln kind of way.

One Saturday night I walked into the family room and saw Wills's corduroy bottom poking out the door of that doghouse, which was now illuminated by the plastic pumpkin-shaped flashlight we'd bought him for Halloween. He was flipping through a stack of train books he'd dragged out of his bookcase.

"I'm putting my smell in here," he explained when I peeked in the side window, "so she'll feel safe."

At bedtime, the Petco catalogue replaced our usual nightly reading of *A Bad Case of Stripes, Richard Scarry's Best Word Book Ever,* and, of course, *Ten Minutes Till Bedtime.* Now we snuggled underneath the white comforter, circling items in the catalogue we would definitely need once Cowboy arrived. For instance, a purple knitted dog vest and an Outward Hound doggie backpack.

At school, Wills was standing by Helen's desk waiting for the bathroom when he blurted out, "I'm getting a puppy."

"A puppy?" she asked. Her patience had won Wills's confidence and affection.

"A golden retriever."

"Those are the cutest dogs," Helen said. "You're gonna love her."

"I know."

"Would you like to see a picture of my daughter's dog?" she asked. "He's pretty cute."

Wills edged closer to Helen. "Is he a puppy?" Wills asked.

"He's about a year old," Helen told him. "Take a look. He's right here on my computer."

There on the screen was a small dog with crazy blond-and-white hair sticking up in spikes all over his body. "Isn't he silly?" she asked.

"Cowboy's zero years old," Wills said. "Her first birthday party won't be until October."

"Can I come?" Helen asked.

"We might only be inviting puppies," he said.

"I see." Helen laughed. "Well, don't forget to bring Cowboy to school. I want to meet him."

"Her," he said. "She's a girl, and she's traveling right now—from Missouri."

"Missouri," she said.

"We have her collar!"

"You're definitely gonna need that."

Wills turned and abruptly headed for the door. "Don't forget to bring her in so I can meet her!" Helen called after him.

Cowboy had actually arrived three days earlier with a cough. The Pet Chalet decided to keep her until she was feeling better, so each day, I drove up the hill to visit her.

On the first day, Amy brought her down this big flight of stairs. Cowboy was the fluffiest, tiniest dog I'd ever seen. I'd pictured a golden retriever puppy to be hearty and full-bodied. Cowboy seemed to be on the thin side with the saddest brown eyes. Amy handed her to me and then went behind the cash register to ring up another customer. The place was packed with pre-Christmas shoppers. I found a quiet corner and tucked Cowboy inside my button-down sweater. She was so precious, I had no idea how I was going to leave her at the store for two more days. I hugged her close and heard a small, throaty cough. I put my ear against her chest, which sounded gurgly and congested. She was sick. Even worse than the cough was a blazing red rash on her tummy. I snuggled her under my chin as she leaned her tiny body into mine.

"What's this all about, Amy?" I asked, walking up to the counter.

"The vet says it's from being in the kennel," she said. "You can speak to him if you'd like."

"I would like to talk to him," I said. "Why is she so sick?"

She dialed the vet without answering me.

I could've called the whole thing off right then, gotten my deposit back, and walked away. I could have waited until after Christmas for a healthier pup from a local breeder, but what would happen to this little girl? I'd fallen in love with her already. I couldn't give up on her because of a pesky cough and a rash. Wills was at home waiting—had his heart set on her. I held her up and looked into her eyes. Yep, there was no way I would ever walk away from this girl.

"Hello? This is Dr. Burke."

"Hi, I wanted to talk to you about Cowboy," I said. "She has this terrible cough, and a rash on her stomach. What's going on?"

"I don't blame you for being upset, but we're going to keep her for a few days and get her back on her feet. That way, it's the pet store's obligation to pay the vet bill, plus, you deserve to be handed a healthy dog."

"She shouldn't have this rash in the first place."

"That's the problem when dogs come in from out of state. She may have been placed in a kennel with another dog who had it. Also, she has a bit of kennel cough, which I'm sure she must have gotten on the trip out here or in the store. It's highly contagious, and very common."

"Should we be buying this dog?" I asked him, just to hear his reaction.

"Look, you need to decide what's best for you and your family. Do I think she's going to be okay? Yes. Is there a possibility I could be wrong? Sure there is, but I see this kind of thing all the time, and it usually clears up."

"Would you take her home to your family?"

"Of course I would. I think she's had a rough time, but she'll pull out of it."

Before I handed her back to Amy, I whispered into Cowboy's tiny ear, "I'm coming back for you, sweet girl. You're comin' home with us." I kissed the top of her head.

The night before Cowboy's arrival, Wills and I were running around the house like maniacs, rearranging her pile of toys, adjusting the water level in her bowl, and making sure all of the items were checked off the to-do list in the back of the golden retriever manual.

Wills finally conked out in our bed at eight thirty, and I lay down with him for a few minutes. He flopped his arm across my face and, eventually maneuvered his body so that he was sleeping horizontally across the bed. Our bodies formed a human T. I attempted to squeeze myself out of the bed when Wills sat straight up. "Mommy, don't go," he said, grabbing my hand.

I lay back down, staring at the ceiling. I had about a thousand

Christmas chores to finish, but I wanted Wills to be rested. He had to participate in the school's annual musical extravaganza—the Winter Sing—with the entire student body performing in a jam-packed church-turned-auditorium. I kept checking to see if he was finally asleep so I could attempt another escape. This dance between us had been going on since his birth.

It wasn't as if we hadn't tried to transition Wills into his own bed. We begged, pleaded, bribed, and, ultimately, failed. It seemed silly to my friends, but after spending six years watching Wills go through one agonizing event after another, having him curled up between us seemed like the least we could offer in terms of comfort. But Katherine knew better. "He needs to sleep in his own bed. Again, you're reinforcing his fear that he can't do this alone." Inevitably, after we'd attempt to get him into his bed, he'd come into our room sobbing, "Why do you get to sleep together and I have to sleep by myself?"

After each defeat, Katherine patiently helped us work up another plan.

The bed war had included one month where Michael, all six-and-a-half feet of him, lay on Wills's floor balanced atop an inflated AeroBed, his ankles and feet dangling off the ends. Lucky for me, Katherine suggested that Michael do the transition because Wills had the most trouble separating from me at night. Probably because I was the one who breast-fed him to sleep and was in charge of bedtime for years while Michael worked.

So, while I slept peacefully in the pink bed, Wills's hand dangled over the side of his bed, clutching the sleeve of Michael's white T-shirt to keep him from sneaking out to watch the eleven o'clock news.

After a week, Michael began steering the blow-up bed out of Wills's room like a slow-moving Goodyear blimp, heading inch by inch, bit by bit down the hallway to where I was engaged in REM sleep for the first time since Wills's birth. It would be four weeks before the AeroBed made the long twelve-foot voyage into our bedroom.

Wills managed to stay in his own bed until three weeks later, when a thunderstorm (extremely rare in L.A.) came rumbling through one night around 3 a.m. Knowing how frightened Wills would be of an unexpected boom, I hurried to check on him, but he was already barreling toward me.

"EARTHQUAKE!" Wills yelled. (He hadn't experienced one yet.)

"Thunder," I assured him.

"WORSE," he exclaimed. "THUNDER'S WORSE!"

"No, no," I told him. "Thunder can't hurt us." I'd been through the 1994 Northridge earthquake. I knew what I was talking about.

Still, he climbed my Nick and Nora flannels like a Rhesus monkey. "Can I get in bed with you and Daddy?" he asked, his hands squeezing my cheeks.

Oh, I was lousy at this. I needed to wake up Michael for emergency intervention.

"Please, Mommy, just tonight?" he pleaded.

I thought of my husband sleeping comfortably in our bed, our intimacy intact for the first time in years. Surely I wouldn't wreck *that*. I couldn't undo everything Michael had spent the last month establishing.

"Of course, you can," I said.

Wills climbed over Michael and I knew the AeroBed would be traveling back down the hallway and that I would be the pilot this time.

CHAPTER SEVEN

The next morning, I didn't need to remind Wills what day it was, but I did anyway. *"Cowboy comes home today!!!"*

Wills shot straight up in bed. "What time?" he asked.

"After the Sing," I said.

"We should pick her up sooner," he said, jumping on top of me. "We should pick her up NOW!"

"They aren't open yet," I said. He threw himself back, flat against the bed.

"It won't be too long," I told him. "Maybe the Sing will make the time go faster." He rolled over, poking my cheek lightly with his forefinger. His eyes were so close to mine they blurred into one gigantic orb.

"I can't go," he announced.

"To get Cowboy?" I asked.

"To the Sing. No can do today," he said, sitting up and waving his finger.

"We *have* to go, Wills." I brushed his hair across his forehead. "I know you don't want to, but your class is counting on you to do your part." I felt like a traitor.

"But my toe hurts." He held his left foot in the air to examine the nonexistent problem.

"I think it hurts because you don't want to go," I said, "but think about this. You made it through performances in preschool, and you can do it at CCS. You've practiced really hard for this. Daddy and I can't wait to see you up there."

"It still hurts," he said, pointing to his foot.

"I'll put a Band-Aid on your toe and fix it right up," I said. "You want to be ready when Cowboy comes, right?"

"I hope I can walk," he said, rubbing it, his eyes welling up with tears.

"I know you don't want to go, but remember, by the time the Sing is over, Cowboy will be coming home! Concentrate on that when you're feeling nervous. Your very own puppy—and wait till you see her."

He smiled as he wiped tears away. "She's great, isn't she, Mommy?"

"She's beautiful," I said, "and so tiny. She can sit right in your lap. You'll be able to carry her into school all by yourself."

Wills was tucking my hair behind my ear. "She's perfect, right, Mommy?"

"She's perfect," I assured him, "and so are you. Let's eat our breakfast and get going, kiddo."

Michael was sitting in the leather recliner reading *The New York Times* and listening to *The Ray Conniff Singers Christmas Album*. Every holiday season he began playing Christmas CDs the Sunday after Thanksgiving and continued all the way through to New Year's Eve.

"Hey, Mr. Wills!" He folded his newspaper.

"We're picking up Cowboy today," Wills announced.

"I know." Michael smiled. "I can't wait."

"Her middle name is going to be Carol," Wills said, "because Christmas carols are playing when she's coming."

"Cowboy Carol sounds great to me," I said, walking in to make breakfast. I had a little bit of a headache and my stomach wasn't feeling that great. Sympathetic nerves, probably.

Finally, it was 8:15 and we couldn't stall any longer. We headed to school for the dreaded Winter Sing, as I silently chanted my morning mantra: *Please let him be okay.*

The place was packed. Parents, grandparents, alumni, and

siblings were stacked in bleachers while the rest of the audience crowded onto the unused stage at the far end of the auditorium. Michael, JoAnn, and I sat near the piano.

This was the worst possible scenario for Wills. Throngs on every side and only one escape route—right down the center. Thirty or more video cameras were pointed toward the students, parents were chatting, and the fourth-graders were tooting Mozart on their recorders. Even *I* was overwhelmed.

Wills was already crying as he filed in with his class. Lynn had given him a good-luck charm, a tiny china dog that was stowed away in his shirt pocket. She walked beside him with her hand on his back as he held a white, neatly folded Kleenex in his hand, the only tidy thing in his world right then.

Wills put his head down on his knees and sobbed. Lynn tried to comfort him, slipping her arm around his shoulder, but he was inconsolable. These were the times I was most angry about the autism—when enduring overwhelming scenarios that crushed Wills to bits was the only means of helping him. And all I could do was sit there, like an idiot.

When the singing started, Ruth had put together another rousing, consciousness-building array of songs for the holiday program, including a tune about Rosa Parks and a delightful melody called "Georgie" about a kid getting his head cut off when a windowsill falls on his neck.

As it turned out, Wills's severe sensory overload was only exacerbated by the fact that he had a 102 fever. But before we discovered that, we were accosted by well-meaning parents in the courtyard after the show asking:

"Why was Wills so sad?"

"Is there anything we can do to help?"

"Is he afraid of performing?"

Amanda just smiled at me condescendingly and made the "call me" gesture.

I wanted to scream, "My son has autism! We're not trying to torture him, we're trying to make him stronger."

But I just kept my eyes on the ground as Michael, JoAnn, and I rushed to Wills's classroom. He looked relieved, albeit pale.

"That was great, Wills," I said.

"You are so talented," Michael echoed.

"I know," he confirmed, holding up the china dog Lynn had given him. His face was still swollen, and his eyes red-rimmed from all of the crying.

"He's a pretty cute doggie," I said.

"Lynn gave it to me," he said. "It's tiny Cowboy."

Wills saw JoAnn and gave her a big hug. She leaned down on one knee. "Hey, you were pretty great in there," she said.

"Did you see me singing?" he asked. None of us had taken our eyes off him the entire time and, no, we didn't see him singing, but in his mind, he saw himself as participating.

"I did!" JoAnn said.

"Everyone was listening," he went on, "and then some kids danced. Did you see that?"

"We saw everything, and loved it all!" I said.

"Did you see the recorders?" he asked.

"Of course." Michael nodded.

"I get to play one of those soon." He held up his arms for Michael to lift him onto his shoulders. "Next year, I'll be the one playing everyone in." He was actually looking forward to the next Sing. Katherine was right—she was *always* right. Wills was happy, proud even, that he'd been there, and was already looking forward to learning the recorder—that was a miracle in itself.

Back home, after making Wills some noodles for lunch, I gave him Children's Motrin for his fever. His nose had begun running and now he had a cough. Still, he was excited about Cowboy's homecoming. Michael took out our Sony camcorder.

"It's December twenty-first and Cowboy is coming home," Michael announced, panning across the room. "This is her crate, and this is Cowboy's pen where she's going to sleep."

The camera dipped toward the carpet as Michael checked his watch. "We're going in ten minutes. Right, Wills?"

Wills seemed a little shell-shocked. He'd waited so long for a dog of his own, and now that the moment was here, he wasn't quite sure how he felt about it. He was pacing around inside the five-by-four wire pen, arranging the new chew toys and her food and water bowls.

"Daddy?"

"Yes?"

"How 'bout we take a movie of Cowboy's Place?" Wills said. "Daddy, take this view."

"I'm filming right now," Michael said. Wills looked up, surprised to see the camera pointed in his direction. He didn't mind being filmed, though he preferred to know before the camera was turned on. He picked up a toy and held it toward the lens. Michael responded excitedly, "What's that?"

"It's Kong," Wills said, rotating the red rubber tube end over end in his hands. He shoved his finger through one of the two holes on either end. "You put a treat in there," he said, holding the Kong up to his eye so he could see directly through the hole to the other side, "and Cowboy tries to get it." He seemed skeptical that a treat would even fit in there.

"I see," Michael said.

"It's for chewing and recreation," Wills pointed out. I'd read that exact description to him off the Kong box the day before. Wills lay down in the pen, just like Cowboy would soon.

"Wow, lots of toys," Michael said, zooming in on Wills. Maybe I'd bought too much stuff. Still, I didn't want a lull in the action on Cowboy's first day home.

"He's a lucky puppy," Michael said.

"It's a *she*," Wills corrected.

"Of course!" Michael said.

"When she gets here, don't make her sad by calling her a boy."

"I won't," Michael assured him. "Are you feeling better?"

Wills nodded his head. "*Way* better."

Despite feeling exhausted and feverish, Wills wanted to get Cowboy today. I wasn't feeling that well myself. I'd barely made it through my shower that morning without needing to sit down.

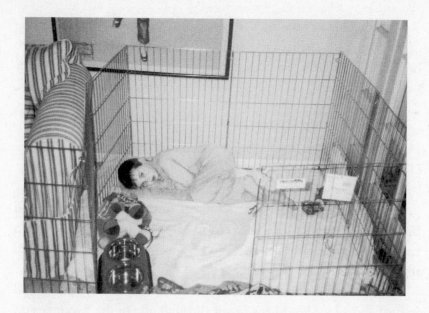

"Michael," I said, walking out of the bathroom with a washcloth against my mouth, "I just threw up." There was no doubt, I had what Wills had.

"Oh, honey," Michael said, "not at Christmas. I'm so sorry." Believe me, I knew what weekend it was, but maybe this would pass quickly. Still, I mentally ticked off the items glaring at me from my hefty list: stocking stuffers to buy, gifts to wrap, a three-foot wooden tree house to build, a Lego pirate ship that still hadn't arrived—all from Santa Claus.

I yanked on a pair of corduroys and looked through the mess on the dresser for my keys. Cowboy was waiting. She had no idea that soon she'd have a home and a family of her own.

Part Two

Cowboy & Wills

CHAPTER EIGHT

The front window of the Pet Chalet was resplendent with swirling, glittery snowflakes and hand-painted holly leaves, reminding L.A. that it was indeed Christmas, despite the heat. Wills stood below a sign that read "Special Order Your Puppy or Kitten Today!" his nose pressed against the glass, hands cupped on either side of his face. Inside were three baby cribs painted white, blue, and yellow. In each one, two or three fuzzy puppies (standard poodles, shih tzus, Labradors) were rolling around chewing on each other's ears or sleeping in piles.

He stayed cemented to his spot, quietly taking in the chaos through the window and listening to the cacophony of "oohs" and "aahs" wafting out the open door. I placed my hand on his narrow back while Michael knelt down beside him, wrapping his arm around Wills's waist. Wills looked up at me. "She's in there," I said. "Once we get her, we can get away from this crowded place."

Tears streamed down his face. "She's waiting," he said.

I pulled a wrinkled Kleenex out of my purse and dabbed his face.

"Do you want me to go in and get her?" Michael asked. "I can bring her outside away from the noise?"

"I'll get her myself," Wills said, taking my Kleenex and handing it to Michael.

As the three of us made our way inside, the clamor escalated: parrots squawking, dogs barking, and people shouting into their cell phones. But Wills held steady. In front of us was a long, tapered staircase.

"Cowboy's at the top of those stairs," I said.

"She's up there, all right," Michael said, giving Wills a little squeeze.

Wills's eyes followed the stairway all the way to the top. "Boy, she's high," he said, repeating the sentence under his breath two more times. "Does she know I'm coming?"

"Mommy told her you'd be here today," Michael said. Wills focused on the top of the steps as one of the employees, eager to help us, ran up to get her.

Wills was pale, his eyebrows practically touching his hairline. Michael picked him up.

"This is pretty exciting, but a little scary, too, right?" he asked. Wills nodded. "It's a big moment," Michael confirmed.

Just then the young employee walked down the steps carrying Cowboy, the most beautiful golden retriever puppy Wills could have ever imagined. She looked so much healthier already. I told Wills as calmly as I could because I really wanted to yell it, "That's her, honey. That's your girl, Cowboy." She looked sleepy with those irresistible droopy brown eyes, her blond hair as fragile and fluffy as new grass. Wills wriggled out of Michael's arms.

The store clerk handed Cowboy to Wills.

"Hold her just like this," he said, tucking Wills's hand under her bottom.

"She's a cutie," Wills said in a clear but timid voice. I placed a hand under Cowboy's warm tummy to help steady her.

"You're a pro," Michael said.

"You're doing great," I echoed.

"Isn't she a cutie?" Wills asked, again, eyes on the top of Cowboy's head.

"She's *perfect*," I told him, and kissed his cheek.

"What's under there?!" Wills called out, alarmed. "There's something under there." He bent his head over, trying to look underneath her. He pulled his hand away immediately. "Oh, no," he said. "Look!" He was pointing to her butt.

"That's her bottom," I told him. "She doesn't wear pants, so it's out in the open."

"Her fur will eventually cover it," Michael assured him.

"It's important," I said. "Everyone needs a butt."

"It's warm," he said, rubbing each hand on the front of his turtleneck while balancing her with the other. "I don't like her bottom." Fair enough.

Michael and I were paying the final bill while Wills stood next to me, Cowboy snuggling against his small chest. The shop had exploded with even more shoppers crowding in to hold the Himalayan cats or buy squeaky rubber stocking stuffers.

"Is that your dog?" a woman with perfect blond highlights and a Birkin bag asked Wills. I instinctively stepped forward to rescue him from the awkwardness of talking to a stranger, but I didn't need to.

"Yes," he told her, turning so she could see Cowboy's face. "She's a cutie."

"She sure is," the woman said. Then something happened. It was so small that nobody in the store would have noticed it. But to me, it was extraordinary. This woman, a complete stranger, patted Wills's shoulder—and he didn't bristle or bolt out of the front door in an absolute panic. He just stood there, staring at us with a shy "what do you know?" smile. Somehow, with this tiny heart beating next to his, Wills had stepped a little further into the world.

We headed out to the parking lot. "I'm just so glad to get a golden retriever," he said.

"Can you hold her really tight so Daddy can get your picture?" I asked.

"She's a cutie," Wills said. "Right?"

"Right," I confirmed.

"I need to sit down." Cowboy and Wills sat on the low curb beside the car. He was looking pale again and his cough sounded like a tin can full of nickels being shaken.

"Let's make this quick," I said to Michael.

"She's cuter than I thought," Wills said. Cowboy wiggled her way out of Wills's arms and plopped into the flowerbed behind him. As she was escaping, Michael and I bumped foreheads attempting to rescue her.

Michael rushed to get her puppy crate opened, and I picked her up. "Wills, climb in the car, honey."

"She's too cute to ride in a car seat," he said, referring to the crate.

"She doesn't have to ride in the car seat on her first ride home. We'll put it in the way-back, and I'll sit in the backseat with you guys." Wills held Cowboy in her new yellow blanket all the way home.

In front of our house, Wills said, "I've got her!" as Michael opened the car door. She immediately began tipping forward.

"Hold her head," I said.

"This is as tight as I can hold her," Wills said, walking carefully with his arms straight out in front of him, Cowboy's tummy drooping down between them, her paws on each side.

Once in the house, Wills and I sat in the pen while Cowboy bumbled around, checking out her new toys and water bowl. Suddenly, she was upside down, stretching out her tiny front paws, displaying three shiny black pads on each one. Her back feet were crossed in midair as she ever so slowly tilted onto her side and promptly fell asleep.

"She's pooped," I said.

"Me, too." Wills laid down, curling himself around her warm little body.

As the day progressed, the blankets and towels we'd laid down to guard against accidents had to be thrown in the washer and replaced several times. We took her outside to potty every thirty minutes like the books had instructed, but our timing was always off by about three minutes.

Wills's cough got worse. By that night his fever had spiked to 103. We paged the doctor, and Michael put Wills into a cool bath. I gave him more Motrin and some chicken broth. He threw up both and went back to bed. I woke him two hours later and he was able to keep the medicine down. At least that would help the fever.

Michael and I took turns, checking on him every thirty minutes until he woke up and said, "Stop touching me. I need to sleep." Enough said.

At midnight, Cowboy kicked into high gear and began rolling all over the family room, dragging her yellow doggie blanket like it was a duck she'd just pulled out of the rushes. She looked up at me, expectantly. She was yummy—adorable.

Michael and I watched her play in the family room, where the construction-paper snowflakes Wills had been making since Halloween were taped all over the windows and a squat, bushy Christmas tree sat twinkling in the corner. Underneath it, winding its way through an Old English ceramic village, was his prized Lionel Christmas train.

It was tradition every year that Wills would pick out his own Christmas tree that was exactly as tall as he was. He'd run through the pine-scented aisles of Douglas and noble firs at Santa and Sons Christmas tree lot, stopping just long enough to back up against one with his arms slapped against his sides, saying, "Is this my size?" "Is this one?" He wasn't worried about running into strangers or the Christmas carols blaring at Santa and Sons. It was an anxiety-free zone and my very favorite part of Christmas, a milestone and a reminder of how it all goes by so quickly. We always tied his tree to the top of the Jeep regardless of how small it was. This year it looked especially tall.

Wills and I spent Christmas Eve in bed. We didn't even get up to play with Cowboy or eat. We were so sick and our temperatures so high, nothing mattered except being on our backs. We wheezed and slept.

It fell to Michael to take Cowboy out every twenty minutes—her first puppy steps to being housebroken. I slept fitfully to the refrain of Michael, just outside the bedroom window, saying, "Potty outside? Potty outside?"

Wills usually spent the night before Christmas checking Michael's computer to find out exactly where Santa was at that moment—time zone *and* city—and making sure that Santa knew he wasn't allowed to come into the house but could leave the presents outside. The idea of a strange man in a fur suit walking around our house while we slept scared the daylights out of Wills. One of the biggest fights Michael and I had early in our marriage was whether or not to do the Santa Claus gig.

"We've always been honest with him," I argued, "and he can't grasp 'magical'—something as illogical as letting a man in our house—down the chimney, no less. It scares him. He needs something concrete, logical."

"But this is like the Tooth Fairy, which he really likes," he said.

"According to Wills, the Tooth Fairy is two inches high and leaves quarters. I don't think she's such a threat. Besides, he hasn't even lost a tooth yet, so who knows how he'll react when she starts stowing loose change under his pillow while he's asleep."

"Monica, I really want to do this. It's something that can only happen when you're young."

"Then find a way to do it so it's not about you reliving your childhood Christmas, which I can understand, but about Wills enjoying his. He's different from you. He has a lot of fears."

Michael's family coveted the Santa Claus tradition, and he relished the tender, happy memories of anticipating Santa's arrival. At his house, Santa not only brought gifts and stockings on Christmas Eve, he also put up the tree. His mom and dad had it hidden away, wrapped in an old sheet and stuffed into the shed where the kids wouldn't see it until Christmas morning.

For me, it had less significance. Christmas at my house had consisted of my mom's attempts to make everything look perfect. For instance, we were not allowed to decorate a Christmas cookie with our own design, we had to follow her original or get up from the table. Meanwhile, my father ranted over the amount of money my mother had spent making everything look perfect, which wasn't really that much. If Santa had put me in his sleigh and snatched me out of there, he might have been significant to me.

Michael came up with a workable compromise. He and Wills would call Santa (which was really my cell phone) every year and tell him to please not enter the house. They'd fax over to the North Pole (JoAnn's fax machine) a map Wills had drawn, indicating where the packages should be dropped off. (Inside our front gate near the mailbox.) Wills placed the cookies and milk out on the front walkway with a hand-drawn picture for Santa of a volcano or hermit crab.

At 5 a.m. on Christmas morning, Wills and I came into the family room, and everything was done.

Michael stayed up all night building that three-foot tree house and the spectacular wooden pirate ship that had finally arrived.

The gifts were beautifully wrapped and the stockings, bulging with candy and presents, were lined up along the fireplace mantel. He had done the impossible! He'd pulled off Santa Claus by himself! There was even a decorated Santa cookie with a bite out of it and a half a glass of milk sitting out by the mailbox.

As Wills stood in front of the Christmas tree, taking in all of the glittering presents, he asked Michael to dial JoAnn's number. JoAnn often called Wills, but he'd usually just sit there, listening. Talking on the phone bothered him, because he couldn't see the other person. He'd listen to JoAnn, excited with whatever plans she was coming up with for the two of them—fossil hunting, a trip to the Aquarium of the Pacific, or a drive out to the desert to look for fallen meteorites. I'd usually be in the background, yelling, "He's listening, JoAnn," so she wouldn't think she was talking into the wind.

"Are you ready to come over?" Wills asked. (This was only the

second time he'd ever spoken on the telephone.) He listened. "I know. Cowboy's here!" he said to whatever she was saying on the other end. "Yeah," he said and then hung up. Wills hadn't yet mastered the art of closing a conversation.

Cowboy was awake in her little pen, staring out at us. She wasn't even crying. It must have been a long night for her as well.

"Hi, Cowboy," I said, hurrying over to squeeze her. "Merry Christmas." I quickly took her outside to potty and then inside for a little breakfast.

"Look, Wills, I left cookies for Santa," Michael said, glancing out the front window.

"He ate 'em," Wills said, peeking outside. "Oh no, it's raining! Did you bring everything inside?" he asked Michael. "All of the presents?"

"I got everything," Michael said. "Nothing got wet." Wills looked out one more time, just to make sure there wasn't a lost package lying on the grass.

Then I heard Wills yell, "HEY, PSYCHEDELIC CRAYONS." We'd gotten these to make bathtime easier for him. They were soap crayons he could use to write on the tub and shower doors.

Cowboy and I walked back into the family room. "Look who's happy to see you," I said.

"COWBOY!" Wills held up his crayons. "Santa brought this," he said, and then stopped. "Santa probably didn't know about Cowboy." His eyes filled with tears. "He probably didn't know she needed Christmas."

"But he *did* leave something for Cowboy!" Michael exclaimed. Thankfully, he'd wrapped two of the squeaky toys from the Pet Chalet and put them under the tree. I never would have thought of it. He'd done everything perfectly.

JoAnn arrived with an overflowing basket of gifts. None of us wrapped presents like JoAnn, ribbons artfully twirled around gold imprinted paper, snowmen and Christmas trees she'd cut out of white card stock and painted herself, sitting on top of white, glittery paper.

"Merry Christmas," she hollered, as she pushed the door open with her foot. I greeted her with a mug of strong coffee. She needed it.

"This is Cowboy's first Christmas," Wills told her.

"I know," she said, enthusiastically. "I have a present for her." Oh my God, everyone was on their toes.

"This is her first Christmas," he said, clasping his hands. "And you remembered, didn't you?"

"I sure did!"

I brought Cowboy around the corner. "Here she is."

JoAnn put down the coffee and hurried toward us. "Oh my gosh, she's gorgeous!" she said. I handed her over. "Wills, what do you think?"

"I can't believe it," he said, turning toward the presents. JoAnn continued to fawn over Cowboy, who was chewing on the end of her finger.

Wills was back in action, as Michael, JoAnn, and I took turns running after Cowboy, who eventually settled on top of a shiny wrapped gift to chew on the corner.

Wills unwrapped a National Geographic–approved block build-

ing set of an authentic ancient Egyptian pyramid. "Hey, it's the Luxor from Vegas." So much for one of the great wonders of the world.

"Look how many cannons are on this boat," he said, scooting over to the two- by four-foot wooden pirate ship with real cloth sails.

"How many?" I asked.

"One, two, three, four, five."

"There you go," I said. "That's right."

With all of the presents opened and Cowboy sound asleep in JoAnn's lap, Wills and I stumbled back to bed. We'd used up all of our energy opening presents, and there was nothing but nausea and exhaustion left.

Two long days passed, as it poured torrential rain. Wills and I could hear Michael outside the window, standing under a drooping umbrella, continuing to encourage Cowboy in an upbeat singsong voice to "Potty outside! Come on! You can do it. Potty outside!" Did nothing rankle him? Michael was so gentle with her. She was so small, and he was so tall. She was barely as long as his size-13 foot.

The toys sat next to the tree, untouched.

Three days after Christmas, Wills and I were perking up. As I stripped the pink bed and put on fresh sheets, Wills sat cross-legged on the floor with his hands on his knees staring at Cowboy, who was tugging on the leg of his striped pajamas.

"What do I do with Cowboy?" he suddenly asked. "She wants to bite my clothes."

"Puppies chew things. It's their favorite thing to do. Get her a toy from the family room," I suggested.

Wills looked skeptical. "Don't chew on *me*," he said, touching the top of her head with his index finger and pushing her back.

Cowboy suddenly bolted out of the bedroom as if she'd been branded, blazing straight through the house and into the backyard, where she began digging a hole.

"Cowboy, don't rip up the grass," I said in a silly voice. (Oh no, goofy baby talk was already taking over.) I lifted her up, pointing her in another direction. She left behind miniature muddy paw prints as she scampered around the corner of the garage, and then gobbled up a river rock from Wills's garden.

"We'll have to pick these up," I said to Wills, prying Cowboy's teeny jaws apart and retrieving the stone.

"What about my Booner trails?" he asked. "Those rocks are for the hamster to walk on."

"Maybe we can put some kind of fence around the garden," I said, setting her back down.

"Let's build a wooden one," Wills suggested. I couldn't even imagine taking on another project right now.

Cowboy reappeared on the patio with a multicolored dinosaur twice her size in her mouth. She was fierce, shaking it violently from side to side and then discarding it for a new victim. The melee ended with her sound asleep on top of a flat of unplanted Irish moss.

The rain was starting to come down again, so I picked up Cowboy, who didn't bother waking up, and placed her gently in her purple bed.

Once I had the laundry going, I sat in the living room staring out at the gloomy, dark sky. Wills was putting his Lego Ferris wheel together. The sky burst open and rain poured down in sheets.

"I have to get out of this house," I said, as Michael snuggled next to me on the couch. I lay my head on his shoulder, and he pulled me closer.

"Let's take a drive," he said.

"With Cowboy!" Wills chimed in. His nose was so chapped.

"Cowboy *has* to come," I told Wills. "You haven't had a chance to get to know her yet. Plus, we can't leave her by herself."

"She needs a sweater," Wills said, worried. "A raincoat."

"Her fur *is* a coat," Michael told him.

"I know," he said, his intelligence insulted. "But there's not much of it."

I stroked her head and she immediately rolled over for a tummy rub. Her hair *was* on the lean side. "We'll bring her blanket," I said.

I took her out and she peed with her eyes closed, rain peppering the top of her head.

Michael and I packed the truck as if we were driving to Utah, including the coats and boots we wore when we traveled back East. Next thing we knew, we were heading to Pasadena, *The Andy Williams Christmas Album* crooning in the background. Cowboy curled into a tiny ball on Wills's lap and slept. He didn't quite know how to touch her so he continued to use his index finger to pet the top of her head.

"She likes me," he said, smiling a real Christmas smile.

"She loves you," I told him. "The two of you are going to be best friends."

He kicked his legs up and down in his car seat and laughed. "She's warm," he said.

The minute we got to the 134/210 interchange, Wills said, "Look at the snow!"

The mountains were covered in white, and the snow line was really low.

"It's beautiful," I said, shocked to see so much snow.

"We *have* to play in the snow, right, Mommy?"

"You've been so sick," I said, "maybe we should wait a few days."

"Then I'll be in school." He was right. New Year's Eve was tomorrow and then we'd all be back to our schedules.

Michael and I looked at each other. Wills had spent most of his holiday in bed. Were we bad parents if we took him up to the snow?

"What if we stay in the car and keep the heater running?" I asked Michael.

"We could do that," he said.

"Let's go," Wills said. "Cowboy?" He gently nudged her. "This is your first snow."

That did it. We started up the Angeles Crest Highway.

We were all together, the flu was gone, Michael had saved the holiday, and Cowboy was ours at last. Christmas had finally come.

In a setting right out of a hokey yet spectacular Currier and Ives lithograph, we pulled off the road, the forest silent and thick with snow. We crunched a little ways into the pine grove, just as the snow, fragile and silvery, began falling. I hadn't seen flakes that big since I lived back East. Cowboy was tucked inside my down jacket with just her eyes and the tip of her nose exposed.

"I should head back to the car and warm her up," I called to them. "Do you think Wills needs to come back?"

"Can I stay for a little while?" Wills asked. He peered out of his tightly pulled hood, looking like Kenny from *South Park*.

"He's pretty bundled up," Michael said. "I think it's okay." Michael's knit Mets hat that we'd gotten him for Christmas now had a small shelf of snow sitting right on top.

"You guys have fun," I said, leaning in for a kiss. "I'll take Cowboy to the car and start the heater." Wills took off running through the snow-covered trees. As I walked away, I turned to see the two people I loved more than anyone in the world. "Don't walk too far back," I said, ever the worrier. They were heaven and earth to me.

Before we headed back down the mountain, Wills and Michael

built a tiny snowman on the hood of our car with two uneven rock eyes and pretzel rods from our snack stash as arms. We made bets on how long it would stay there for the thirty-minute ride back down the mountain.

Unfortunately, the snow stayed put, but the rock eyeballs blew in two different directions, one of them creating a ding in the center of the windshield. I didn't care, I was happy.

I crawled into the backseat and handed Cowboy to Wills. "No can do, Mommy," Wills said. "I have to sleep."

It was the first chance I'd gotten to really snuggle with Cowboy. She sat in my lap as I kissed the tiny hairs on the crown of her head. She licked my wrist and looked around, noticing, maybe for the first time, that she'd found a new family . . . one that had waited and wanted—only her.

CHAPTER NINE

After Christmas break, as Wills's class sat in their morning circle, Terri asked if anyone had something they'd like to share. Wills's hand shot straight up. Lynn said it was like all of the air went out of her lungs, she was so taken aback. Terri called on him right away.

Once he'd been chosen to speak, he seemed less sure.

"Wills, I'm dying to know what you're holding in your hand," Lynn said.

Wills looked down at the photograph in his hand. "It's my new puppy," he said, remembering why he'd raised his hand in the first place. "It's Cowboy."

The children moved in closer to get a better look, but Wills didn't back up.

"Would you like to walk the picture around the circle so everyone can see her?" Terri encouraged. So Wills leaned down and walked around the interior of the circle, holding up Cowboy for everyone to see.

When he got back to his original spot, he said, "Cowboy was born on October nineteenth but we got her on December twenty-first." Standing there with everyone staring at him in anticipation, he was unsure and thrilled by how good it felt to be the center of attention.

"Would you like to tell us a little bit more about her?" Terri encouraged.

"She's a golden retriever, that's for sure, and they like to hunt. Only Cowboy doesn't hunt because we feed her Science Diet. She goes to the bathroom in our bed sometimes and sleeps upside down."

Lynn whispered into Wills's ear. "Questions or comments?" he asked the class, which was protocol for all of the kids after Sharing. Eighteen small hands went up.

It was mind-blowing, according to Lynn; Wills standing alone, in front of the class, answering questions and enjoying himself!

While Wills was at school, I began to see that Cowboy would need my undivided attention. Puppies were needy and too cute for me to be distracted by bills or phone calls or writing. Wherever I took Cowboy with her floppy (and unusually large front paws) resting on my arm, we were inundated with smiling faces full of gushing compliments—even at the bank. I understood. I couldn't take my eyes off of her either.

When I picked Wills up at the end of the day, I carried Cowboy into school. The children were gathered in the play yard for carpool and they exploded in ahhs and ooohs over this gorgeous, roly-poly puppy with the stick-thin tail. I lowered her onto the grass, but before I could attach the leash, she took off running in all directions, zigzagging across the schoolyard, which thrilled everyone except me, who was fumbling around after her.

I waved for Wills and handed over Cowboy's leash, which was finally attached to her collar. She galumphed toward the circle of kids with Wills right behind her.

He wasn't sure what to do with an even larger group of people, most of them he'd never met, staring at him and cheering, but Wills moved from group to group, letting the kids hold up Cowboy and rub their hands all over her bunchy little body. Cowboy was clearly basking in the glory and the chaos.

"Can we hold her?"

"Did you get her for Christmas?"

"How old is she?"

"Is she *yours*?"

Again, with Cowboy in between himself and the crowd, Wills was able to answer most of their questions. Everyone suddenly knew Cowboy, which meant that everyone now knew Wills. We'd hit an unexpected gold mine. Wills was making his social debut. Cowboy, on her purple leash, was leading Wills into the world of his peers, one that both terrified and beckoned him.

Suddenly, he and Cowboy ran past me.

"We have to go to the office," he said, darting up the steps and heading straight for Helen's desk.

"Don't tell me this is *Cowboy*?" Helen clasped her hands together.

"This *is* Cowboy," Wills said, beaming.

"She's just beautiful," Helen gushed. "I think I'm in love."

"She peed on our bed," Wills told her.

"Puppies do that," Helen said in a serious tone.

"Mine did."

"Can Helen hold her?" I asked Wills. He put her gently into Helen's arms. She nuzzled Cowboy's neck.

"She's so cute," Helen told him. "Can I be her grandma?"

"Oh, yes," Wills said, smiling. I had to laugh. Helen was my age.

From that day on, Wills carried Cowboy's picture in his pocket and a photograph of the two of them taped inside of his lunchbox.

Two months later we began playing "school" in our family room, dragging dining room and patio chairs inside to form a semicircle. He arranged three stuffed turtles, Baby Wertheimer, the hammer-head shark, two Beanie baby hamsters, three stuffed snakes, and about ten other animals on the chairs and the floor around the foot-stool where he (the teacher) would sit.

Jerry, the Panda, sat near Wills because he was scared of the potty. Wills walked him into the yellow bathroom while the other students were instructed to line up outside the master bathroom.

"Jerry doesn't like the boy's bathroom," Wills told me. "He uses the one in the office."

Wills insisted on pushing Cowboy's neck (and each of her front paws) through the holes of his Southern Pacific Railroad T-shirt so she could spend an entire day at school with him.

"You have to wear *something,*" he scolded. "You can't go to school naked!" She seemed oblivious to being dressed for the first time.

Cowboy was a lousy student, wandering around chewing on the other kids' tails and plastic eyes, then flopping down in the middle of Sharing to gnaw on the hair between her miniature toe pads.

"Cowboy, do you need a time-out?" Wills asked with authority, but the minute she heard his voice, she ran to him.

"That's okay," he'd say, "you just need to stay in your group."

When she peed on the carpet because we forgot to take her outside, Wills said, "She's afraid of the potties."

"She's like Jerry," I said.

"Jerry needs privacy," Wills said, "Cowboy wants company. She doesn't like to go to the potty alone."

I'd bought felt squares at an arts and crafts store, and cut out people shaped like gingerbread men—exactly like Terri had in her class—except we also included a cutout figure in the shape of a golden retriever.

At CCS, Wills was not able to stick his felt man on the board, which would indicate that he was present at school that day. Nicholas did it for him, but at home, it wasn't a problem.

When it was time for music or hot lunch, the stuffed animals were arranged in a straight line, heading toward the piano or the kitchen, waiting their turn. By then, Cowboy was lying on the couch snoring like an old alcoholic sleeping one off.

"You're allowed to nap at school," Wills told me. "She's not in trouble."

Wills slipped his guitar strap over his head just like Ruth. It was time for music. He turned on his boom box and lip-synced to "Sail On, Sailor" by the Beach Boys while strumming the guitar.

For reasons we were still trying to figure out, Wills was unable to

address a person by name. He easily used "Mommy," "Daddy," and "JoAnn," but that was it—except for his animals, of course.

This was a big hindrance for Wills in kindergarten, where one of the main lessons was to learn to socialize, which included calling the children by their names. If Wills was sharing in front of the class (talking about Booner or his model of the space shuttle) and a child raised their hand to ask him a question, he was supposed call on the student by name. Terri agreed that he could whisper the name in her ear, and then she'd say it aloud.

After writing the students' names on slips of cardboard, I'd point to one and Wills would say, "I already know that one."

"The teacher has to say them *out loud,*" I'd say. Wills, who never broke a rule, said them aloud. No surprise, he knew every name by how it was spelled. He just couldn't bring himself to do it in class.

On Monday, Lynn called. "Wills was able to put up his felt figure today," she said, excitedly. "Nicholas stood up and said, 'Wills, come with me,' and the two of them put up his orange felt man together. I could not believe it!"

With Nicholas by his side and a felt cut-out of Cowboy in the pocket of his sweatpants, Wills counted himself "present" that day. He was ready to join his class in a way he'd never done before—as one of nineteen felt figures—a member of his group.

* * *

We were at Longs Drugs waiting for a prescription to be filled when over the loudspeaker, a pharmacist announced: "Would Benjamin Lawrence please come to the pharmacy window? Mr. Lawrence to the pharmacy."

"He needs to hurry," Wills said, looking around.

"They'll wait," I assured him.

"Mr. Lawrence must be far away," he said. "They might give his things away if he doesn't hurry."

"Mr. Lawrence, please come to the pharmacy window."

"They won't give up on Mr. Lawrence," I explained. "There's nothing to worry about, sweetheart—really." By the time we looked up, there was a sophisticated older man, à la Paul Newman, wearing a plaid Pendleton wool jacket, standing at the pharmacy window talking.

"LAWRENCE IS HERE!" Wills announced. The gentleman looked back at Wills and gave him the thumbs-up.

On the way home we were stopped at a red light in Brentwood, and Cowboy was sitting on Wills's lap in his booster seat, with her head sticking out of the window. An Impala with five or six young guys pulled up beside us. They were laughing and pointing at Cowboy.

I looked over, sizing them up, hoping they weren't planning on causing trouble. The one in the back yelled, "Hey, what's that, a poodle?"

"Golden retriever," Wills replied.

"What?"

"Golden retriever," he said a little louder.

"What's her name?" the guy asked, lifting his chin.

"Cowboy Carol Lawrence," Wills said, articulately.

"Ride 'em, Cowboy!" the kid yelled, as they sped off.

I looked back at Wills. "What in the world was that?" I laughed.

Wills just shrugged and continued stroking Cowboy's head, his bangs blowing across his forehead.

Cowboy had become one of us. We were no longer surprised to find a pair of underpants lying in a defeated heap with the crotch chewed out or teeth mark patterns on the side of the leather chair.

With Wills in school, I spent my days throwing her Frisbee and picking soft yellow hair off my tongue. I didn't know how it got there: it wafted, it tumbled. Soft, furry hairballs rolled across the dining room floor like tumbleweeds in an old western. Cowboy's coat made every piece of clothing a "hair shirt," a "hair jacket," or "hair sneakers."

She'd grown into an awkward adolescent—her paws almost as big as her head—and very tall. When the two of us ran errands, she'd sit next to me in the car looking straight ahead, as if she were the one driving. I was madly in love with this little girl.

One night, after Cowboy had been with us for three months, I was giving Wills a bath when the bathroom door flew open and there she stood like Clint Eastwood in *High Plains Drifter*. I jumped up to shoo her out, but she wriggled between my legs and before I could stop her, she leapt into the tub, landing like a sack of flour in a sink of dishwater right next to Wills. Water splashed up the sides of the shower wall, out the bottom of the glass doors, and onto the floor.

I braced myself for the scream, but instead came giggling, which quickly erupted into laughter so exuberant that I had to peer into the tub to make sure that it was coming from Wills. Cowboy was consumed by the absolute thrill and good fortune at being in close proximity to everything she loved: Wills, water, and a chance to wreck a room.

Wills slid the shower doors shut, and all I could see through the fog was wet, brownish-blond hair the full length of Cowboy's body smushed against the glass. She was rubbing back and forth, kicking up water, and then disappearing into the steamy depths of the tub. Wills's head was thrown back in a fit of unadulterated joy. It was a sound I'd never heard before—Wills roaring with laughter, and then trying to compose himself only to erupt into an even louder fit of giggles.

I sat on top of the counter with my legs crossed, snapping pictures of the two of them.

"Can we have bubbles?" Wills asked, as if they hadn't tortured him for the last six years of his life. I stood there, flabbergasted, silently staring at him. "Cowboy's dirty," he explained.

"Sure," I said, snapping to—careful not to break the spell. "Bubbles for everyone!" I rummaged under the sink pushing aside sticky, yellowed tubes of Neosporin and dusty jars of unused face cream, searching for what I prayed would be there—an ancient

bottle of Mr. Bubble. I'd bought it over three years ago when I'd still imagined Wills greeting me in the bathtub with a fake bubble beard.

Thankfully, I found Mr. Bubble's pink molded-plastic body right behind some cotton balls. His overly delighted smile seemed to suggest that he'd known this would happen someday. I warmed up the bathwater and poured in the bubbles as Wills slathered them all over Cowboy. In return, she stuck her nose under the spigot, snorting and sneezing.

After an hour, I pulled out one exhausted hairy kid and an even hairier dog, who was anything but tired, trying her damnedest to jump back into the tub. She had a straight barbershop quartet part where Wills had poured water over her head. "Your hairdo is dated," I told her. "You look like Jan Brady."

"Cowboy needed that bath," Wills professed, wrapping Cowboy in the towel I'd laid out for him.

"She really did!" I said, as Cowboy shook herself, splattering water all over the walls and cabinets. Wills covered his face with his hands.

"She's happy," he said. "She was hoping I'd shampoo her."

"Well, thanks to you, she got her wish," I told him, wiping water droplets off my face with my sleeve.

Cowboy shook a second and then a third time.

"I gotta get outta here," Wills said, tearing off naked down the hallway. Cowboy was right on his heels.

"Good job in the bath," I yelled after them.

I picked up the phone and dialed Katherine's number. I always called her with the great ones.

At six months old, Cowboy pooped with the fierceness of a miner, eyes fixed on the pear tree near the fence, ass barely hovering above the ground as foaming tan goop swirled out of her. A solid poop was cause for celebration; a Carvel foamer, not so much.

At our house, a *foamer* was also called a *hoser*. After Wills witnessed a liquid poop, he'd run through the house yelling, "Mommy, it's a *hoser*, HURRY!"

That was my clue that a simple plastic bag would not do the job. I unwound the green hose and blasted the crap off our grass like Dan Aykroyd zapping ectoplasm in *Ghostbusters*.

I telephoned our vet, Dr. Burke, who we'd met at the Pet Chalet. "Cowboy's stools are loose," I told him, "like barley soup."

"She's still a *puppy*," he said, "they eat everything. Maybe she ate some dirt or small rocks or something."

"Wouldn't that make her constipated?" I questioned. "Wouldn't soil and stones dam everything up?"

"Actually, it makes the stool soft."

"Like water?" I asked. "Her poop is actually like water."

"Bring her in, and I'll take a look," Dr. Burke said. "Maybe I can give her something to make things more solid."

I hung up the phone, unconvinced of his rocks and dirt theory. It couldn't be her diet. I watched everything she ate, wrenching open her jaws and swiping the inside of her mouth with my finger.

"We have to take her to Dr. Burke's," I told Wills, who was in his room. "You'll have to come with us since Daddy's not home."

"She doesn't want to go," he complained, walking around the corner with Cowboy's thickening body bulging out of his arms, her skinny tail wagging.

"She *loves* Dr. Burke," I told him. "You can't believe how happy she is when she sees him."

"NO!" he said. "Doctors scare her."

"Doctors scare *you*," I said.

"She told me she hates it," he said.

"I'm telling you, she loves it there. It's a good thing you're going so you can see for yourself," I told him.

"She's really sick," he said, "if she has to go to the doctor."

"Cowboy has a little diarrhea," I told him. "Nothing to worry about."

"THE DIARRHEA?" Wills asked as if I'd said "polio."

"Diarrhea is no big deal," I assured him. "Everyone has it once in a while."

"She still has to go to the doctor?" he asked, sitting down with Cowboy on his lap.

"I'm not used to having a puppy," I said. "I just want to give her the right medicine."

"Oh, Cowboy." He put his face in her blond fur and sobbed.

"Wills"—I sat down beside them—"when you get frightened at Dr. Todd's, what do Mommy and Daddy do?"

"Hugs," he said.

"And what else?"

"Pay the bill."

"Yes, we pay the bill, but the most important thing we do is love and support you. We stay right by your side." I ran my hand along the top of Cowboy's head. "She's going to need you to do the same thing."

He disappeared into the office, which was now officially the toy room, leaving Cowboy with me. There were loud bangs and drawers being opened and closed. Finally, Wills came out carrying the plastic doctor's case we'd bought him in a feeble attempt to soften his fear of going to Dr. Todd's. I'd never seen him play with it.

"What's that?" I asked.

"I'm going to help Dr. Burke," he said. "Cowboy will feel safer if I examine her, too."

"Good idea," I told him.

The three of us drove over the hill with a red plastic stethoscope hanging around Wills's neck.

He carried her into Dr. Burke's, and the staff came running.

"Look at Cowboy!" they gushed. "She's growing so fast."

"She's so sweet," Tammy, who ran the front desk, said to Wills. "Are you the one who got her for Christmas?"

"I did," he said. "She's afraid of the doctor."

"Well, it's a good thing you came along to help her out," she said, winking at me.

Dr. Burke was very patient as Wills took out the tongue depressor from his doctor's bag and followed along. Forty-five dollars later, we went home with instructions to give her a quarter of a teaspoon of Pepto-Bismol.

"She's so happy to be going home," Wills said.

"You helped her by being calm and supportive," I told him.

"She's my sister," he said simply, as if that's just what big brothers do.

Wills was an only child, so I could understand the "sister" reference. My friend Ellie told our entire first grade that she had a sister named Cindy, but she turned out to be her standard poodle. She was embarrassed that she didn't have siblings. I hoped Wills was okay with his only-child status, because Michael and I had decided several years earlier that we wouldn't be having more children. It was less about Wills's diagnosis and more about us. We hadn't expected parenting to be all-consuming, but since it was, we decided to direct our focus onto one child—Wills.

* * *

At CCS, with Terri and Lynn gently nudging him toward the crowded lunch line, the tether ball game, the soccer match, Wills was beginning to look forward to school. He especially loved having Cowboy arrive at the end of every day. As soon as we walked on campus, someone would yell, *"Wills!! Cowboy's here!!"*

He'd turn toward me with this smug, gorgeously confident expression, wrap her leash around his hand, and begin making the rounds.

Wills's movement teacher, Kathleen, pulled me aside one afternoon. "Wills is doing very well in dance."

"Thank you," I said, my hand immediately flying up to my heart to calm it. Even with all of Wills's improvements, I still found myself bracing for bad news. This was the first time Kathleen and I had spoken.

"It's very good he has Lynn," she continued. "She helps him immensely, not to dance, but to have the confidence to try."

"She's a terrific influence on him," I said.

"I've seen kids with special needs become more and more lost without an aide present, and that's just heartbreaking, as you can imagine."

"We went through that in preschool," I said, feeling the sting of her word choice—"special needs." I'd been living with those two words and their implications for more than five years and, still, when someone used them to describe Wills, it was as if I'd just heard the news. That's how jolting they were—not at all familiar, as someone might obviously assume.

Kathleen seemed to be lost in her own thoughts. "The thing is, he's *wanting* to dance," she said with conviction, "not that he can always participate due to the anxiety, but the desire is there, which is very exciting."

"He likes to dance—he dances with me," I said.

Wills enjoyed putting the Wiggles CD into his boom box and clicking to track 4, "Toot toot, Chugga Chugga, Big Red Car."

"I'm gonna do a really fast one," he'd announce. "It's going to be the best ever."

Once the music began, he'd grab both my hands and jump up and down in place, tossing his head back and shaking it. "I *know* this one," he'd announce, practically bent over backward. Cowboy would bark and try to hump us.

Kathleen looked at me intensely. "Autistic children often take things one step at a time, don't you think?"

I nodded. "Sometimes." She smiled, not understanding—waiting for more—but I couldn't say anything else. I was thinking about the steps he still had to master—using a public restroom, sitting in a restaurant, withstanding loud claps of thunder, pulling up a zipper, eating food with texture and color, saying the words "I love you."

But she wasn't wrong either. Sometimes he'd hold my face in his cushiony hands, stare directly into my eyes, and say, "Hello, Good Person." There'd been those shooting-star moments like when he built a wooden lemonade stand from scratch and sat behind it with his dad near our front gate. He'd timed it perfectly, opening for business just as the Catholic church across the street was letting out—4:30 p.m. I was in the kitchen making pitchers of lemonade and before I knew it, I was WAY behind. He was standing next to the booth, his hands crossed in front of him, clearly pleased. He was smart, all right, making fifteen dollars at twenty-five cents a glass. They were only out there twenty minutes.

Kathleen continued. "I get the feeling he's watching and waiting for the right moment. When he breaks through this barrier it will be so freeing for him. You know, to tell his stories." She smiled, not at me, but at the thought of what that might look like. "I think he'll be brilliant."

And I knew that he would be.

CHAPTER TEN

Cowboy's arrival had signaled the beginning of many firsts for Wills, but none was more significant than allowing other children into his life—opening him up to the possibility of having really close friends.

The transformation began with kids calling to ask Wills if they could come over to play with Cowboy. (I spoke to them, relaying the messages back and forth since Wills still refused to talk to anyone but JoAnn on the phone.) Knowing they wanted to play with Cowboy made him feel safer, because it was once removed from them wanting to play with him.

All of a sudden, he had playdates lined up a week in advance, but the kids no longer came over just for Cowboy, they came over for *Wills*. Wills still needed Cowboy beside him, but no one minded.

As Wills's circle grew, so did mine. I started making friends with other mothers. Meeting Bethany Strickland was like discovering someone from another galaxy. Here I was, in my jumpy, isolated, paranoid world when just over the icy black tundra appeared a woman who was my exact polar opposite—someone who breathed deep into her diaphragm and exhaled genuine peace. And it wasn't like her life was any easier than mine or that she hid her messes, like I so clumsily attempted to do.

Bethany carried her mess around with her—people could look at it, ask questions, talk behind her back—she didn't care. She wasn't going to hide anything or adhere to some social norm. It was a real shocker to meet someone so open.

"You match," she said the first time I met her.

"What?"

"You match." She smiled. "Everything you're wearing matches." It sounded like a put-down but it wasn't. She was curious as to why I wore only one color—beige.

Bethany, on the other hand, was wearing purple pajama bottoms under a mesh fuchsia skirt and her black curly hair was pulled up with a thick, hairy rope you might tie around a scarecrow's waist. On top she wore a black, cotton camisole with lace accenting the plunging neckline and a short navy blue sweater over that. It sounds horrible, but it was strangely wonderful. She was holding the most adorable reddish-brown King Charles spaniel.

"I'm Wills's mom," I said.

"Sacha's mine," she said. "She talks about Wills. This is Murphy." She held up the tiny dog.

"He's adorable," I said. "We have a golden retriever puppy named Cowboy."

"Ohhhh, I love puppies, they're my favorite."

"Would Murphy want to play with another dog?" I asked, setting up Cowboy's first playdate.

"I'm sure he would, and I know Sacha would love to play with Wills. We should get together."

"How about Thursday?" I asked, surprising myself.

"Thursday's great," she said, "since school gets out at two o'clock, that'll give us plenty of time."

"Sounds good," I said, thinking four days would give me plenty of time to indulge my cleaning obsession—even though Bethany wouldn't have cared if my house was lying on its side.

The minute Bethany, Sacha, and Murphy stepped through the front door on Thursday, I knew it would be fine. There was nothing in my house, in my past, or in my future that was going to ruffle her. She accepted people as they were—and thought the very best of them. And Sacha was the exact same way.

Murphy, however, was still sussing things out when Cowboy, who was three times his size, came running out of the kitchen and chased him around the outer perimeter of the front yard, through the house, out the back door, around the pool, back through the house, and out the front door again. In an about-face, Murphy chased Cowboy, taking the exact same route. This continued for several minutes as the four of us watched from the front hallway.

"They love each other," Wills announced.

"They're going to be very good friends," Sacha confirmed. "I want to see your room," she told Wills.

"Cowboy can show you," he said, and on the third lap through the house, I grabbed Cowboy's collar and corralled her into Wills's room. Murphy tailed them.

"I brought hermit crabs," Sacha offered, showing him the box she'd been holding.

"I have hermit crabs," Wills said.

The two of them sat on Wills's floor with their legs crossed, examining each multicolored crab with his magnifying glass before hauling out the wooden ramp Sacha had built for hermit crab races. After a couple of hours, they snuggled on the couch wrapped in Wills's steam engine blanket, watching *Pink Panther* cartoons on DVD and eating macaroni and cheese. Bethany and I hung out in the kitchen with the two dogs, chatting like old friends.

Laughing with Bethany, I realized that I'd been as isolated as Wills, except I didn't have a Katherine to point it out to me.

* * *

We were still trekking to Dr. Bauman's office for testing every Wednesday. Wills grew to be more relaxed with Dr. Bauman, as long as I was sitting on my stump where he could see me, even though the testing continued to be overwhelming for him. Wills would try to avoid answering by saying his "eye hurts" or by telling the doctor that he needed to "mark" something. This meant he wanted to get out a piece of paper and scribble all over it—even though he was pretty good at drawing pictures—and then he would staple the whole thing together and proudly present "his book" to me at the end of the hour.

Dr. Bauman attempted to accommodate Wills by giving him extra time to answer or by explaining multiple-choice questions in more detail than the testing required, but it was still an awkward climb straight uphill. Later, when I read the notes from one of his sessions, I couldn't help but feel that Wills was expressing himself correctly, he just couldn't adhere to the rigid confines of the test itself, which required very specific answers.

When asked to explain what the stomach does, Wills offered only, "It gets your food when you eat." When asked to explain what a fossil is, Wills offered, "It's something you see on the ground." When asked if he could explain more, he stated, "It's something that was there. It's something that got there. It's something wet and went away and all you see is the marking on the ground."

To me, these answers were typical of Wills's fabulousness. He knew what he was talking about, but Dr. Bauman had to adhere to the boundaries of each particular test. So these answers were unacceptable.

Yet there were other instances where I could see Wills was struggling with the language:

Wills's difficulty in comprehending language seemed particularly apparent in his response to this question, "Why is it important for police to wear uniforms?" His initial response was, "Because in baseball games, you look nice." When the question was reread to him, he next offered, "In case something is dangerous, and they have to take care of it." Similarly, when Wills was asked what one should do if one finds a wallet or purse in the store, his initial response was only, "Look at it." When he was asked to explain further, he offered, "Buy it." When the question was again reread, he stated, "Give it back to them." He was unable to consider the more abstract concept of turning it in to a store employee, the lost and found, or the police.

When Wills wanted to "mark" something at the end of a session, it was suggested that he come out from under the desk "because it's hard to draw on car-peting." Wills responded, "I won't draw on the carpet. I'll draw on the paper."

This was why my heavy use of slang, or "sloppy talk," as my informational books called it, was very unhelpful to Wills. I already knew this, and had been working on it whenever I was around him. Still, if I told him I was going to "crack a window," he'd start crying. "I mean open the window, honey. 'Crack' the window is just an expression people use because they are only opening the window a 'crack,' which is this much," I said, indicating about two inches with my fingers.

I was so casual and Wills needed someone structured. Or maybe he needed someone like me to loosen him up, as well as someone structured. Either way, it was a good thing JoAnn lived nearby. She was exactly like Wills. (And Michael was somewhere in the middle.) JoAnn and Wills were similar in temperament and had a lot of the same interests. JoAnn was certainly the first great friend he'd ever had, and no surprise, since she was actually standing there cheering and waving to him as he slid out of the birth canal.

When Wills was four, JoAnn began taking him on adventures in her little red sports car. When she picked him up on a Saturday morning, I usually didn't see them again until well after dark. They were gatherers, rock people. Coming home, their pockets and fanny packs bulged with fossils, agate, and stones they'd found interesting because of their shape or color. They'd dig out the *Rocks and Minerals* book JoAnn had given him, lay out their treasures on the picnic table outside, and try to figure out just what they were holding.

They loved building anything out of wood. JoAnn bought him a sawhorse and wood clamps for his birthday, which tickled him to death. When she was helping him with the saw, he wore safety goggles, which he'd then wear for the rest of the day.

One morning they decided to go to Soledad Canyon. Wills greeted JoAnn at the door with a half sheet of white paper folded over like a book. On the front was a soft foam turquoise flower taped right in the middle with a squiggly *S.C.* written in red marker in the center. Next to the flower, was *J.P.*

He had one, too, with a *W.P.* next to his purple foam flower.

"Oh, this has my initials on it," JoAnn said, very pleased.

"That's for you. They're our reports for today." He was holding his with both hands.

"What's the S.C. stand for?"

"Santa Clarita," he said.

"I love it!"

At the end of the day, their reports were filled with the trains they'd seen: Metrolink 12:55, Union Pacific freighter 1:30, rattlesnake 1:45, Union Pacific, four engines with intermodels 4:05 (neither JoAnn nor I knew what an intermodel was), and Santa Clarita Station 4:28.

On one of their many trips, JoAnn had taken Wills to watch the trains in the Tehachapi Loop out past Mojave. It was one of the only locations in the world where trains went through a pretzel-like formation and the track actually passed over itself. This "lessens the angle of the grade," according to the Tehachapi Railroad Museum, and made it one of the "prime train watching enthusiast areas in the country." And heaven knows those two were enthusiasts.

After JoAnn and Wills came home raving, not just about the excitement of seeing really long trains rumbling up that enormous spiral, but also how the sloping mountains and green meadows made them feel like Los Angeles was a million miles away, I decided I had to see it for myself.

Wills, Michael, Cowboy, and I made several trips to Tehachapi in the ensuing months. Cowboy and I ran up and down the trails, wearing ourselves out, while Michael and Wills sat in lawn chairs with binoculars and a box of club crackers. From high up, the little farm that sat right in the middle of the loop looked like a scale model from one of Wills's train sets. I could see (what looked like) miniature horses dotting the meadow.

One afternoon, Cowboy, Wills, and I were at the Tehachapi Loop by ourselves watching the trains when Wills suggested that we also check out Caliente.

"Where's Caliente?" I asked.

"Straight up the highway, but before you hit Bakersfield." I never questioned Wills when it came to directions, but I always wondered how he knew these things. At six and a half years old, he didn't look old enough to know where Caliente was—especially since I was almost forty and had never heard of it.

He must have known what I was thinking. "I saw it on Huell Howser," he clarified. "That's where the construction base was for the Southern Pacific while they were laying track in the Loop. Some of the buildings are still there."

"Let's do it," I said, folding up our lawn chairs. My boy remembered *everything*—especially if it had anything to do with the railroad. I yelled for Cowboy to hop in the car, but she was standing stock-still staring at that little farm.

"Those horses are too far away, Cowboy, let it go." She didn't budge. "COWBOY!" Nothing.

I walked over and gently nudged her collar to lead her to the car. The next thing I knew, I was holding a collar with no dog in it. Cowboy was hurtling down the hill and across those tracks where fourteen unsuspecting horses grazed on the other side of a flimsy barbed-wire fence.

I almost had my own foamer as I frantically looked up and down the tracks to make sure there were no trains coming. I lifted Wills out of his booster seat, put him on my back, and we ran, his sneakers bouncing against my sides. "We have to get Cowboy!"

Miraculously, we got to her just as she was writhing under the fence. The only thing slowing her down had been the sharp barbs pulling at the fur on her back. Lowering Wills to the ground, I quickly grabbed Cowboy's tail with one hand and the fur on her back with the other, wincing as I pulled her back toward me, lifting the bottom of the fence as high as I could with my knee, which wasn't very high.

"OH NO!" Wills cried, slapping his hands against his ears.

"I have to get her," I said through gritted teeth as I peeled her back from underneath the wire.

"She needs the horses," he said, "and you're hurting her."

"She doesn't *need* the horses," I promised him. "She wants to chase the horses."

"You pulled her tail."

"I couldn't let her go under that fence," I said, completely out of breath. "I'm sorry about the tail pulling."

"If she got under the fence, we couldn't have saved her," he bawled.

"We would have saved her," I said, "but you and I would have had to climb over." I sat down in the dust, scooping Cowboy onto my lap as an apology for the hair pulling. "Come here," I told Wills. He sat down beside me, rubbing Cowboy's head and resting his forehead against hers.

"I need her," he cried.

"I know," I told him, watching the dust blow off of Cowboy's filthy head. "And she needs you."

"Whoa, something's wrong," he said, jumping to his feet, pointing. "She ate an animal!"

Cowboy tilted her head toward me, as though she were about to say something witty, when I saw a huge hunk of horse dung hanging out of the side of her mouth like a soggy brown cigar—Groucho Marx–style.

"Drop it!" I demanded, attempting to maneuver her collar back over her head so I'd have something to grab onto. "DROP IT!" Cowboy held onto that dung as if it were the last horse turd on planet Earth.

"She wants to eat it," Wills hollered, backing away from us.

"I *know* she wants to eat it, but it's horse poop," I told him.

"Horrible," he agreed. "*That* is just horrible."

"Yeah, and we get to ride home with poopy breath blowing all over the car!"

I started laughing. It was funny, until the stench began to smell three-dimensional. Wills started to gag, bent over at the waist and spitting onto the chalky ground, while I stuck my fingers into Cowboy's mouth and swiped out most of the horse crap.

After pouring water over my hands, which only exaggerated the horse perfume, and cleaning my hands with baby wipes, we all piled into the car. "I smell it," Wills yelled, "I can definitely smell it." He put the tip of an index finger against each nostril. That's how Wills held his nose. I reached back and patted his grimy leg. He was even more gorgeous when he let himself get dirty.

Cowboy was now lying on the passenger seat with her chin on the center console, saliva dripping from her mouth. As I drove off, I stroked the top of her dirty blond head with the burrs sticking out the sides of it. She looked up at me through half-open eyelids and then fell back into a deep sleep. Dreaming of horse poop, I supposed. She was getting tired faster these days, but she was still a puppy. Maybe it was the old run-and-poop-out routine. I made a mental note to keep an eye on it.

* * *

I was brushing Cowboy the next day when I noticed brownish-black polka dots all over her stomach. I rushed her to Dr. Burke's.

"I'm sure this didn't just happen overnight, but I swear I didn't see it until today," I said, panicked.

"Skin discoloration is common in dogs," Dr. Burke said, "but she has giraffe skin."

"Giraffe skin?" What in the hell was he talking about?

"If you shave off a giraffe's coat, its skin mimics the spots on its fur. Giraffe skin is spotted," Dr. Burke said.

"Should I be worried?" I asked.

"Not unless she develops a rash or the area becomes inflamed. I think it's just the way her skin is." He shrugged his shoulders. "I've never seen anything like it."

"There's nothing to treat it?" I asked. "It's no big deal?"

"Not really."

Later that night, I told Wills, "You aren't going to believe this! Cowboy has giraffe skin!"

He pulled out his magnifying glass and took a really good look at her tummy.

"That's what makes her special," Wills said after poking it gently.

We were still having a terrible time getting Wills to go to restaurants with us. The noise, the other diners, and the waiters who startled him by plunking down plates and glasses onto the table, were more than he could tolerate. To Wills, the amount of time it took to sit down, order the food, eat it, pay the check and, blessedly, leave, was the equivalent of twelve trips to Dr. Todd's for shots.

Michael and I loved to eat out. Loaded up with toys and games, we picked low-key restaurants and took Wills on the off-times when there wouldn't be many customers. Still, he sat there rigid and blank. If he actually popped back into the present, he shrieked and tried to scram, making us very unpopular.

My inclination, of course, was to eat at home or pick up something to go and sit in the car. Katherine had other ideas, and believe me, her ideas were really getting on my last nerve. She'd never once been proven wrong, but my instinct was always the opposite of hers. Nonetheless, *she* had the Ph.D.

"You need to take him once a week to a restaurant," she said. "If you can't do it, Monica, then Michael, you're going to have to."

"More torture," I mumbled.

"I know, I know," she laughed, "but, again, if he doesn't get the practice, if he isn't required to go, then he'll assume you think he can't do it either—and this will only debilitate him more. He needs to know he can survive this. It's part of being a social person— of being in the world." *Why didn't* she *take him out to eat,* I wondered.

We needed reinforcements. Cowboy would have to come. All three of us needed her there.

We chose California Pizza Kitchen, because it was casual, with food Wills would eat and had a patio that allowed dogs.

"We're taking Cowboy out to eat," I said.

"She hates that," Wills said. "I'm telling you, she hates it."

"She's never been," I said.

"Trust me." He was shaking his head confidently.

"We're going."

On the way there, Wills held Cowboy's leash and walked along casually, even though he knew where we were going.

"Are you doing okay?" I asked.

"I'm just worried about Cowboy," he said, seemingly unruffled, but he was repeating himself under his breath.

As usual, whenever Cowboy was with us, there was a human stampede to pet her or ask how old she was. Wills was an old pro, answering each question as if he'd heard it a million times (and he had) and gently pulling her leash away. "Let's go, Cowboy. We've gotta eat."

Michael and I were practically cartwheeling down San Vicente Avenue. This was going to be great! Maybe I'd even have a glass of wine.

Scott, our favorite waiter, who'd delivered endless cheese pizzas, light on the sauce, to our car when Wills was unable to wait inside, was smitten with Cowboy.

"Are you kidding me?" he said. "Is this your dog?"

"It's Cowboy," Wills said.

"Oh, man, I could fall in love with this one," he said, grinning.

Wills was checking out the patio area. "We need a table where Cowboy can eat," he said, repeating it twice under his breath.

Scott shot me a knowing, *this is very good* look. I held up my crossed fingers over Wills's head.

"It just so happens that I have the perfect table for this little guy," Scott said, leading us through the maze of black wrought-iron furniture.

"Cowboy's a girl," Wills told him.

"I see." Scott sat us at the far end of the patio, leaving Cowboy in Wills's lap. "I'll get some menus."

Wills made it through ordering, the drink arrivals, and the kiddie mat and crayons. When the food arrived, he was still in his chair, alert and calm. He was so relaxed that he wished us, "Boing Appetite!"

"Boing Appetite, to you," I said, taking a sip of my wine.

I slipped Cowboy's leash around the bottom of my chair. After I'd taken two bites of my tostada pizza, I was jerked to the right. Cowboy had spied a gray schnauzer three tables away and was pulling toward him. The schnauzer barked. Oh, hell.

The next thing I knew, a delighted Cowboy, who'd taken the barking as an invitation, was lunging toward the other table. She ripped the leash from the bottom of my chair leg and was gone before I could react. The owners of the schnauzer scooped up their dog as if a rabid raccoon was heading in their direction.

"I'm sorry," I said, racing to grab Cowboy's leash.

"You should have better control over that animal," said a woman with skin stretched so tightly across her face, she looked like she was wrapped in cellophane.

"*Your* dog was the one who barked," I countered. "Mine was practically asleep."

"Still, this is a restaurant. You must have your dog on leash at all times." She gave a smug smile as if she'd just delivered the coup de grace.

"*It slipped out of my hand!*" I practically screamed, visualizing my relaxed son, my wine, and my dignity swirling right down the toilet.

The patio fell silent. I strode back to our table with Cowboy in my arms.

"Well, that was fun," I said, reaching for my wine.

Wills was laughing like a funhouse clown. He'd spit out wet doughy pizza onto his plate.

"Funny, right?" I said.

"Killing me," Wills said.

"Oh, really?" I said, teasing him. "Well, the next time that schnauzer tries to bring down Cowboy, I'm going to wrestle his owner to the ground."

More guffaws. Michael was laughing, too.

"You hold Cowboy," I told Michael. "I'm going to eat."

Somehow the hand-off went terribly wrong and Cowboy was,

once again, on the loose. Her leash wrapped itself around another chair leg and she was flipping around like a fish on a hook, much to the disdain of the other diners. Michael gathered her up in record time.

"We've gotta go," I said, feeling boxed in and aggravated.

"I'm not done eating," Wills said, smiling.

Oh, if I could count the number of times I'd used that line on him.

"We have to stay?" I asked.

"You have to find a way to make yourself comfortable," he said. "I will help you." He gave me his kiddie mat with the coloring activities.

"Thank you," I said.

The rest of the meal was a little better, with Cowboy squirming, snorting, and making a general fool out of all of us. But Wills had eaten everything on his plate, and was leaning back in his chair. Pleased.

Cowboy began riding with us to Dr. Bauman's every week. The six weeks Bauman had hoped for in the fall had turned into three months with no end in sight. Financially, it was devastating. Between Bauman's weekly remuneration, Katherine's modest fee for two sessions a week, the astronomical cost of private school, and having Lynn with Wills full-time, we were getting our monetary butts handed to us. But we knew how fortunate we were to be able to afford it.

At Bauman's one afternoon, I was sitting on my stump with Cowboy sleeping at my feet when the skies cracked open and rain poured down in cold, steady sheets.

I huddled under a navy umbrella, my leather boots soaking wet and mascara running down my cheeks. Cowboy, a leggy, wet ninja, loved the rain and started launching herself into the air, chomping at raindrops and attempting to chase every leaf that blew by. I clung to her mushy, undulating leash.

After one particularly forceful tug I fell backward, and the umbrella blew inside out. What in the hell was I doing out here?

I knocked on Bauman's door with a soggy Cowboy in tow. "We're freezing out here," I announced in response to Bauman's surprised look. "We're going to the car to start the heater." Cowboy was pawing the air and emitting a high-pitched whimper. She'd spied Wills. "We'll be back when you're done, honey," I told him. "It's only twenty minutes."

Wills's hands flew up and slapped against his cheeks like the kid in *Home Alone.* He shook his head, his eyes welling up with tears. I needed to be firm. "Wills, it's pouring down rain. I can't sit out there anymore."

"Count the thunder," Wills said.

"What?" I asked.

"Count the thunder. It's the only way."

He was talking about something we'd read a couple of months ago. If a person counted the seconds between a flash of lightning and a peal of thunder, you could determine the number of miles to the center of the storm.

"I'll try that," I said, stepping back out into the waiting room, "but there's no thunder right now."

Wills turned to Bauman, simultaneously shutting his workbook. "We're going home."

"It's up to you," Bauman said, turning to Wills.

My expression froze. I wanted to say to the relaxed, dry man whom I resented for not manning up and letting Wills know he'd be okay: *Look, we've paid for three months of something that was supposed to take a few weeks. I did not just drive this kid all the way out here in the rain in bumper-to-bumper traffic so you could give him permission to go right back home!*

But I stayed calm. After all, Dr. Bauman was doing everything in his power to accommodate Wills—including contorting his body into a Downward Dog pose to present material to Wills, who was on the floor with all of the couch cushions on top of him. He'd never complained, he never seemed frustrated or short with Wills. Why was I so angry with him?

"Wills," I said, Cowboy writhing in my arms like a Guinea worm, "you can do this. You've been with Dr. Bauman a long time now. I'll be really close by. You know where the car is, right?"

Wills didn't answer. He was staring down at the table in disbelief.

"You're okay," I said, proud of the new, reasonable me. Perhaps the fall off the stump had knocked some sense into me.

Wills vomited onto the table.

I had two choices: I could put the drenched puppy down on Bauman's gold wool carpet and clean up the vomit, or I could hold Cowboy and let the doctor clean it up.

"You can put the dog in my bathroom for a second while you clean this," he offered.

I will, I thought. *I hope she craps all over your linoleum.*

Bauman watched as I closed the bathroom door, came back to his office with a wet paper towel, cleaned Wills's face, and then the table. When it was tidy again, I said to Wills, "Honey, let's get outta here. This day has been a disaster."

"I'll see you next week," Bauman said cheerfully.

I looked at him, wondering what the hell we were even doing here. This testing was taking a toll on me—and on Wills, of course, but I was the one feeling sorry for myself. I was putting us through all of this so Wills could hide under tables and run his toes along the baseboards of Bauman's office. Nothing seemed to be getting accomplished.

"I'm not convinced we should continue this," I said.

"It's up to you," Dr. Bauman said. "I honestly do believe that Wills is doing the very best he can. This is where he is in his development."

If this was his "very best," we were in more trouble than I realized.

I retrieved Cowboy, and the three of us sloshed to the parking lot. While I rifled through my purse for the keys, Wills and Cowboy waited for me under a magnolia tree.

"It's open," I yelled, and as soon as they walked in front of the parked car beside us, someone inside accidentally pressed on the horn. Wills and Cowboy did a fright take like Scooby-Doo and Shaggy, jumping into the air.

I looked over to see an older woman sitting behind the wheel— and here's the rotten part—she was laughing. Laughing at how much she'd scared them as they stood there in the rain. I stormed over and stood right in front of her parked car.

"SHAME ON YOU!" I screamed at her. "DO YOU LIKE FRIGHTENING SMALL CHILDREN?" She quit laughing and stared wide-eyed at the dripping lunatic in front of her. I might as well have been limping through a snowy hedge maze with an ax given the look on her face. "DON'T YOU EVER DO THAT AGAIN— TO ANYONE!" She turned on her car, threw it in reverse, and tore out of there.

I was expecting my son to be staring at me slack-jawed and horrified, but he was bent over at the waist—laughing.

"Whoa, I totally lost it," I said. "What's so funny?"

"SHAME ON YOU!" he yelled, wagging his finger at me. "You told that lady, SHAME ON YOU!"

"And that's funny?" I asked, tickled and a bit confused. "Well, she honked at my sweeties, so I told her what I thought." I corralled them into the car, with Wills snorting and carrying on.

"SHAME ON YOU," Wills yelled, again. "You were *so* mad!"

"You're darn right I was mad. She scared you guys, and when you jumped, she laughed about it."

"She laid a patch," Wills said, "and a skid mark."

"Where did you hear about 'laying a patch' or leaving 'skid marks'?" I asked.

"JoAnn." That made sense. JoAnn was always peeling out in her hot rod.

Wills asked if he could call Daddy on the cell phone—another first.

I dialed Michael's number. "Hi. Wills wants to talk to you." I handed the phone over the backseat.

"What a wonderful surprise!" Michael said, but all he heard was giggling. "Wills? Are you there?"

"Mommy just told an old lady, SHAME ON YOU," he said.

"Why did she do that?"

"Because she honked her horn and scared us," Wills said, giving into a laughing fit all over again. I could hear Michael laughing, too.

Wills refused to express anger—would not acknowledge that he even had angry feelings except when Katherine pressed him to talk about it. Watching me erupt—my outrage unchecked—obviously released pent-up tension in him that came out in the form of laughter. I had freaked out, in an absolute rage, and the world didn't end. Wills needed that laugh. *I* did, too.

Later that night as we climbed into bed, Cowboy sauntered up and stood on her hind legs next to the bed. Wills squealed with delight.

"Cowboy wants up! Can she sleep with us?" The loss of even more space in our bed was unacceptable.

"Sure," I said. And she did.

The next morning, we had a discussion over cinnamon toast and cereal.

"Isn't it great that Cowboy slept with you?" I asked.

"She was really happy."

"It might be time for you to move back into your own bed again,

now that you have Cowboy to squeeze. What do you think?" He dropped his spoon into his bowl. "Cowboy likes the pink bed," he said, looking up for my response.

"She does," I said, "but she's pretty good with transitions. It's going to be an adjustment for both of you."

"When?"

"Today is Monday, so let's try it on Friday," I said. "How does that sound?"

"I don't know."

"We can talk about it this week and get ready," I said. "Katherine will have some good ideas on how to make it easier for you."

He put his head down on his arm and dissolved into tears.

I swear I couldn't take these moments. If that were all he was up against, I could deal with it, but he'd been pushed and shoved into uncomfortable situations his entire life. The pink bed felt like his safe haven, but I hoped that his own bedroom would be the next safe place. Katherine was sure of it.

As the week unfolded, reliable Cowboy continued to stand on her back legs, begging to sleep in the pink bed. It was cemented. Wills would have his sidekick for the four-poster transition.

When bedtime came on Friday, we put Wills in his own bed. He was fairly pissed off and wanted us to leave him alone.

"Don't you want to read?" I asked.

"Just go," he said, turning toward the wall. His light-up globe, a white noise machine muffling sounds from the rest of the house, his new down comforter, and the pillows he personally picked out from the pink bed did nothing to relax him.

Cowboy meandered down the hall toward our bedroom.

"There goes your buddy," I said. Wills didn't move. Cowboy was probably standing on her back legs beside the pink bed wondering where everyone went.

"COWBOY," I called, "WHERE'S WILLS?" She came back around the corner, her ears cocked and nostrils flaring. "WHERE IS HE?" I teased.

She broke out in a run, sliding on her butt the last two feet. Spotting the Wills-size lump shoved against the wall, she jumped onto the bed without needing to be lifted and began digging for Wills.

"Cowboy, stop it," came the muffled voice beneath the blankets. Hearing his voice made Cowboy more determined to unearth him. She tunneled more vigorously. "SHE'S AFTER ME! HELP!"

Soon Cowboy was licking Wills's face and pushing herself against his stomach, settling in for a long night. Wills didn't look so sure.

"Stay here, Mommy," he said, sniffing back tears.

"I'm not going anywhere," I told him, lying on the floor.

He reached his hand down and patted my arm. Then he wrapped it around Cowboy.

I lay there, looking up at the ceiling fan with the glow-in-the-dark stars stuck to the bottom of every paddle. When it turned, each glowing star blurred into a solid circle, and it looked like Saturn was twirling above us. I'd put those up so many years ago, I'd forgotten they were even there.

Later that night, Michael and I snuck quietly into Wills's room to find him sound asleep in the bed we'd ordered for him four years earlier, his freckled cheeks rosy from the heat of Cowboy wrapped around him like a sarong.

"What if he's too hot?" I worried, realizing exactly what this moment meant—Wills was separating from me. I'd imagined I'd be giddy, relieved, happy for all of us, but I was overcome by a sense of grief that I hadn't expected.

"If he gets too hot, he'll wake up," Michael assured me.

Cowboy lifted her head as if to say, *I've got him. You guys get a life.* Right. That.

"Let's inaugurate our bed," Michael whispered, pulling me toward a place where we'd never once had sex. (We'd bought the pink bed after Wills was born.)

I looked at my husband, who was suddenly unfamiliar—not someone with whom I slept *in a bed*—that was way too intimate. At some unknown point, our lovemaking had become date sex—on the family room floor or the desk in the office or against the refrigerator. We'd become creative with furniture and heavy appliances, but now our bed was the new and exotic place. Was this the guy I wanted to have husband-and-wife sex with for the next forty years of my life?

"You look worried," Michael said.

"I'm not," I lied.

I gazed back at Wills, nostalgically. It hadn't all been a walk in the park. We'd been vomited on countless times, and kneed in our groins and stomachs. Michael was accidentally squeezed out of bed one night, and ended up at St. John's Emergency Room at 4:30 in the morning getting liquid stitches in his cheek. There were countless farts, colds we passed around to each other like paper plates at a picnic, and snoring so loud I actually had to wrap a pillowcase around my head, until the two of them informed me that I was the snorer.

I followed the man I'd loved way before my stretch marks down the hallway to our room. I'd underestimated the value of privacy—and, of course, a firm mattress. Michael and I were back in the saddle.

The night before Wills's dance recital with Kathleen at CCS, he lost his first baby tooth. I put on Styx's *The Grand Illusion* CD in celebration. Every summer Wills had one band he'd listen to repeatedly. We'd just retired They Might Be Giants, and Styx was his new love. Wills came running out with Cowboy right behind him.

"Let's dance," he said, grabbing my hands. He started swinging my arms and twisting his body, which was way too much fun for Cowboy. She stood on her back feet with her front paw against Wills's leg.

"She wants to dance!" he said. I danced us around the room a little bit and Cowboy followed.

"She must know you lost your first tooth!"

"She's funny," he said.

"She loves to dance just like you," I told him. I lifted Cowboy up and danced around with her in my arms.

"I'll do that," Wills said, taking her from me. With great effort, the two of them whirled around the room together, Wills's flushed cheeks and Cowboy's maturing long, skinny body bouncing like a pogo stick.

Lynn called later that night to discuss the recital.

"He's doing really well with his dancing," she said. "He knows all the moves."

"So he's participating?"

"He gets up there with everyone else," she said. "I think you're in for a big surprise."

"I can't wait," I said. "Michael's coming too."

"Well, I hope so!" Lynn said.

"Wills finally lost that baby tooth that was hanging by a thread," I told her.

"His first tooth!" she exclaimed. "He's getting so big!"

At bedtime, I asked Wills, "Do you want to put your tooth on the windowsill or under your pillow?"

"How big is this fairy?" Wills wanted to know.

"Well, the Tooth Fairy is only about three inches tall," I said.

"I don't want her to take my tooth, so let's write her a memo." I ran to get some paper. "Okay, shoot."

To the Tooth Fairy,
For the Tooth Fairy,

This is Wills Price. Do not take my tooth with you tonight. You can admire it, but please leave it behind. Thank you.

From Wills
About Wills

After he went to sleep, JoAnn came over to help me with the Tooth Fairy—not that it was complicated, but she had a great idea. She brought over finely ground, sparkly fairy dust she'd purchased from the Bodhi Tree in West Hollywood and sprinkled it on his pillow, leaving a trail that led all the way to the outside window ledge. This was where JoAnn prevailed—creating magic. She had a little dust left, so she sprinkled a tiny bit on Cowboy's back. I laid out fifty-cent pieces I'd been collecting, but JoAnn pulled gold coins out of her pocket. "We have to use these, don't you think?" I wasn't going to argue.

"Sacajawea coins!" Wills yelled when he woke up. "And magic gold!" He bent down to examine the glittering dust. "Look, she came in under the window here." His hair was sticking up in a swirl right in the back where he'd slept on it. Cowboy came padding in. "Oh no, she stood on Cowboy!" He giggled. "Look, Mommy, she stood right on her!"

JoAnn was brilliant.

At his dance performance the next morning, thankfully, only the kindergarteners and their guests were invited, so the auditorium was spacious and quiet. The children were sitting in a circle, and Wills, dressed in an orange T-shirt and bright orange beachcombers, was somber, but not crying. Kathleen began, "To all our moms and dads and friends sitting over there, let's wave at them with our elbows." They waggled their elbows at us, even Wills.

"Now wave with your eyebrows." Everyone laughed. "Can you wave with your eyebrows?" She started out so small, moving at *their* pace, and the parents were charmed.

"Let's wave with our shoulders.

"Let's wave with our spines—our backs all loose. Good work.

"Let's say hello with our pinkies, and our noses." She laughed and the kids broke into laughter. She asked them to stand. As she recited the following lines, the children repeated them.

> *Ain't been to college.*
> *Ain't been to school.*
> *Ain't been to Frisco.*
> *But I ain't no fool.*

They continued repeating after her, but now they were moving their bodies. Wills looked around as they shifted their positions.

Stand right up.
Take a step back.
Jump front-back-front
Jump out-in-out
Hop on one foot
Hop on the other foot
Hop jump hop
Out cross out. (They jumped with their legs apart,
    crossed them, then jumped back into place again.)
Do your own jump
FREEZE! (The kids stop mid-move.)
Take one step back.
And sit right down.

Wills followed along nicely, mostly jumping in the air with his hands at his sides, but he was performing. I wouldn't have said he was relaxed, but he was in front of us, and he was a part of his group. Michael and I were smiling—*huge.*

Kathleen went on: "Now we're going to do our Mexican Hat Dance."

Terri called out names and each child joined their partners.

Wills walked toward Lidia, but when she reached out, he didn't take her hand. She didn't seem to mind and they took their places. He was focused and serious. As the kids stood in two lines facing their partners, the music began.

Wills's hands were behind his back and Lidia's were on her hips.

Wills jumped up and down, keeping his hands in place, but was unable to clap with the others. Who cares? He was *dancing*! When Kathleen announced it was time for the swing, Wills and Lidia entwined arms square dance-style and walked around in a circle, then they reversed. Lynn was right there, but standing away from Wills, watching the group, ever present.

Michael and I were enchanted. That's the only word. Wills looked over to see if we were watching and a shy grin crossed his face. At that moment, the room fell silent for me. All of Wills's challenges and my worries fell away as I watched him, my boy, moving in slow motion, twirling and dancing to the music, his feet kicking to the beat. He *knew* the dance and had given in to the music, to the idea of all of us watching him—he was enjoying himself.

The next thing I knew, Wills was standing in front of me, taking both of my hands and leading *me* onto the floor. As I danced the Mexican Hat Dance with my son, everything around us blurred until it was just the two of us. For the first time ever, I didn't have the urge to take his hand and run.

Wills was happy.

We *belonged.*

CHAPTER ELEVEN

In spite of my doubts about the effectiveness of Wills's sessions with Dr. Bauman, he had continued seeing him weekly. Now it was March, and Wills was heading into his last appointment.

Wills was terrible at good-byes. He didn't let anything or anyone in his world fall by the wayside. For instance, after each session, Dr. Bauman had rewarded Wills with a Baskin-Robbins gift certificate. Wills had collected more than twenty-five of them, but when I encouraged him to use them, he broke down into sobs. We paid cash for the bowl of Quarterback Crunch while Wills shoved the gift certificate back into his pocket.

"Then they'll be gone," he said. "They're *gifts.*"

"Yes, the certificate is a gift so that you can buy a better gift: ice cream!" He'd been stacking them in an old wooden jewelry box I'd given him and that's where they remained.

At the beginning of his final appointment, on March 13, Wills quickly removed his shoes and socks, throwing them behind a stack of toy containers where they would be difficult to reach. Dr. Bauman's efforts to administer the final test were hindered when Wills started saying, "I'm not feeling good AT ALL today. I have butterflies in my stomach." When he was told that the test would not be continued, he stated, "My stomach feels a little better, but not much."

Bauman's stump and I had weathered thunderstorms, hot Santa

Ana winds, smoggy Pasadena afternoons, and Cowboy knocking me on my ass and gnawing on the bark. I wouldn't miss it.

Still, I dreaded the next step—reading Bauman's report. I quietly prayed it would contain a map—an overview—a clear shot at a safe passage toward a bright future for our Wills.

After his last session, Wills came out of Bauman's office with red swollen eyes holding a package.

"Just a parting gift," Bauman said, creating more tears.

"Good-byes are difficult for Wills," I said.

"When you watch that," he said to Wills, pointing to the gift, "you can think of our time together."

"Thank you for everything," I said, dragging Cowboy (whom I think Bauman secretly despised) toward our car.

I looked in the rearview mirror to see Wills holding up a National Geographic DVD box with an ominous-looking tornado tearing across the cover.

Wills's new obsession with weather had begun several months earlier, when he discovered The Weather Channel. He now had countless books on everything from hurricanes to ice storms to why erupting volcanoes created their *own* weather. Wills slaved over drawings of tornados, making more than twenty of them in one week—he had his own barometer and digital weather station from Brookstone. Dr. Bauman's gift was perfect. He held it on his lap all the way home.

I made popcorn, and Wills, Cowboy, and I settled onto the couch. When I flipped on the DVD player, the first thing we saw was a dead woman in a filthy housecoat being carried out of a demolished house on a wooden door. Her lifeless arm was swinging down—and this was before the credits. Wills sat frozen, staring blankly at the screen.

I scrambled over the top of the coffee table, knocking over my Coke, to turn off the TV, but could still hear the howling wind and the screaming. I crawled all over the bookshelves trying to silence the storm.

"You have to turn off the TV *and* the DVD," Wills said, the

untouched popcorn bowl tilted on his lap. What was Bauman thinking?

"That certainly wasn't meant for little boys," I said, trying to catch my breath.

"Terrible." Wills began to cry. "He's *terrible* for giving that to me. It's a good thing I'm not seeing him anymore." I could tell that he already missed Bauman.

"We can stop by and say hello," I told him.

"Not after this," he said, pointing toward the television.

"Dr. Bauman wanted you to have a nice gift," I told Wills. "He bought it because he knew you love weather and tornados. He just should have watched it first."

"Terrible." Wills popped out the disc, walked to the kitchen, and stood by the trash can.

"You can throw it out if you want to." Again, more tears.

"I can't, Mommy, I can't throw it away."

"I'll keep it for you," I told him, "But we're not going to watch it, okay?"

"Certainly not."

I tossed it into the top of my closet.

"How about *Lilo and Stitch*?" I suggested, and we snuggled up.

Bauman's written report cost us a stunning $4,000. I must have stared at that invoice for more than twenty minutes in complete disbelief. No parent or therapist we'd ever talked to had heard of such an exorbitant amount. He justified the bill by tallying the number of hours it took him to analyze the data, come to his conclusions, and detail them on paper. Our insurance covered only a small portion of this, so Michael and I were in a panic. It seemed that everything we were doing to help Wills was cleaning out our checking account—forget our savings, that money had long since evaporated—but we had to get our hands on the critical information that would help Wills.

We put off reroofing the house, which could probably wait until winter, L.A.'s rainy season. But it had been worrying me since we'd found a leak early in January.

Dr. Bauman's conclusions were crushing—$4,000 to get the worst news of our lives, far worse than the dead lady lying on the door in that DVD. The information came in waves, a few of the surging crests being:

Wills, at times, has difficulty perceiving and interpreting the stimuli of his environment in a realistic and accurate manner. Such distortions could lead not only to misperceptions, but misjudgments and faulty behavioral responses.

Wills has an aversion to the expression of anger and aggression, stating that he does not like boys or girls who fight and stated that he does not like "to fight." He identified the thing that his friends do not understand about him is that, "I don't like to fight. They love to fight. They just go for it and never say 'no.' "

Wills can tolerate cognitive and academic challenges only for brief periods of time before becoming cognitively and emotionally overwhelmed. Wills also evidences some significant difficulties with oral language at both the listening and expressive levels.

His language, which was expected due to his autistic qualities, is extremely concrete. He responded to the item, "I dream about . . ." with "Genie." When he came into the office with sand in his shoes, and I asked him to "dump your shoes in the trash can," he took them off and threw them in the trash. Although Wills has benefited greatly from his psychotherapy, his presentation during this evaluation makes it apparent that he remains quite anxious and fragile. His anxiety would be best understood in the context of the challenges that Wills encounters socially, emotionally, and cognitively.

Diagnosis: *High Functioning Autism*

Recommendations: Educational Therapist
                      Social Skills Group
                      Occupational Therapy
                      Speech and Language Specialist
                      Continuing Psychotherapy

The diagnosis was expected, but reading paragraph after clinical paragraph, forty-eight pages of what Wills could not do—how ill at ease he was with the world and himself—was crushing and, in its formality, conclusive.

Michael and I read the report separately. I could feel it pulling us

apart. The strain that had been put on Wills's future was so debilitat-
ing that Michael and I didn't know how to even admit to each other
how devastated we were. Wills had endured so much, he'd come so
far in the six months since beginning kindergarten and putting up
with the weekly testing. But for every small triumph, every shining
moment, he was still tiptoeing through a minefield of difficulties.
And that report detailed every single one of them, like pinpoints on
a panzer map.

Later that week, Michael joined me at Katherine's to discuss
Bauman's findings. We were both deflated. How could a child who
built spaceships from old scraps he'd found in the garage not be
capable of re-creating simple drawings on a page? How could someone who looked at the night sky and pointed out the International
Space Station, barely visible, flashing by, someone who asked to go
to Dutton's bookstore to read about what stars were and what made
the moon, not be considered curious? Our baby, who was spouting
information about how the engines of a 747 were assembled after
I'd read it to him only once, was not able to learn? It wasn't possible.
I didn't want to believe Bauman, but there it was in wallet-busting
black-and-white.

We blamed ourselves, how could we not? We hadn't done
enough or provided all of the support he needed. Wills's promising
future had snapped in two.

"First of all, there's a lot of information here," Katherine said,
calmly. "We need to take it slow. We also need to remember that
these reports are far from perfect. They serve as a device, that's all—a
way for us to have a sense of where Wills is so that we can get him
the specialists he needs. This is not written in stone," she assured us,
"it's a tool, that's all."

"Where's the hope in this?" I asked. "It looks hopeless." I threw
my copy, with my underlined sentences and illegible notes scribbled
all over it, onto her coffee table.

"I know it does," she gently assured me. "I know it's hard, but
think of it this way: the more information we have to sort through,

the quicker and more specific we can be in helping Wills. This is not an ending, it's a beginning."

To me it felt like the beginning *and* the ending of the whole world.

That weekend, Wills and Cowboy spent hours playing in a tent he'd built using every chair in the house and some metal folding chairs from the garage as well. Our beds were stripped of blankets and sheets that had become ceilings and walls.

The meandering patchwork tent wound its way through the front room, down the hallway, and out into the backyard. There was much discussion, tinkling of dog tags, and a few unfortunate ripping sounds as they bumbled their way through. Cowboy bullied her way ahead of Wills, pulling down the sides of the tent with her teeth, exposing the two of them.

"DON'T LOOK!" Wills yelled, frantically rehanging the wall. "IT'S TOP SECRET IN HERE!"

Wills didn't know the report had come back and wouldn't have cared even if he did. He was too busy dragging a laundry basket filled with stuffed animals into the tent.

"Cowboy's chewing up these animals," Wills informed me through the blankets. "They are really mad."

"Bring them back out," I suggested.

"She'll follow them," he said. There was some rustling around in there. "I'll give her Johnny." Johnny was a raggedy, old polar bear.

I stared at the Cowboy-and-Wills-shaped bulge on the side of the tent. The innocence of that bump in the blanket, of the stuffed animals that were now being hurled out of a small gap between the sheets "for their own safety," as Wills put it, only made me sadder. I wanted to keep them just where they were—safe, forever.

I couldn't assure Wills that life was going to get easier, that he wouldn't always have to work harder than his peers. That there might be a day when he wouldn't need therapy, or be confused socially. I couldn't protect him from everything. Someday he'd be taller than me, he'd be twenty and then thirty. What would that look like for him? How would we get him ready?

At school, Lynn was blunt. "Bauman is wrong! It's like he's talking about another kid! I don't know the child in this report, that's all I'm saying." She held the folder above her head, jabbing the sky.

I was too exhausted to be indignant. So I started at the top of the list of recommendations and called Vanessa Platis-Silver, an educational therapist who came highly recommended, and set up an appointment. She'd named her company Silver Lining Educational Services, which sounded good to me. Wills asked to bring Cowboy to Vanessa's, but I was concerned that she'd erupt into a drooling Tasmanian Devil. At home when she pulled a teak end table across the yard and then chewed it to bits or unearthed my box shrubs, I found it forgivable, fun-loving even. It was lazy of me, not teaching her better behavior, but I was tapped out in all directions. Yet, Cowboy was getting so much bigger and harder to handle, that when we brought her to unexplored places with pristine lawns and new faces in need of licking, she was nearly impossible to control.

Still, I wanted this to go well with Vanessa, which meant Cowboy needed to come.

"I can't go without her," Wills cautioned.

"We can bring Cowboy, but she has to wait in the car," I told him.

"I need her *inside*," he urged.

"She'll be right outside of Vanessa's house," I told him. "You can look out and see her whenever you need to."

"She can't sit in the car when she's all crazy," he argued.

"We'll take a walk before we go, and she'll be fine with the windows down." Wills looked skeptical. "I'll check on her while we're there," I promised. I'd never left Cowboy in the car. It was only sixty-four degrees, so the temperature would be fine, but I could easily picture the chewed leather seats and deep fang marks on the steering wheel. I packed lots of treats.

* * *

"Hi, Wills. I'm Vanessa," she said, extending her hand. He shook it, shyly. "After talking to your mom, I couldn't *wait* to meet you."

Wills stood with his back against her front door. Vanessa looked at me, "Wills can play with my boys until we're done talking." She began walking toward the back of the house. My internal alarm sounded, *Didn't I say he was autistic? He can't just walk into a stranger's house and play with kids he barely knows.* Two adorable mop-headed boys came running down the hallway with walkie-talkies. One was about nine years old and the other was about Wills's age.

"Where are *we* going to be?" I asked.

"I have a little schoolhouse out back," she said. "Wills, do you want to see my schoolhouse?" He followed us. The boys came too, tumbling out the back door, curious.

There beside an enormous pine tree sat a small schoolhouse with a brick walkway leading up to the front door. Inside, it was just big enough for a wooden table (Vanessa sat on one side and the student on the other) and bookcases built into all four walls. I knew immediately that this safe, adorable little schoolhouse and this charming, down-to-earth woman would be a haven for Wills—a place he could relax, a person who would hold him in high esteem, so that he could do his work. She looked like she knew exactly what she was doing.

Vanessa and I sat down in the schoolhouse, and Wills went back into the house with her boys. I was ashamed for thinking he couldn't handle it. Were my expectations so low? Was I holding him back because I was too cautious? I made myself a promise to regain the optimism I'd felt before reading Dr. Bauman's report. Hope would be somewhere in front of us, not behind.

"Did you read the report?" I asked Vanessa.

"Yes," she said, looking at me with an open, smiling face, "I did."

"Do you think you can help him?" I asked.

"Yes, this report doesn't scare me at all." She held it up and threw it in the trash. I was flabbergasted. You don't throw out a $4,000 detailed report! Or do you? I just might love this woman.

Suddenly, three boys ran by the window with Cowboy on her leash. Oh, crap!

"Is it okay that Wills took the dog out of the car?" I asked, looking at her manicured lawn and imagining it post-Cowboy.

"Oh, sure," she said, "it was probably my boys who convinced him to do it." I hoped she had a hose handy.

She continued, "I don't know the kid in this report, I only know that there's a terrific boy at my house right now who needs support and love and attention. That's all I need to know."

Another angel had appeared, this time on a cul-de-sac in Granada Hills.

A few weeks before kindergarten ended for the year, I pulled up behind the playground midday to help decorate the bulletin board for the CCS Health Fair. I was curious to see Wills interacting with his class. I spotted him pulling four little girls around the blacktop in an old wooden wagon. He was in front with his arms stretched out behind him, his upper body pressed forward, to compensate for the heavy load.

"Go faster," Sacha squealed.

"We *have* to get to the store," Lauren said. "It's closing."

Wills put his head down and pulled harder. It was hot, and his bangs were plastered against his forehead. I felt a pang of uneasiness. Was he having fun or just being bossed around by the girls?

A few seconds later, the five of them arrived at the imaginary store and the girls jumped out of the wagon and hugged Wills with such exuberance that they accidentally knocked him down—all five of them in a small pile on the blacktop.

"Oh, my," Wills said, untangling himself from the girls and hurrying to his feet. Sacha wiped him off.

No doubt that Cowboy had loosened him up. Her natural instinct to rough-house allowed Wills to recognize that he was safe even if he got knocked around a little by an excited bullet of fur (or an overenthusiastic gang of girls).

"Thanks for getting us here *so fast*," Lauren said, in a baby voice. "You're a good daddy." And the game was back on—Wills had rebounded.

As I locked the car, I overheard one of the girls say, "I'll be the mom."

His grin said it all. Pretend play, just as Katherine promised, was finally here.

Just as Wills's social life on the playground was heating up, kindergarten was winding down. Had we really made it through the longest, happiest, strangest, and most rewarding nine months of our lives?

Wills turned seven in May, and we celebrated by having a certified paleontologist come to the house and do a dinosaur presentation for the kids. This was as extravagant and ridiculous as it sounds, but Wills had only celebrated two birthdays with parties, so in our excitement, we overdid it.

Wills was alert and fairly relaxed at the party, holding Cowboy on her leash the entire time. When the cake came out, despite our announcements that we would not be singing "Happy Birthday," the children broke into song. Michael and I ran to Wills's side, but we didn't need to. "They sing that at school all the time," he said, waving us off.

When everyone was gone and Cowboy was sacked out on Wills's bed, he opened his gifts.

"Hey, there's another gift from Lynn," I said. He'd already opened a kit from her where you dig plastic dinosaur bones out of hardened sand. I looked in the gift bag. "She knitted you a hat, Wills."

"She did?" he asked. "She knitted me a hat?" I pulled it out and showed it to him. It was orange—one of his all-time favorite colors—with white edging. "Now I saw this before . . . getting made," Wills said. "You know what she did at rest time when she was watching me rest?"

"What'd she do?" Michael asked.

"I saw her knitting something that looks like this." He twirled it around on the end of his finger. "I saw this." He laughed. Lynn was the best.

After surviving yet another traumatic end-of-the-year sing-along—this time wearing giant ear cuffs from the shooting range to help block out the sound—he greeted us outside his classroom. Standing right in front of the gate where he'd cried so hard that first day of school was an undeniably gorgeous, grinning first-grader.

We rushed home from school that day to pick up Cowboy. Michael had to return to work after the Sing, but Wills and I decided to take a drive to Sycamore Cove Beach, where dogs were allowed off-leash. We were ready to celebrate.

We had just set down the cooler and Wills's brand-new boogie board when Michael surprised us by walking across the sand, smiling.

"Daddy!" Wills yelled, running to him. "Cowboy wants me to swim with her."

"She does?" he asked, giving him a kiss. Wills was leery of big waves and usually avoided wading in the ocean, but lately, with Cowboy sprinting in and out of the surf, he'd been testing the water more and more.

"I can't believe you're here," I said, grabbing a kiss too.

"I got your message saying where you guys were going, so I thought I'd duck out and join you." He held up a bottle of champagne in one hand, and a Coke for Wills in the other. "It's a big day," he said.

"I'll say," I agreed. "I love it that you brought champagne!"

"You deserve a crate of it," he said, leaning over to put the drinks in the cooler.

Cowboy created a mini-sandstorm racing over to Michael.

"LOOK OUT!" Wills yelled.

"Okay, Cowboy, okay," Michael said, leaning down to scruff her neck. She jumped up, paws against his knees, raced away, and then tore back again. Michael turned to Wills. "You want to go in the water, buddy?"

"Maybe," Wills said, shrugging his shoulders.

"What's this?" He picked up the boogie board.

"It's mine!" Wills said. "We bought it at Big Five Sports across from Katherine's."

"Do you want to try this out in the water?" Michael asked.

"No!" Wills said.

"Do you mind if I try it?"

"Really?" Wills laughed.

"I'm not *that* old," Michael teased. The two of them walked down to the water's edge, with Cowboy racing back and forth between them. Wills personified the classic California kid with his blond hair and shiny black wetsuit. He didn't go very far into the water, but *always* had on his wetsuit. His behind looked like two little bears in a bag wrestling.

Michael walked right in, wearing only khaki shorts, as if the water wasn't sixty-two degrees, and rode in on a wave.

"Nice goin'," I called out. "You had a foam wreath around your face."

"Attractive, I'm sure," he said, smoothing his hair back. "Do you want to try it?"

"The water's too cold for me today," I said. "You go ahead."

On the next wave, Cowboy raced back down the beach and ambushed Michael as he plowed into shallower water. When he stood up, she backed up and started barking, but it wasn't her usual high-pitched puppy bark, she sounded like a *huge* dog! Her voice had changed. Wills and I were squealing and jumping up and down because she was killing us. Maybe the competing sound of the crashing waves had forced her to really make herself heard, or maybe she just wanted Wills to pay attention, but it was the funniest (and deepest) sound coming from such a petite, gangly eight-month-old puppy.

"Wills, she found her true voice," I gushed. "She's definitely a Price."

Cowboy, oblivious to the excitement she'd whipped up, paced back and forth along the shoreline, eyes glued to Michael. When he rode back in, she crashed through the water and jumped on his back. He carried her in one arm and the boogie board in the other.

"I want her to chase *me*," Wills squealed.

"Sure," Michael said, winking at me. Our pool was still uncharted territory, but here was our son, willing to take on the Pacific.

Michael walked out with Wills until he was almost up to his waist, and then ran along beside him, holding onto the board. Every single time, Cowboy came running out to greet him, knocking him into the water. When he got back up on the board, she'd back up and bark.

"She's got the crazies," Wills said.

"She's a beach dog," Michael said.

I watched the three of them dig holes in the sand until just after the sun had set and the light was finally gone. This was one of the first worry-free days I'd had since September. I hated to see it end.

* * *

June was gone in a flash, as Wills made up for the lost time he'd spent indoors at school. He replanted his garden, jumped on his trampoline, and built train setups that wound around the patio and under the shrubs.

Whatever he did, Cowboy was right beside him.

Their most ambitious project was the pond Wills decided to dig right beside the back walkway. One trip to the Home Depot for a prefab pool liner, a pump, and a fountain, and we were in business.

When we got home, Wills turned the pond liner upside down and asked me to trace around the outside with chalk. He would have done it himself, but chalk gave him the "chills." Textures were still a problem, but nothing like before. Now he was wearing shirts with tags, and I'd gotten him into his first pair of jeans the other day. He still wore protective gloves in his garden but not when he painted or played with clay. Those days were long gone.

It took us three days, and several visits from JoAnn for technical support, to get everything in place. But the pond was finally complete . . . except for the koi. After a pet store run (I know, I know), Wills released the fish, flashing orange and silver, in the water. I had to admit, Wills's little koi pond looked pretty good.

Cowboy, of course, *loved* it—she was barking and jumping around, positively gleeful. No one loved water more than Cowboy.

On a hot July afternoon, Lynn called. "What's up over there?"

"We miss you," I said. Putting my hand over the receiver, I whispered to Wills, "It's Lynn."

"Can you bring Wills over to school tomorrow?" she asked. "I was thinking it might be a good time to show him the boys' bathroom while nobody's there."

"Sure," I said, "we can come."

"Can I bring Cowboy?" Wills asked, not even knowing where we were going.

"Can he bring Cowboy?" I asked.

"Probably not Cowboy, but one of his smaller animals can come," she said.

I put my hand over the receiver again, "No Cowboy because we're going to stop by school. You can bring a hermit crab or a hamster, though."

When we showed up, Lynn had a large bag of BBQ potato chips (Wills's favorite snack), a camera, and her twelve-year-old son, Ripley, who'd just graduated from CCS and was as calm and funny as his mom.

"Ripley's going to show you the ins and outs of the boys' bathroom," Lynn said, "and then we're going to have a snack."

Wills took three steps back. He was holding his plastic box filled with seven hermit crabs.

"Your crabs can come," Lynn said, waving him in. "I can't go into the boys bathroom because I'm a girl, but Ripley's an expert. He's been using that bathroom for seven years!"

Ripley gave Wills the thumbs-up, but Wills was on the verge of tears.

"No one's at school today," said Lynn, "so you can look around without being interrupted."

"My eye hurts," Wills said.

"Well, that's not going to keep you from hanging out in the bathroom for a minute or two." I smiled at Lynn. "We can keep the door open."

"Go ahead, Wills," I said. "Check it out."

"Mom, why don't you come back in half an hour," Lynn said, shooing me away. She was mighty for being so tiny.

Wills gave me his please-don't-leave-me-here look, but he was in excellent hands. "I'll see you in half an hour," I told him.

The next morning, Lynn brought a small photo album to the house. She sat on the couch with Wills and they looked through the pictures from the day before—the solitary toilet that sat in the only stall, Big Jake the hermit crab balanced on the back of the urinal, and a picture of Wills looking miserable, pointing to the MEN'S ROOM sign. She'd gone to the one-hour photo place and filled this little book with pictures for Wills to look at all summer long.

"This will help you prepare for first grade, and a whole new bathroom experience," she said.

"Can't I still go in the office?" he asked, closing the book.

"We'll see, my friend," she said, eyes mischievous. "You might grow up a little over the summer and want to be with your friends in the bathroom. You never know."

Lynn was right, Wills was growing up, and he was about to pass a major test: saying good-bye to Cowboy and me for an entire week.

It was finally time for the long-planned, much-anticipated, Daddy and Wills Chicago-to-L.A. Amtrak trip. Not only was Wills able to get past the sadness of leaving home for a week, he also handled the bathrooms on the train with aplomb. Well, he did attempt to pee with his hands covering his ears, which didn't fare well for the front of his pants, but he managed nonetheless. He didn't let his bathroom fears keep him from enjoying his big trip—just the guys.

I picked them up at Union Station with a homemade "Welcome Home" sign and Cowboy by my side. She and I had gotten there two hours early in our eager anticipation to see them. When Wills came off that train, he looked like he'd grown two inches, and emotionally, he had. I squeezed the daylights out of him while Cowboy jumped up on him and made silly, happy growly sounds. I didn't stop staring at that kid for weeks.

The second big summer leap was Wills's sudden interest in our pool. When his friends came over, they'd jump right in, especially Sacha, who swam like a fish. Wills would sit on the side and throw in sinkers shaped like sharks or striped beach balls. He also had a plastic remote-controlled boat he'd cruise around on the water, leaving a small V-shaped wake. But he'd always been uneasy about going in himself.

We had a small pool party and even Amanda came. By now we knew most of the other parents, and they were so fun and supportive that whatever she had to say, and there was always something, it just rolled right off my back. But the best part was, I no longer worried about laying out Spode platters or whether my house was clean enough. It was just nice having other families over. I hoped Wills would relax enough to at least dangle his feet in the water.

He used to hate the pool. At least now he tolerated it. When he was two or three, he'd have a screaming fit if I tried to swim. Now that he was much older, he didn't care if Michael or I swam, he just preferred to sit on the dry tiles near the shallow end. Now, during Cowboy's first summer with us, everything changed.

If I dove into the deep end, Cowboy would run to the exact spot where I'd been standing and fling herself into the water. With her front legs arched and her head slightly lifted, she usually glided in, but there was the occasional belly-flop. When I'd emerge two seconds later, Cowboy was already there, her face just inches from mine.

"Don't do it, Cowboy," I'd warn, but she couldn't help herself. She'd lunge at me, her front paws pushing on my shoulders, and down I'd go.

"She's a real swimmer," Wills would say. "Did you see that?"

"Did I *see* it?" I'd ask, climbing out. "She practically drowned me."

"Not really, right, Mommy?"

"Not really, honey." I was looking for my towel. Cowboy was shaking off water—not once, not twice, but an even four times. Wills pulled a towel up over his head and just left it there.

"Thanks, Cowboy," I said. I was covered in thin blond porcupine quills.

Cowboy was beginning to lose quite a bit of body hair for some reason. I grabbed a towel and gently wiped her face, careful not to rub off any more of her coat. Maybe she was shedding because of the heat.

I rolled her onto her back to check out the fur on her stomach when Wills, who'd been sitting with his feet tucked under his butt, fell into the pool. In less than three seconds, I was pulling him up off the bottom, even though he was in only three feet of water. Cowboy followed. Before I knew it, the three of us were floating around in the hairy blue water, Wills coughing, Cowboy wheezing, and me, gasping.

I held Wills around the waist with his back against my chest. My heart was pumping, and I was hiccupping through my sobs. What if I hadn't been right there? What if he didn't know that all he had to do was stand up?

"Are you okay, buddy?" I asked as calmly as I could, not wanting to scare him more than my sobbing was all ready doing.

"I'm swimming," he said.

"Yes, you sure were," I said.

Wills abruptly pushed off my thighs and was out of my arms. Startled, I rushed to grab him. Cowboy was already there, dog paddling in a circle right above him.

I pulled Wills up again. This time he was mad. "Don't stop my swimming," he scolded.

"Your swimming?" I asked.

"Quit stopping it," he said, again.

"Okay," I told him, hesitant about stepping back.

The next thing I knew, Wills was near the towel rack yanking my yellow goggles over his head. He splashed back into the water with Cowboy shadowing his every move.

Wills was *swimming*!

"Did you want to swim," I asked when he came up for air, "or did you fall in by accident?" His straight bangs had become a series of small, upside-down triangles dripping across his forehead, and the yellow goggles magnified his already enormous eyes. He looked like a cross between Swifty Lazar and Coco Chanel.

"Cowboy wanted me to help her swim," he said.

Everything came easier when it was for Cowboy. "I love it," I said. "Now we can have fun together in the pool."

I couldn't wait for Michael to come home from work. He'd called twenty minutes earlier, so I knew he was only minutes away. Cowboy and Wills were circling the shallow end, Cowboy's legs pumping up and down as if she were in the Sherman Oaks High School marching band.

Michael appeared around the corner of the garage just in time to see Wills dive underneath Cowboy's stomach and come up on the other side, the goggles shielding his eyes and nose from the water.

His canvas bag dropped onto the tiles.

"He's swimming," I said coyly, scrunching my shoulders up around my neck as if to say, *You tell me.*

Michael was flabbergasted.

"I can see that," he said, clearing his throat. "Hey, Wills, when did you start swimming?"

"Cowboy was having trouble, so I came in!" he yelled back.

"You're so good!" Michael said.

"I'm excellent."

He certainly was excellent.

Michael sat down beside me near the shallow end with his feet on the first step of the pool, his sneakers and the legs of his jeans soaking up the water.

Wills resurfaced.

"Hi, Daddy," he said, playfully.

"Hello, Mr. Wills," Michael said.

Cowboy had suddenly noticed Michael and began a quick water march in his direction. I jumped up and backed away, but Michael was too slow, as she'd already reached the stairs. Climbing out to smother him in kisses, she firmly pressed a front paw into his groin. Cowboy never missed an opportunity to step on someone's crotch if she could help it.

"Daddy, look at this!" Wills shouted, keeping his body rigid and falling backward.

"That's it!" Michael said, "I'm comin' in."

"No!" Wills said, pointing. "You have clothes on."

"I don't care," Michael said, "I'm swimming with my pal."

"And Cowboy," Wills pointed out.

Michael slipped into the pool, his jeans and shirt glued to his body. I joined him and we swam with Wills and Cowboy for almost two hours.

In the pink light of the sunset, I watched Cowboy, now lying asleep on the wet tiles beside the pool, her lips blowing in and out with each snore.

"You did it again, girl," I told her, running my hand along the side of her face. "You're superdog."

I wrapped myself in a thick towel and relaxed in a lounge chair, sleepy and content.

The pool lights came on, and I could see the wavy shadow of Michael and Wills cast long against the side of the pool. My sweethearts.

Part Three

Only Dogs Have Tails

CHAPTER TWELVE

Cowboy's hair loss was continuing to accelerate. Her blond eyelashes were falling out, and I noticed a small bald patch in one of her armpits. I took her to see Dr. Burke.

Cowboy, the canine star of Burke's office, couldn't wait to get in the door to see who was working that day. With her butt shimmying faster than her tail, she sashayed down the hall, heading straight behind the counter where we weren't allowed. China, a beautiful African American woman who worked the front desk, was Cowboy's favorite. When Cowboy saw her, she made low happy, growling noises as China leaned down to hug Cowboy's neck.

"Cowboy's here!" she said, taking Cowboy's head in both her hands. Cowboy licked her on the mouth. "Oh, I love you, too," she said in a lovey-dovey voice. "How's our girl?"

As Cowboy wiggled in delight, I noticed white flakes floating to the floor, and realized that I'd seen them floating in the pool for the past few weeks, not knowing what they were. In the examining room, I asked Dr. Burke about them.

"I'm not sure why she's developed such scaly skin," Burke said, placing both of his hands around her torso and pushing his fingers around on her stomach. "It's probably just dandruff."

"These flakes are the size of nickels," I said.

"She has dry skin."

"She's *molting,*" I told him.

"I'll send you home with a conditioning shampoo. It'll take care of that." I pictured myself rubbing Head & Shoulders on a naked golden retriever. "I don't understand this hair loss, though," he said. "And there are tiny sores all over her stomach." He was now looking inside her mouth and ears.

"Really?" I asked. "She has sores?" This was moving in the wrong direction.

"I don't understand what's happening here," he said, shaking his head.

"Maybe it's related to what she had when we first picked her up at the Pet Chalet," I suggested.

"I doubt it," he said, "but let's not rule anything out. I thought her skin problem was from being in the kennel."

"Maybe she should see a specialist," I suggested.

"You could do that, but she's still so young. She might outgrow this." I looked at her balding eyes and peeling, spotted skin with dubious concern. Something was obviously wrong with our girl.

Burke cleaned waxy black crud out of her ears and took her temperature, which was a little elevated. He sent us home with shampoo and an antibiotic. She had some kind of an infection, but Burke didn't know the cause.

When we got home, Wills was on his swing, pumping his legs back and forth. This was another new development—learning how to keep himself going without needing a push—and now he was sailing so high!

"COWBOY!!" Wills yelled. That was all it took to get her wild with enthusiasm. JoAnn, who was babysitting, ran inside the house to keep Cowboy from licking her knees. I don't know why she only did this to JoAnn, but it was Cowboy's special greeting just for her—and JoAnn hated it.

Our neighbor, Tina, walked across the street to say hello. Cowboy hurried to the front gate and stood on her back legs to see over the top.

"I'm happy to unlock the gate so you can come in, but she's fired up for a love attack," I said. "I can see it in her eyes."

"I still have my work clothes on," Tina said, rubbing the top of Cowboy's head. "I'll stay out here."

"Can I come out too?" I asked, jokingly. "Since this morning, she's knocked me down twice, destroyed a window screen, dug up both of my sweet pea shrubs, and chewed the face off Wills's stuffed kangaroo."

Tina noticed Cowboy's face. "What's going on with our girl here?"

"She's losing hair around her eyes," I said, not wanting to admit that there was a litany of other problems—especially within hearing range of Wills.

"Oh, poor baby," she said, reaching over to scratch Cowboy's head. "What's happening with you?"

Tina's love of dogs was unmatched. She owned two vizslas—Tess and Chloe—and vizsla sweatshirts, vizsla coffee mugs, needlepoint vizsla pillows, and a rug with a vizsla woven into it. Tess and Chloe were prominent on Tina's Christmas card photo and she even gave them doggie birthday parties.

"My mother-in-law, Connie, knows an excellent canine dermatologist," Tina said.

"I didn't even know there was such a thing." But hey, if there were private-school agents, just about anything could exist.

"I'll call her and get his number," she said, smoothing Cowboy's ears with both of her hands. "He's right down here on Ventura."

"That would be great, because Dr. Burke has no idea what this is."

Cowboy and I went to the doggie dermatologist the next day. In the corner of the waiting room, on a thick tree limb rigged up by green twisted wire, sat a brilliantly colored, extremely alert parrot. He was so large he dwarfed the tree limb and the man who was waiting in the gray metal chair below him.

Cowboy became all goofy and drooly, as if she'd either seen the man of her dreams or spied a gigantic bird-shaped liver treat.

She slowly initiated her serpentine shuffle—tummy on the ground, butt moving back and forth, her front paws pulling her in a zigzag across the concrete floor. I tugged and yanked on the leash but her curiosity was stronger than I was.

The woman behind the counter stood on her tiptoes and peeked over. "She's adorable!"

"Thank you," I said, faking a smile as Cowboy dragged me sideways toward an increasingly agitated parrot.

"She loves birds," I explained, a little too politely. It was clear now that she wanted to eat one.

When Cowboy was within two feet of the parrot, she sprung up, her front paws slapping against the wall next to the tree limb. The parrot swooped down and eradicated Cowboy's intent with one shrill, ear-piercing screech. Thankfully, the bird was tethered to the branch, but Cowboy didn't stick around to see. She whirled through the waiting room, slipping and sliding on the painted floor, making a beeline for the front door. In her panic, she ripped the leash out of my hand, leaving stinging red welts across my palm.

"I can't control my dog!" I felt like shouting. What Cowboy lacked in body weight, she made up for in sheer determination. I intercepted her just before she made it to the front door, throwing my body in front of her. She curled into an oversized blond Ho Ho, petrified. I sat down with my legs wrapped around her.

I couldn't have imagined, when I was single and dreaming about having a family, that I'd spend most of my days tackling them. *Clearly, I need a trainer,* I thought, as Dr. Graham stepped out of the back to welcome us.

"The parrot scared her," I explained, my body draped over hers like a pro wrestler.

"I can take her," he offered, and I gladly handed him the leash. He pulled her, head down, butt planted squarely on the floor across the concrete for a second and then bent down and gently picked her up.

On the way to the examining room, I spied plastic card holders containing all kinds of recommendations for trainers: Mutt Manners, Doggie and Soul, Dot's Dog Training, and Pawsitive Dog. I crammed them into my pockets.

Dr. Graham fawned all over Cowboy, which won me over immediately. "What a beautiful dog you are," he said, placing his hand under her chin and lifting her head to kiss it. "What a doll!"

"She's so sweet," I said.

"I can see that, yes I can," he said to her in that you're-so-yummy doggie-tone that had become my second language.

"I'm worried there's something wrong with her," I said. "She's not even a year old."

"Let's take a look," he said, rubbing his nose on the top of her head. I'd never seen a doctor treat a patient with such love—Cowboy and I were smitten.

Apparently this was Dr. Graham's first experience with canine giraffe skin, and he took a few too many Polaroids of it. Sitting cross-legged on the floor, he examined Cowboy, pushed on her sides, and fingered underneath her armpits, jawline, and neck. "Who's this pretty girl?" he'd say, looking into her ears and pulling her jaws apart to check her mouth and throat. "What's going on with you, Cowboy? Can you tell us?"

"If only," I said.

"She's a sweetheart," he said, again. "Given the sores and the balding, I think this could be an autoimmune problem."

"What does that mean?" I asked. It sounded chronic, threatening.

"I'm not going to speculate," he said. "I want to keep her for a few hours and draw blood. With your permission, I'd like to take about half an inch of skin from her stomach and send it out to be tested. She'll only need about four stitches."

"Okay," I said, wincing.

"We'll numb it," he said, rubbing her ears. "She won't feel a thing."

Cowboy pawed Dr. Graham's pant leg. He wrapped his hand

around her snout and kissed her right on her black, leathery nose. This sent her into a spinning, huffing, fur-flying frenzy of ecstasy.

"Should I be worried?" I asked.

"She should be a healthy, fuzzy nine-month-old puppy, but she's not." He stood up. "Something's definitely wrong, but I don't know if it's just allergies or something more serious." He turned to Cowboy. "We're going to find out, aren't we, girl? We're going to take good care of you."

I walked to the car holding a leash with no Cowboy attached. He did say "allergies." That didn't sound so bad. So why was I already in tears?

I sped up 405 North to the Antelope Valley Freeway without my sidekick, got off at Placerita Canyon, and threw the car in park on a pull-off near a small waterfall. I would need to pick up Wills from a playdate at Sacha's in an hour and Cowboy after that. Through my windshield, I saw the familiar, winding trails where Cowboy, Wills, and I hiked on Saturdays. If she were with me, I'd have been covered in saliva by now while she happily waited for me to attach the leash.

I thought of Wills, anxious about spiders and rattlesnakes, braving the woods so that Cowboy could get her exercise until, eventually, he was the one running ahead of *us,* yelling for her to follow.

I remembered the afternoon Wills was stung by a bee and I ran to the car with him on my back to grab his EpiPen that I'd foolishly forgotten to throw into my backpack.

We'd just discovered a few weeks earlier that he was allergic to bees when he was stung near the pool. The swelling came on so quickly that I had him in the car within minutes. I was on the phone with Dr. Todd's office because he was closer than the hospital. He told me to come there, and met us in the parking lot with a shot of epinephrine. We got there in under four minutes but Wills's entire arm, shoulder, neck and even his upper back were swollen and red. Dr. Todd's did not think Wills's allergy was life-threatening because Wills's throat was itchy, but not very swollen. Still, he gave me an EpiPen just in case.

That day in the woods, I was counting every second it took to get back down that mountain trail, my only solace in the abject terror that Wills's throat would close this time was Cowboy, who led the way, barking the alarm.

That was only two weeks ago, and now *she* needed something from the backpack—only I had no idea what it was.

When I picked up Wills, he and Sacha wanted to know where Cowboy was.

"She's at the doctor getting a checkup," I told them.

Wills was not happy at all. "We're going to get her right now," he told me, as harshly as I'd ever heard him speak to anyone. "Why did she stay?" he asked, repeating the question two more times under his breath. I knew his anxiety was escalating because Wills hadn't repeated himself in a long time—not since Cowboy had arrived.

"Because of her giraffe skin," I said. "Dr. Graham, who specializes in dogs with irritated skin, had never seen anything like it. It was so unusual, he wanted to take pictures and show her to the other doctors there," which was partially true. "Let's go get her."

When we picked her up, the doctor wanted to see me alone—not a good sign. Plus, I never left Wills alone anywhere—ever. I surveyed the waiting room: an older man with a dachshund on his lap, and a teenager on her cell phone, her husky asleep beside her chair. Seemed okay to me.

"I need to talk to the doctor for a minute," I told Wills. "We'll be in that room right there," I said, pointing, "and we'll leave the door open so if you need me, you can come in or just say 'Mommy' and I'll hear you. Okay?"

"How long will you be?"

"Four minutes," I told him, trying to be specific and reassuring. I turned to the woman behind the counter who had checked us in. "I'm sure he'll be fine, but would you mind keeping an eye out?" I asked.

She looked at Wills and smiled. "No problem."

Wills sat stiffly on a gray plastic chair holding tight to Cowboy's leash, which I'd also tied to the Wellness food rack right beside him. Cowboy sat on Wills's foot, giving the parrot the hairy eyeball.

"The door's open," I reminded him. He nodded. "I'll be really quick!"

"We won't have results back until next week," Dr. Graham said, leaning forward, Cowboy's file in his hands. He looked like Tom Selleck, sort of. "Cowboy's immune system is suppressed. I don't know why, but her ears are yeasty and infected, her skin is *definitely* infected—very itchy. She's scratching a lot, which only causes more sores."

"What could cause something like this?" I asked, covertly moving to the doorway to peek out at Wills. Now *he* was staring at the parrot and Cowboy was sleeping.

"She could have an allergy of some kind," he said.

"I have my son with me, and he's uncomfortable being left alone. Can I call you from home?"

"That's fine," he said, "but I want to send some medication with you and also shampoo."

"How often should I shampoo her?" I asked.

"Every day."

"Oh my God! You've got to be kidding!" How would I find the time?

"I know it seems like a lot, but we have to get her skin problems under control right away," he explained.

"I'll call you tomorrow," I said.

I looked at the bill and was jolted by the $350 fee. We were hemorrhaging money we no longer had.

"We take credit cards," the receptionist offered, politely.

"That's good." The pressure behind my eyes was mounting and my throat was dry. This was only the first visit. How many more would there be? I looked back at Wills sitting patiently on the metal chair and Cowboy next to him. She looked dopy—spaced out—from the procedure. Wills stroked her back, sending fine golden hair wafting around them, twirling in all directions. We would find a way to pay it. Just like with Wills's therapy, we would do anything to make Cowboy healthy. We would never neglect her.

I reached into my wallet and pulled out the brand-new MasterCard we'd just gotten, the one we said we'd never use. I stepped outside to call the 800 number on the sticker to activate the card. While I was waiting for the operator to verify, I thought about getting a part-time job to help us out financially. Surely there was something I could do while Wills was in school and still get my writing done.

I took care of the bill, and the three of us walked out, exhausted and feeling a little off. Something had changed that day. There was something lurking just below the surface, but I had no idea what *it* was. I couldn't shake that feeling for the rest of the night.

CHAPTER THIRTEEN

One morning Wills saw me picking little skin flakes (now the size of quarters) off of Cowboy.

"You can't stop doing that, can you?" he asked.

"No, I can't," I said. Busted. "I'd like to stop but it's hard for me. I'm compulsive. That's the name for it. That's why I clean a lot and pick up leaves all over the yard. Sometimes I can stop and sometimes I can't."

"I do that," he said.

"Yes, you must have gotten that from me," I told him.

"How?" he asked.

"In the same way you have my eyes and Daddy's nose, you can also inherit other things from us; like being compulsive. I think you probably got that from me," I said, my shoulders sagging in defeat. How many flaws had I passed on to this child?

"Can you stop picking at Cowboy?" he asked. "Or do you have to do it?"

"I don't *have* to do it, but it's hard to stop, especially when I see all of these flakes just hanging off her." Wills looked at me expectantly. Just like we'd asked him to do on countless occasions, I would make a plan. "I'll pick off flakes for five more minutes and then, no more trolling for flakes. Okay?"

"Okay."

And that's what I did.

Sitting there in my Adirondack chair with the bird poop that needed to be cleaned off the armrest, I decided to go back to the therapy that had helped me years before when I'd first moved to L.A. I didn't want to worry my son, who was watching me and wondering about himself. I needed to get my own compulsions under control so I could give him the hope that he would also be able to control his. Between Wills's therapies and worries, Michael working late, and Cowboy's health, I was stretched a little thin.

Dr. Graham finally called with Cowboy's test results. They were inconclusive in terms of a diagnosis. Her immune system was unable to fight off the skin infections, which were causing the sores and the flaking, but he couldn't pinpoint why.

"It could be that she's still too young to diagnose," Dr. Graham hypothesized.

This sounded eerily familiar.

"She definitely has allergies, but nothing extreme enough to warrant these skin infections."

"What do we do?" I asked.

"Wait until she's a little older," he said. "Meanwhile, we'll keep her comfortable with medication and then test her again in three months," he said. "I'd like to see her in two weeks for a checkup."

"Okay," I said, resigning myself to watching and waiting—two things I was terrible at. Meanwhile, I took my shower every day with Cowboy standing in the tub right behind me, covered in her shampoo that smelled like tar. She was so dear, sitting with that awful gunk all over her, staring up at me as if I were St. Teresa. It was worse for her than for me, and it was pretty crappy for me. There was no room in there for me to shave my legs, so as Cowboy got balder, my legs got hairier.

As if Cowboy hadn't been through enough medical procedures, in July, at nine months old, she needed to be spayed. Dr. Graham was the disease expert, but Burke still got the ovaries. She had to stay overnight after her operation. We played it down for Wills. "Just remember how much she loves Dr. Burke," I said. "And he'll tell her she's coming home tomorrow."

"Can I sleep in the pink bed?" Wills asked.

"Sure," I said. With no Cowboy to hug, it would have been a long, dogless night.

The next morning, Michael, Wills, and I were up early, sitting in Burke's parking lot with hot chocolates and croissants as if we were on a stakeout. When China opened the office, our faces peered back at her through the heavy glass door.

"Missing somebody?" she asked, smiling.

"Can she go home?" we said in unison.

Michael carried a very groggy Cowboy to the car. A slick, white plastic cone was tied around her neck with a white ribbon, to keep her from biting her stitches. I looked in at her. Her little head was way down inside.

"She's too sleepy to worry about this cone right now," I said, untying it.

Wills and I rode in the backseat with Cowboy draped over our laps.

"She's happy now," Wills said.

I wasn't sure about that, but at least she was on her way home.

Cowboy had done well with her surgery and, despite the white plastic cone around her neck, was chewing underpants again. I'd never been more pleased in my life to see a pair of expensive Calvin Klein boxers with the crotch missing. She was back to her old self.

The phone rang: "Hi, Monica, this is Dr. Burke. How's she doing?"

"Eating underpants."

"That's a good sign." He laughed.

"Not mine, thank God."

"I wanted to call you about her skin," he said. "It's worsening for some reason."

"Really?" I'd been caring for her stitches and ignoring her skin.

"I noticed it during the surgery."

I pushed aside the hair in her armpit, which was usually where the trouble started. "It *does* look inflamed," I said.

"I want to give you Dermacool Spray with Lidocaine. It should relieve some of the itching and inflammation," he said. "I also cleaned out her ears, and noticed another ear infection. I want you to use Nolvasan to clean out the ears and Otomax to clear up the infection. I don't think it's anything serious. Just a pain in the butt, really, and it's uncomfortable for her, which we don't want. I'll give Dr. Graham a call right now. Maybe we can put our heads together and figure something out."

"Well, let me know," I said. "I don't want this getting worse again."

"I'll call you as soon as I talk to him," he said. "Keep the cone on so she can't get at her stitches, and I'll take a look at her next week."

I looked down. Cowboy was chewing on my shoelaces.

* * *

Unlike kindergarten, first grade began with a bang!

On his first day, Wills and Sacha walked through the front gate chattering.

"It's easy," she said. "You just have to make sure your foot is on the right limb."

"But how do you get up there in the first place?" Wills asked.

"Your mom has to put

her hands like this"—she demonstrated by entwining her fingers and leaning over—"and then you have to step on them while she boosts you up." Sacha flipped her hands up in the air as if to say, *"Ta-da!"* Wills wasn't sure about it.

"Is it the tree in the front yard," he asked, "or the back?"

"The back! I got so high up, I could see Patrick's house." Sacha laughed. "I could even see him walking around *inside.*"

Wills did an exaggerated double take.

"I know," she said.

"Cowboy climbs those cliffs behind Sycamore Cove now," Wills said. "She follows me all the way up."

"Seriously?" She shoved her long brown hair behind her ears. "We have to go there."

"We should."

Sacha ran off to see who else was at school. Wills was looking less confident all of a sudden. We stood outside his classroom, silently taking in the other kids dodging in and out of the door.

"Everyone's here," he said, whispering it under his breath two more times. He was pulling on the neck of his striped T-shirt.

Lynn hurried over. "Hey, Wills! What's up, man?" His shoulders relaxed a little. "Are you ready for first grade?"

He nodded, not so sure anymore. He'd forgotten the crowds in the hallway and the threat of having to face the boys' bathroom.

"Hey! You're big man on campus now," she said. "Those kindergarteners are going to be looking up to you!" She pointed toward Terri's class, which was overflowing with new parents and impossibly young children. Was it only a year ago that Wills stood outside the front gate, devastated and pale? Could he have ever been that small?

"Bring Cowboy," Wills said, "at pickup."

"You got it," I promised.

"Can she wear her scarf?" he asked. Wills and JoAnn had tie-dyed everything in the house a few weeks ago—including Wills's white underpants and athletic socks. Wills made Cowboy a special bandana cut out of my white scooped-neck tee.

"Of course!" I said. Wills was overwhelmed—a little blank. "Are you nervous?" I asked him.

"No," he said, quietly.

"Katherine said you'd feel a little anxious at first, remember?" He nodded. "She said that it might take a couple of days to get used to school again."

"I know." He wasn't looking at me. I gently lifted his chin so I could look into his eyes.

"Do you remember what else she said?" He shook his head. "She said that this year you could ride a horse to school instead of driving in a car."

"No she didn't." Wills smiled, having caught the joke. "She said this will be an easier year because it's not new." He was present again.

"It's a good thing you have a good memory," I said.

"Wills and I are going to take a little stroll around campus and see what's going on," Lynn said, putting her arm around his shoulders.

"Have a great day!" I said, my jawbone tightening. "I love you."

Wills's new teacher, Seth, was active in the California Audubon Society, and would be teaching Wills's class about birding. Math, science, and social studies would all be taught through the study of birds. Similar to being unsettled by Ruth's politically charged songs, I wasn't used to the concept of spending an entire year of school relating everything to birds. But I decided it was time to trust Neal again. Besides, this could not have been a better topic for Wills.

At the end of last year, we were hiking with Cowboy up in the Angeles National Forest, and he asked, "What's that?" as a small yellow bird with red streaks on its chest flew out of the brush.

"I have no idea, but we can look it up," I said.

On the way home, we bought the *Peterson Field Guide to Birds of North America* and discovered it was a yellow warbler. That night, Wills used a thin black Sharpie to circle the American kestrel, the Western bluebird, and the peregrine falcon—birds we might see in Southern California. JoAnn bought him a pair of high-powered binoculars, but with Cowboy tromping through the underbrush and splashing across streams, bird-watching was difficult at best. They took flight before Wills could even focus the lenses.

He came home from first grade bursting with news. "California condors live in the mountains behind Fillmore!" he told me so fast I could barely understand what he was saying. "Can you believe it?"

"I had no idea," I said. We'd been to Fillmore at least a dozen times to ride the Fillmore & Western antique trains.

"If we sit on that mountain behind the depot, we might see one!"

"We should bring your binoculars."

"And we're each getting our own owl pellets," he continued.

"What are owl pellets?" I asked, imagining the turds rolling around the bottom of Ruby's cage.

"Dried owl poop. It has hair and tiny mouse bones inside," Wills said, swinging his arms up and down.

Turds; I was right.

That evening, as Cowboy and Wills made up for lost time by setting up the nylon tent maze in the family room, Ruby the Rabbit began thumping away.

"She wants to run around the yard," Wills said.

"Keep Cowboy in the house," I told him. "I'll let Ruby out."

Cowboy, whose baby teeth had fallen out long ago, no longer seemed harmless to Ruby. Still, Cowboy fawned over her. Ruby, being a rabbit, understood that Cowboy, on some level, wanted to eat her. Cowboy would stick her long pink tongue through the wires of Ruby's hutch to lick her downy fur. Ruby just eyed her skeptically, as if Cowboy saw her as a drumstick with ears like in a Road Runner cartoon and was cleaning her next meal. But when Ruby and Cowboy were in the yard at the same time, Cowboy lay down with her back feet splayed out behind her and, using her front paws, slowly pulled her body in Ruby's direction. She made low muffled love noises, which Ruby ignored.

I opened the hutch and watched Ruby leap out and bounce around the corner of the garage. She was heading to her burrow, where there was work to be done. Cowboy was no longer tearing through the tent maze with Wills. Her face was pressed, longingly, against the windows of the sliding doors.

"Ruby's got a tweezer in her foot," Wills said through the glass. He was still inside with Cowboy.

"A what?" I asked. Neither of us would dare open the door because Cowboy would definitely bolt and Ruby would probably take a chunk out of Cowboy's ear—like Mike Tyson fighting Evander Holyfield.

"A tweezer. In her foot," he said loudly, as if it were my fault. "She won't hop on it."

Ruby wasn't all the way down in her burrow, so I carefully pulled her back out and felt between her toes. There was a sharp piece of hay stuck in her back right paw. "You were right," I said, holding up the culprit as Wills squeezed himself out the back door.

"You've got to start taking care of these animals," he said, walking back to check on his garden.

I was just about to snap back with a "Hey, get off my case," when I stopped to realize what had just happened. Wills was giving me shit! I couldn't believe it! He had gained enough confidence to have an attitude. Soon he'd be embarrassed to be seen with me. I couldn't wait!

A week into the new school year, profound separation anxiety set in—only now it was Cowboy who was struggling with separating from Wills. She'd had him to herself all summer long, so spending her days without him left her mopey and sad. In the morning, Cowboy rode along with us to drop off Wills, crying a mournful good-bye out the passenger window like Chewie to Han Solo, as Wills stepped away from the car.

"It's okay, Cowboy," he'd say, looking to see if any of his friends were coming down the sidewalk. "I'll be home soon. Don't worry."

Inevitably, another child would walk up and try to comfort her.

Today it was his friend Lauren. "Cowboy's devastated," he sighed. "She *hates* being home without me."

"I can tell," Lauren said, rubbing the top of Cowboy's head. "He'll be home soon, Cowboy."

"Sorry, girl, gotta go!" Wills said, with the authority of someone who really had business to attend to, and the best part was, he did.

How good it must have felt to be the confident one for a change—the one who could finally say good-bye knowing that nothing was lost, the kid who had good friends and interesting things to learn.

During that first week, Vanessa, who was still working with Wills on word recognition and addition, suggested that a "Scheduler" might relieve Wills's anxiety about not feeling in control of his day. If the Scheduler was keeping track of what was coming next, Wills didn't have to.

"I do this for my boys," Vanessa said. "All they need to do is look up on the wall to know exactly what's expected of them. This means that I'm not bugging them about getting their chores done, but more important, it gives them a sense of independence. It's getting to the point where they're changing the schedule around to accommodate sports or weekend activities. I'm not even in charge of it anymore."

I bought a long nylon banner with clear plastic cardholders at Education Station and hung it on the family room wall. Every morning I'd sit with Wills to write out the events of the day on index cards, and he would insert them into the Scheduler.

Cards with the seven days of the week ran down the left side, on the far right were cards with the time of day, and in the middle were longer cards on which I wrote an activity to slip into the appropriate time slot: BRUSH YOUR TEETH, EAT LUNCH, or GO TO THE SHOE STORE.

After a couple of weeks, Wills began inserting his own cards scribbled with backward letters and misspelled words: "Goto the—bate rom." He reminded himself not to "pick the nose" at 10:30 on Tuesday (the card included a stick figure with wobbly arms covering its nose), to have a "Coke without ice" on Fridays at 3:00, and to record the space shuttle launch on Thursday at 2:30 p.m.

Katherine had been making calendars for him since he was three, drawing pictures in the squares to represent "Going to Catalina Island" or "Time for bed." But now that he could recognize words on sight and understand what "3:00 p.m." meant, the Scheduler changed everything. His entire day was structured right there on the wall. This gave him much more stability.

Even on weekends, if we were supposed to leave for the beach at 11 a.m., and it was pushed back for some reason, instead of getting anxious Wills would take out the beach card and put it in its new time slot without so much as a whimper—because he had control over his day.

In November, I was a parent volunteer for a field trip to Malibu Lagoon, one of Southern California's premiere sanctuaries for birds. Seth, decked out in his khaki wide-brimmed birding hat and vest, told the class that "two hundred and seventy-six native and naturalized bird species have been reliably recorded at Malibu Lagoon State Park." He gave us a list of birds to look for: the American white pelican, the double-crested cormorant, a great blue heron, the egret, a northern pintail, a killdeer, and about ten others. It was going to be a great day.

As we were getting out of the car in the parking lot of the sanctuary, Wills turned to me. "I have to go to the potty!" he said, his eyes welling up with tears.

"That's okay," I told him. Indescribably embarrassing restroom disasters clicked through my head like a film reel. "There are bathrooms here."

"I can't go in there," he said, pointing to a Porta-Jon in the parking lot.

Of course, I already knew this, but I leaned down and took both of his hands in mine. "Wills, you can do this. You can go to that potty. I'll go with you." There was no other option, he *had* to go in. He tried backing away from me.

"I'll do a bush potty," he said, which was what he did in the back of the parking lot at Target or on a rocky hillside in Tehachapi. He was pulling hard now, and I knew that if I lost my grip, he would run.

"You can't do a bush potty," I told him. "There are too many people walking around."

"I CAN'T GO IN THERE!" he screamed, trying to cover his ears. "I CAN'T, MOMMY!!" Seth continued to explain the nesting habits of the greater yellowlegs. I was looking around frantically, trying to figure out Plan B, when Wills bolted in the opposite direction. I followed him down a dusty dirt path toward the beach, yelling, "Wills, we'll figure it out. You have to stop."

I tackled him by Lifeguard Stand #14. By then, he'd peed a little in his shorts and some of it was now running onto the leg of my jeans. I spoke quickly. "Let's go into the dune grass, buddy. Hurry."

I was ashamed of myself, tearful, as I led him to the grass. I felt completely incompetent. I knew he wasn't ready for a Porta-Jon, who was? His future rushed toward me like a freight train—someday I wouldn't be there for him. He had to learn to function in the world. Katherine and I had been working on this forever, it seemed. Michael was the point man, carrying/dragging Wills into men's rooms across Los Angeles with him screaming and sobbing, his hands clamped over his ears. At school, he was still using the faculty bathroom. Surely he would make the leap, but for now, after he finished peeing in the grass, I held him in my lap. I rocked my traumatized son, who was doing the very best he could.

Luckily, I had extra clothes in the car. We quickly walked to the parking lot, where he awkwardly changed in the backseat.

"I'm really sorry, Wills," I told him, "but I know you're going to be able to do it soon."

He was unsuccessfully trying to put his foot through the leg of his dry shorts while I held a towel up over the back window.

"When we're not at home, you need to use public bathrooms. You'll feel much better if you don't have to worry every time we go out."

"No, Mommy."

"Yes, Wills. I know you'll be able to do this sometime, and I hoped it would be today." He pulled his shorts up way too high, the waistband hitting below the middle of his chest. "But it wasn't and that's okay too," I said. "But soon. . . . No more running away, Wills," I said sternly. He didn't respond. "Did you hear me?" I asked, gently titling his face toward mine.

"No more running," he repeated. When he looked up, he didn't have tears anymore, his expression was blank, shut down, far away from the wet shorts crumpled on the backseat.

"I'll always be right behind you, Wills. But I'm an old lady. You have to take it easy on me."

I could no longer see his class. They'd headed toward the lagoon.

★ ★ ★

At school, Wills was still struggling with saying people's names out loud. Saying a person's name was like standing too close to them—it was too intimate. Lynn and Seth were trying to help Wills feel casual enough to address his peers directly, so they told him that when he wanted to call on someone during Sharing, he could go over, pull their name card off the wall, and hold it up. It was one step closer to verbally addressing them.

Everyone who worked with Wills—Lynn, Vanessa, Seth, Kathleen, and Ruth—was beginning to understand the importance of the written word for him. Katherine had known this all along, instructing us to dictate letters or journals for him since he was very young. If something was written down, like on the Scheduler, he could grasp it—and it wasn't too personal.

By the same token, Wills had trouble receiving compliments.

Block building was an integral part of the CCS curriculum. Neal believed that using materials like blocks, wood, and paint, helped students increase their powers of observation, reconstructing what they see, and also deepening their understanding of the world around them. By building it, they understood it. This activity sat squarely in Wills's comfort zone.

When Wills was working on his blocks one afternoon, Seth knelt down beside him. "Good job," he said, putting his hand lightly on Wills's back. "You seem to really enjoy block building."

"I do," Wills said without looking up.

"You're really great at it," Seth said.

Wills didn't respond. He stopped working.

"Did I interrupt you?" Seth asked, but by then tears were running down Wills's face. Seth was at a total loss.

When Cowboy and I came to pick up Wills later that day, Seth asked to speak to me.

"When I complimented Wills today in block building, I think I hurt his feelings," Seth said. "He cried."

I explained to him that Wills cried when *anyone* complimented him. "It isn't out of sadness," I said. "I think, just like saying someone's name or touching another person, being praised or singled out feels too intimate to Wills. Or maybe he's just too shy and sensitive to accept it, I don't know. But it's *so* good for him. Don't stop telling him he's doing a good job," I told Seth, "even if he cries. Inside, he's proud. I know he is. And we need to build his confidence."

"That's good to hear. I didn't want to do something to upset him," Seth said.

"No, you did the right thing."

If Wills had trouble with compliments, criticism was like a knife in his chest.

Once, when I came into the family room, there were muddy foot (and paw) prints all over the light gold carpeting.

"Wills," I called, and he and Cowboy came tearing in. "You guys are tracking mud in from the backyard."

"OH NO!" he said, wounded.

"It's no big deal," I said, "but you guys need to either stay inside or out so there's no more mud."

"Inside," Wills said, beginning to cry.

"Honey, it's okay. Kids track in mud. I'm not mad at you."

"I need a time-out," he whimpered.

"You don't need a time-out. You didn't know. I just don't want to clean the rug anymore, that's all." I lifted him onto my lap. "Look at these," I said, holding up his feet. "We have to wipe off the bottoms."

"I can do it." He jumped up, ran into the kitchen, and tried to haul his leg up to the sink but could barely get his foot up to the counter.

"Let's do it in the bathroom, pal," I said. "I can help you." I carried him through the house with his feet sticking out in front of him.

Wills was in between being a little boy and a bigger boy. We were all confused. There were still many things Wills was unable to do, so we did them for him—zipping his coat, getting the shampoo out of his hair, engaging him in conversations with people he didn't know, zipping his jeans, buckling his seat belt. But there were many things he *could* do, only we weren't sure, so we did those for him, too.

But we were learning to step back and let him try and, most important, he was showing us that he was ready.

Kindergarten had been a time of enormous social growth, and first grade was just what it sounded like—a year of "firsts." Wills was chosen to be Leader of the Week at school, and was asked to pick two kids to join him to walk over to the kindergarten class and make an announcement. Wills knocked on the door to Terri's classroom and said to the kids, "I have an important announcement. Please stop making a big mess in the tree house. NO MORE MESSES. Thank you." As he was walking out, he turned and said, "Please learn the rules." These were the three things Seth had told him to say, and he always followed the rules. Still, it would have been impossible for him to do this last year.

When he got home that night, he and Cowboy were in his room with the door closed. Even from the kitchen I could hear him telling those kindergarteners to "Stop messing around with the hose" and "You know better than to leave sand all over the place." He was giving Cowboy the low-down. I ran for the phone to call Michael. Another milestone.

The trick, now, was for him to communicate that way with kids his own age—to stick up for himself, tell them what *he* wanted to play, and, in general, express his needs without worrying that there'd be bad consequences. The kids wouldn't turn away from him or become angry if he was true to his own feelings.

He was doing this more with adults, and now it was time to help him with his peer relationships.

Michael had recently introduced Wills to *Bugs Bunny* and other Looney Tunes cartoons. The two of them sat on the couch with a bowl of popcorn, laughing and laughing. The comedy was so broad, Wills really got the jokes. Also, in *Tom and Jerry,* the characters are so mean to one another, that this gave Wills a chance to relax a little about really bad behavior. He could see that anger didn't kill any-one, not really. It might make a bomb go off in your pants or twist your head off, but he could see that getting yelled at didn't bring on Armageddon, and that pulling a prank on someone else wasn't the worst thing anybody ever did. You apologized and moved on. Unfortunately, seeing these things on TV hadn't yet transferred to the real world for Wills.

One day in November, Wills took his carrots out of his lunch box and began peeling the plastic off the sealed top. This was not an easy job for him—he had difficulty separating the clear wrap from the plastic bottom.

He'd bought the carrots from the grocery store because there was a picture of Bugs Bunny on the wrapper, and thank God for marketing because this was the first time he was excited about eating a vegetable. His meals had been an ongoing battle because he craved an all-white, carb-filled diet. The textures of fruits and vegetables freaked him out, so I snuck them in—pureeing veggies and adding them to his spaghetti sauce, giving him different kinds of salad dressings for dipping his carrots. But the things I relied on the most were great big multivitamins.

Ryan, the boy sitting next to Wills as he struggled with the wrapper, said, "You stole those carrots from Bugs Bunny." He was only teasing, but Wills still didn't understand the joke.

"No I didn't, I bought these at Ralphs with my dad."

"No, you stole them and Bugs Bunny wants them back." Ryan laughed and looked around to see if the other kids were watching.

Wills took the accusation literally. "I don't steal things," he said, tearfully. "Why would you say that?"

This just egged Ryan on more and he ended up chanting, "Wills is a thief! Wills is a thief!"

Wills placed the carrots back in his lunch box and sat there not knowing what to do. He was mortified that anyone would think he could rob Bugs Bunny. Lynn gathered up Wills and Ryan and the three of them had a discussion about how Wills needed to speak up and say, "Are you joking or are you hurting my feelings?" And Ryan needed to recognize when a joke turned into something cruel. Who knew if either of them understood, but Wills threw the rest of his carrots into the trash.

Wills came home with red eyes, and re-created the scene that Lynn had already relayed to me over the phone two hours earlier. I listened carefully as Wills told me the story in his own words.

"Wills, you know I would never stick up for Ryan because he has been a jerk in the past. And he did get carried away with this. But I have to say that when he started saying that you took the carrots from Bugs Bunny, he was joking. Because Bugs Bunny is a cartoon character, there's no way you could take anything from him. That's why Ryan expected you to laugh."

"It's not funny," Wills said.

"No, to *you*, it's not funny."

"I don't like to be teased."

"Of course you don't, and Ryan took it way too far. Once he saw you were upset, he became a jerk about it."

Wills was sobbing now. This was when I wanted to "wrap him

in bubble wrap," as JoAnn always said, and never let him out of my sight. I knew this incident was small compared to what awaited him in the future. I wanted to spare him and toughen him up at the same time. But how do you explain the subtleties of teasing to a kid who takes everything at face value?

When Wills was anxious or sad about something, he confided in Cowboy. Sometimes I'd hear him in his room or the backyard telling Cowboy all of his troubles. I couldn't make out what he was saying, but he cried with his face pressed into her soft blond ears. She loved the attention and sat perfectly still, tail thumping away, her soggy ears slicked back against the sides of her head, her skin flakes drifting onto the carpet. Wills found great relief in getting his troubles off his chest, but confiding in a person was nearly impossible. Cowboy was different. She didn't offer solutions. She just listened, and there was no one he was closer to than Cowboy.

One day when we were driving back from Katherine's, as the car climbed a hilly, congested road, Wills said, "There's a stomach-wide water shortage back here."

I looked at him in the rearview mirror. Cowboy was sitting next to him on her purple suede dog bed. He softly banged a Nike Velcro tennis shoe on the back of my seat.

"I know you're thirsty," I said, translating for him, "but I can't do anything right now, buddy. Sorry."

He sighed and rolled down his window, letting the wind blow his thick blond bangs off his forehead.

"This is like the Mojave Desert, I'm telling you. I need rain back here."

"Wills, I can't move any faster with this traffic," I told him. "We'll be home in five minutes."

"In five minutes, I'll have no body fluid. I'll be dust on the seat."

I looked in the rearview mirror again and he attempted to wink at me. He'd been learning to wink. I winked back.

He settled back into his seat and hauled Cowboy onto his lap. Now her hair was blowing, too. She leaned her tiny back against his chest, and he hugged her tight.

We were turning down our street when I heard it. "I love you, Cowboy."

Three simple words. He'd never said them to another living soul.

One Saturday morning, Wills woke up and told me that he had another mosquito bite—raising the number of bites he'd had in the last week to seven.

"I think there's a colony making their home under the house," he said, walking around the bedroom with his hands in the air as if he were trying to get God's attention.

"You do get a lot of bug bites at night," I said, "but I don't think there's a colony under the house. I don't even know if mosquitoes live in colonies."

"I'm afraid they do," he told me. "Please call the exterminators."

"I'll call them and have them spray front and back, okay?" I assured him. "I just need to find an organic company. I don't want Cowboy or any of us near any harsh chemicals."

"And do the sides, too," Wills said.

"And the sides, too," I repeated.

"And inside, right?"

"Of course," I assured him.

"And don't forget that black widow we saw in March by the garage," he reminded me.

"Okay, but it's been months, I think he's moved on by now."

"You can't be too safe," he said, walking out of the bedroom, irritated.

Wills had been intent on keeping everything neat and safe since his toddler days. With my scrubbing and cleaning all the time, it's not surprising. But I wanted to tell him that a person *can* be too safe.

That *he* is too safe, and I am, too. That he needs to roam into chaotic territory—cut loose a little, give the wrong answer, tell a white lie, ride his scooter too fast, tease Ryan. But he was too busy straightening the cushions on the sofa.

That spring of first grade, Wills, facing yet another damn sing-along, wore Michael's red ski ear warmers with earplugs underneath to help shut out the noise.

He walked in with Lynn, who led him up to the stage and sat him down in front of the metallophone. He was fighting tears as Lynn handed him two wooden mallets with soft round tips. I sat up in my chair.

His classmates gave an introduction, and while the children spoke, Wills pushed the soft ends of the mallets against each ear to block out the sound. But when they began to sing "Star Bright," Wills kept time with the music, hitting the vibrating metal bars in perfect rhythm.

Wills was weeping now, but didn't miss a single beat. He cried *and* played the hell out of that instrument. Ruth had done it! She figured out that Wills could relate to something concrete like counting out a beat, and that he was more comfortable behind an instrument than standing out in front of everyone. She got it!

At the end of the Sing, he walked out calm and composed, and when we went to pick him up from the classroom, he didn't pay any attention to us. He was busy talking to Patrick about coming over for a playdate.

"Then you have to come to my house," Patrick said. "I have two dogs."

Wills's friend Benjamin tapped my arm. He wanted a playdate with Wills, too.

"He needs a social secretary," I said to Lynn, laughing.

"No kidding, man," she said. "I think the kids are drawn to him because he's so kind."

"You did a great job, Wills," I told him. He laughed.

"Thank you."

"What was your favorite part?" Michael asked him.

"*My* part."

Terri had called it way back in kindergarten when Abigail coaxed Wills outside to play for the first time: "Never underestimate the kindness of children," she'd said. And now, with the Scheduler full to bursting with playdates, Wills's sweet nature had earned him a whole host of friends who loved him like Michael and I did—just for being Wills.

A few weeks later, I called Dr. Graham because Cowboy could not stop scratching her ears and shaking her head. He did a microscopic examination of her ear canal, and she had what he described as "an ear infection so bad that there's thick, yellowish oozing inside the ear." I held both of her ears flat against her head, and gently rubbed them. How did she put up with all of this? My sweet girl.

"I want to analyze another skin punch," he said.

After the exam, Dr. Graham sent us home with ResiSooth to help with the dry skin and itching. When the results of the skin punch came back, the prognosis was worrisome. Dr. Graham did an ANA (antinuclear antibodies) test checking to see if Cowboy had SLE, systemic lupus erythematosus. He sent us home with Trental, a substitute for Prednisone that gave her some relief from the itchy skin and healed some of the sores while we waited for the test results. We'd been around this bend so many times, I was losing track of what had helped and what hadn't.

When the biopsy came back, Dr. Graham was reluctant to diagnose Cowboy with lupus, but suspected that's what we were dealing with. Lupus. The word itself sounded phlegmy and terrible, like a lump in the throat. I didn't know dogs could even *get* lupus.

Immediately, Cowboy began a full regimen of pills and *weekly* visits to Dr. Graham. This was getting very expensive. What had come to be known as the Graham MasterCard was filling up quickly, and I had no idea how we would pay it back. But worse than that, our Cowboy was in trouble.

On the way home, she rode shotgun as I made a beeline for In-N-Out Burger—Cowboy's favorite place to eat. She loved their Double-Double burgers. Today, she could have two.

CHAPTER FOURTEEN

The summer between first and second grade, Wills began occupational therapy—a Dr. Bauman recommendation. He hadn't tested Wills's ability in terms of gross motor skills, but knew Wills needed help with fine motor skills—holding a pencil correctly, buttoning shirts, tying shoes, zipping his pants, using a fork. I didn't even know what OT was at first. It sounded more like a place where an ad executive might go to learn better marketing strategies than like a colorful gym with sunny, warm classrooms.

Wills and I drove into the parking lot of Therapy in Action in the heart of Reseda. The concrete building didn't look like a place of healing, there was gang graffiti on the walls. Wills immediately began humming, which was something new that he did when he was nervous. I was nervous, too.

I wanted him to get better, though, and to have every chance for success, so I parked the car and walked around to open his door. He was sitting in his booster seat, staring straight ahead.

"Hey, pal, this place looks interesting," I said, starting to unbuckle him.

"What's wrong with me?" Wills asked, looking at me beseechingly with those huge blue eyes.

I stopped. Stunned.

He'd never asked me this before, and yet it was a moment I

suspected was coming—sometime. My mind raced. I didn't know what to say to him, how much information to give without revealing too much. But I knew from Katherine that I needed to answer his question.

"Your brain doesn't always tell your body how to move correctly or balance itself. This place will teach your body to listen to your brain. There's a big gym in there with all kinds of really fun equipment that will help you learn to balance on a bike, button your shirts, catch a ball, and tie both your shoes," I said.

"Why doesn't anyone else come here?" he asked.

"It's true that there aren't other children in your class who come here, but there are many, many children who do. Every child, including everyone in your class, has something that they struggle with, but it's not always the same thing. You need to learn how to hold a pencil so you can write neat letters and numbers. Jason is getting help from a tutor so he can recognize his numbers, but you already know yours."

"Let's go in," he said.

I held his sweaty hand as we walked toward the front door. There were about a thousand ways I could have comforted my child at that moment, but I couldn't come up with a single one. We walked to the entrance in silence.

This was only the first time the question had come up; there would be many more times. Would I ever have the courage to tell Wills the truth? That he wasn't just imagining the world was a more difficult place for him to understand than for some of his buddies— that it was, in fact, more difficult for him. That he'd been dealt a rotten hand in that regard, but only in that *one* regard. Because I wouldn't change one freckle, one misunderstood moment, one tiny piece of him for anything in this world. I would change *myself.* I would change the things that other people said or thought out of ignorance or fear. I would change so many things, but I would absolutely never, in a million years, change him.

Once inside, there were instructions in the lobby to "Pick up a white phone, dial 54, and say the patient's name." I dialed 54 and said "Wills Price" in a loud voice. Wills was pale and whispering to himself. I picked up the phone again. "Is anybody in there?" I asked in a really spooky voice. We could hear it echo throughout the office. "No one's answering my zombie voice," I said.

Wills started laughing. "Why did you do that?"

"That lets them know we're here, I guess."

"Pick it up again and say 'Nobody home,' " he said, his lips pressed together.

I picked up the phone, and said, "NOBODY HOME?" into the receiver. Wills cracked up laughing.

"That's a crazy phone," he said.

A door opened behind us and his therapist walked out. "Hi, Wills, my name is Heather. Wanna come play with me?" She was about twenty-five years old, with the sweetest, most inviting smile. Wills looked at me. "Your mom can come, too," she said.

We walked down a couple of steps to a gigantic gym. There were trapezes, round leather tubes, rope ladders that led all the way up to the vaulted ceiling, a gigantic pit of colorful plastic balls, and wooden swings with the seats covered in carpet.

I helped Wills untie his sneakers, and he ran onto the thick red mat with Heather right behind him.

"What do you want to do?" she asked, swinging open her arms to indicate that the whole place was his. He couldn't believe it. He thought she'd be the one telling him what to do.

"Build an obstacle course," he said.

"Let's get goin'."

For the next hour they shoved oversize, soft square benches, nylon tents, and rubber human-size tubes into different configurations. Wills's cheeks were flushed as he ran all over the gym pointing to what he wanted to add, and then helping Heather shove it into place. This sure beat lying under Bauman's table.

"When are we coming back?" he asked, running toward me.

"Next Tuesday," I told him.

"Can't we come sooner?"

"Sorry, next Tuesday is our time to come."

The following Tuesday I spent his entire OT session sitting outside in the ninety-seven-degree Tarzana sun with Cowboy looking through the big sliding glass doors that led from the gym to the parking lot. It was Bauman's stump all over again.

Wills stole glances in our direction, making sure Cowboy was paying attention. I held a blue-and-white–striped umbrella the size of our patio over our heads and refilled Cowboy's water dish about six times. Meanwhile, I absentmindedly picked and flicked skin flakes off of her.

When Wills finally came out, he said to Cowboy, "Did you see me?" He bent down to take her leash. "I climbed high, didn't I?"

Cowboy pounced onto his chest as Wills yelled, "SHE'S HUMPING ME!" I quickly surveyed the parking lot to make sure no parents were watching my son be assaulted by a horny dog.

"Cowboy, down," I ordered, wrapping my arms around her middle and hauling her backward until she was once again on all four paws.

"What *is* humping?" Wills asked, once we got into the searing hot car. I started the air-conditioning, buying time.

"It's what dogs do when they mate," I said, and, miraculously, this seemed to satisfy him. Again, I'd learned from Katherine to provide the information he asked for, but not to "overexplain it." Wills had no idea what mating was. He concentrated on Cowboy.

"Who's the good girl?" he said in his Cowboy voice. "You! Yes, you are. You're the good girl. You stopped humping, yes you did."

Come September Wills was raring to go back to school so he could be with his buddies full-time, to be in the thick of all the activities and chatter—he was *dying* to start second grade. Lynn was waiting for him when he arrived the first day, but she and I ended up standing on the playground alone while Wills took off with Patrick and Sacha.

"This is very, very good!" I said.

"Pretty soon," she said, "he won't even want you hanging out with him."

"Isn't that the best?" I said, slightly taken aback. "That would be such a leap." But from the looks of things, the leap had already taken place.

I tried to stay away from the school, giving him the space and independence he needed, and he was thriving. He still leaned on Lynn academically, and for transitions into new activities, but socially, it would have been nearly impossible to single him out as having severe difficulties.

This was the first year that there were younger children in the same class with him. (At progressive schools, two grades are often mixed into one classroom.) This year, Wills was the second oldest in the class. It quickly became clear that he was more at ease playing with kids who were at least a year, if not two years, younger than he was. He was about seven, but his social age was more like five or six. He and Sacha were still as thick as thieves, but she was playing more with the girls, and Wills had met his first, very best friend.

Cowboy had held that title for almost two years, but Cole was now in the picture. He was a slight, curly-headed sprite of a boy, extremely smart and very gentle. When it came to playing, he was a perfect match for Wills.

On playdates, I'd hear Cole say, "Now *you* say, 'Don't burn the building down.' "

Wills would repeat, without intonation, "Don't burn the building down."

"Wills, they're coming to take your kingdom. You can't let them do it. Tell them not to burn it." Wills just stood there. "You have to stop them!" Cole, who was at least five inches shorter than Wills, was jumping up and down.

"DON'T BURN THE BUILDING DOWN!" Wills yelled, startling himself.

"That's *it*!" Cole said. "You can't let them win."

These two played for hours. I checked on them, but I barely knew they were in the house, they were so involved in putting together Bionicles or laying out their Chevron car collections.

One afternoon I was picking Wills up from school when Jeffery, another parent in his class, asked me, "Is Lynn here to help Wills?"

"Yes." I was so surprised. No one had approached me about this issue in such a long time, and his daughter had been in Wills's class since kindergarten.

"Wow, I can't believe that. Someone told me she was shadowing Wills, and I was puzzled. He seems fine to me."

"Well, he's doing pretty great now. Lynn has helped him so much and now he's used to the school."

"Why does he still need her?" Jeffery pressed.

"Wills has high-functioning autism."

"I heard that, but I gotta tell ya I just don't see it. What's the deal with people diagnosing these kids?" Jeffery shook his head. "Right now, it seems like every kid I know has autism. It's like a fad or something."

Jeffery wasn't the first person to voice this opinion to me. People thought if they said, "Wills doesn't look autistic," that it would make me feel better, or maybe they honestly didn't see it. Regardless of the intent, comments like these always came out sounding like a criticism—as if I was just overreacting, a nervous mother who needed to loosen up. Trying to persuade someone that your child is autistic when it's the last thing in the world you want for him really sucked. Why would I want him on the spectrum if he wasn't?

And then I realized that I should take it as a compliment. I should have simply said thank you—like you're supposed to do when someone admires a haircut or a new outfit, instead of blurting out, "Oh, I hate it—I look like Bea Arthur," or "Target—forty-nine bucks!" Wills was doing so great that Jeffery had no idea he was autistic. And suddenly the only thing that mattered was that Wills was *here*—and not *there* anymore.

Wills's appointments with Katherine continued on Tuesdays and Thursdays; then we reduced his visits to once a week so he would have more time for playdates. She thought, and we agreed, that spending time with other children might be more therapeutic.

He was still seeing his Educational Therapist Vanessa in her little backyard schoolhouse two times a week, after taking a short break over the summer, and Lynn went to his sessions on Wednesdays to observe. Michael and I wanted to make sure that Wills wasn't missing anything academically.

We continued reading two or three small books a night, but now Wills was interested in reading on his own. Michael and I were ecstatic, though in the back of our minds lurked the pronouncement of Bauman's report. We worried, for instance, about Wills's ability to scan words left to right. Vanessa suggested he begin reading the Mr. Putter and Tabby series, for six- to nine-year-olds, about a man who found a true companion in his adopted cat. Wills could relate— he *loved* that series.

In October, I had what I thought was the brilliant idea of bringing home two bales of hay from a local feed store and flinging it all over the backyard to make our own pumpkin patch. Wills and I prepared by spreading a blue tarp from the Home Depot over the grass, which was fruitless, because every time we tried to shake it out, Cowboy, who was experiencing another period of good health and tons of energy, pounced on top of it, pinning it to the ground. When I attempted to spread out the piece she wasn't protecting, she leapt onto that one. We'd finally brought her a toy she could really use.

I gave up on the tarp, and proceeded to push the heavy hay bales off the top of the truck. My metropolitan neighbors watched in wonder as I grunted, cursed, and rolled first one and then the other hay bale, end over end, up our slanted driveway. Eventually I disappeared behind the back gate, a hay trail fluttering in my wake. Wills ran alongside clapping and asking questions I couldn't begin to answer due to my shortness of breath and the tiny particles of yellow dust that had lodged themselves in my throat.

Cowboy had never been so deliriously happy to see anything in her life. The delectable tarp paled in comparison. She took one look at me, red-faced and swearing, and streaked across the yard, barreling full-on into the side of the hay bale. The blast knocked me backward and the bale landed across my chest. Then Cowboy got into the action and stood on top of me.

"Get her off!" I managed to squeeze out.

"What, Mommy?" Wills asked, leaning over my head.

"GET HER OFF OF ME!" I yelled in a smashed-lung kind of way.

"She's happy," he said.

"Her big butt is hurting me," I said, unable to move.

"She's lying down," he announced.

"ON *ME*!"

That was it. I used my feet to push my butt up and began rocking back and forth to throw her off-balance. For Cowboy, this only added to the fun. She glanced over the side of the bale, and furiously shook her head, ridding it of all debris, then did a Ukrainian folk dance with the agility of a logroller.

I eventually managed to tilt her off-balance and roll them both off of me. My neck was burning, as if it'd been scrubbed with an SOS pad, and my arms and legs had red, wormlike scratches crawling up and down my skin.

I took Wills inside so he could change into sweatpants and a long-sleeved shirt and then we clipped the strings and watched the hay bales unfold like a slashed bag of Jiffy Pop. Wills and I began tossing the hay all over the yard, with Cowboy skipping around like Gene Kelly in *Singing in the Rain*. And the two of them played for hours.

Wills, who'd never even skinned a knee, took Cowboy's lead, sliding on his butt and then turning around on his stomach to stop himself. He wasn't worried about the yellow dust or the possibility of bruising an elbow. He was just playing with Cowboy.

When he got up to run, Cowboy was only too happy to trail him, Wills squealing with laughter. At one point they ran toward the house and when Wills stopped abruptly, Cowboy crashed into the back of him. Together they slid, Cowboy's chest shoved against Wills's back, across the yard and slammed into the white wooden fence.

Wills turned toward Cowboy, who was now blissfully rolling upside down, her legs kicking the air, and said, "Thank you, Cowboy. Thank you for knocking me into the fence." No reaction from Cowboy. Wills tried again, "Hey! Thanks for practically *killing* me." Cowboy looked up mischievously. Clearly, "the crazies" had resurfaced.

"RUN FOR YOUR LIFE!" Wills yelled, but Cowboy was too

fast. She chased him around the yard while he yelled, "HURRY, MOMMY!! COWBOY'S CRAZED." He was, once again, howling with laughter and a little worried. I opened the window and leaned out.

"Need help?" I asked.

"HELP!" he yelled, panting as hard as Cowboy. "She only just tried to *kill* me." I hurried out the back door, even though I could tell Wills was enjoying himself, and joined in the chase.

"She's nutty," I said. "If you need a break, we can go inside."

Instead, he took off again, knowing that Cowboy wouldn't be able to resist. She managed to grab the leg of his gray sweatpants and began tugging and pulling him backward. Wills was no match for her weight and strength. Hay and skin flakes were flying just above the two of them.

I waded through piles of hay. "Don't tear his sweatpants," I said, laughing. Wills was giggling and clawing at the ground to get away. I straddled Cowboy's body and tried to pry her mammoth jaws apart. "Those are *new* sweatpants," I reiterated through gritted teeth.

"She loves me," Wills declared.

"She does," I said.

"She's my sister," he said. By now Cowboy had accomplished her mission and the sweatpants were off. She took off galloping around the pool, shaking the life out of them and praying that one of us would chase her.

"I'm pooped," I said. "No more for me."

"I'm itchy," Wills said simply, without any of the fear that dirt and texture and roughhousing usually incited.

I noticed that his legs were covered in crisscrossed red lines from the hay. Cowboy moseyed by, having deposited the sweatpants back by the garden and plopped down next to Wills. I brought out cold water for both of them. They drank like camels after a trek through the Sahara.

Next, I spread a quilt on top of the hay and they snuggled up together—Cowboy sound asleep, her head rising and falling on

Wills's tummy. Wills was lying flat, watching the leaves of the pear tree swirling down around him. It was the first time I'd watched the leaves fall without the urge to pick up each and every one. We were both getting more comfortable with messes.

Friday night, after the pumpkins had been carved, and the novelty of the hay had worn off, it was Cowboy's first Halloween. She'd turned one on October 19 with a doggie treat cake from Bones Bakery and a visit from Sacha and her dog, Murphy.

Around four o'clock, Wills began preparing for the evening. He meticulously filled the orange and black plastic bowls with Snickers bars, Hershey Kisses, and all of the other candy he'd picked out at Long's Drugs down the street. Each brand had its own bowl so that the Milky Ways never touched the Jolly Ranchers. He artfully arranged them on top of two beige card tables he'd draped with sticky, purple cobwebs, leaving in the bag the creepy plastic spiders that came with them. The tables stood on either side of the front door for maximum convenience when it was time for Michael and me to dole out the treats.

Wills and JoAnn went into the office where he dressed Cowboy in a Mets T-shirt and a pair of his nice blue shorts with a tail hole cut out. Suddenly, Cowboy bolted out the door and down the hallway, realizing there were kids at the door.

"Look out!" I yelled, as ghosts and witches scattered in all directions. Michael, JoAnn, and I tried to corner the party-wrecker while the kids ran down our front walk. We slammed the front gate shut just in time.

Cowboy stood on her back legs, front paws resting on top of the gate, gazing at the trick-or-treaters, despondent.

Looking out our bedroom window, Wills said, "I guess she wants to go trick-or-treating." He sighed, like an exasperated parent. "I guess we'd better go."

Without a moment to waste, Michael snatched Cowboy's leash off the dryer, JoAnn helped Wills put on his Spider-Man suit over his striped pajamas, I grabbed his mask, and we ran out the front door. We'd waited seven years to go trick-or-treating; we weren't going to give him time to change his mind.

We squeezed through the front gate in one tight bunch, Cowboy leading the way. Michael and Cowboy accompanied Wills as he went up to the doors with Wills to say "trick or treat" while JoAnn and I stood grinning on the sidewalk, flashlights dangling from our wrists. Wills could not believe people gave out candy for free, even though we'd been telling him about this tradition for *years*.

"I have six pieces," he called out to us, as he scampered off to the next house, Cowboy close on his heels.

Wills was trick-or-treating. It's the little things that always got me.

Part Four

Cowboy Sings
Good Night

CHAPTER FIFTEEN

D r. Graham called me the next morning while I was making French toast for Wills. He'd finally gotten enough information from all the tests he'd been doing on Cowboy to confirm a diagnosis.

"I can definitely tell you that Cowboy has lupus," he said. "It's what I'd suspected, but it's tricky to diagnose."

"Why?"

"The initial symptoms can mimic other diseases. They also come and go, which is confusing." I didn't say anything. "I wish I had better news."

"Canine lupus?" I asked just to confirm.

"Systematic lupus erythematosus," he said. "I think I'd mentioned the possibility of this early on."

"Is there a cure for this?"

"No, I'm sorry, Monica," he said.

"Is it fatal?" I whispered, walking out the back door so Wills wouldn't hear me.

"Unfortunately, about forty percent of dogs with SLE die within one year of diagnosis, due to either the disease itself or complications from therapy." I sat down on the back step.

"What complications?"

"The drugs we've been using to treat Cowboy are rough on her organs. It doesn't help that she presented symptoms at such a young age. She's been irreversibly affected by these drugs, there's just no way around it."

"Will we lose her soon?" I asked, my blood pressure shooting through the ceiling.

"I don't think she's in danger at the moment," he said. "I can't give you anything specific in terms of a timeline. You just never know. The most important thing is that we keep her comfortable—give her the best quality of life possible."

"Could she go into remission?"

"Definitely," he said. "It wouldn't surprise me at all. The only problem is, once they come out of remission, their symptoms are usually worse."

After hanging up, I sat down on the back step. Cowboy wandered out and I wrapped my arms around her. "You're the best girl," I told her, speaking directly into her ear. "We love you so much." I was too disturbed to dwell on what Dr. Graham had said. It would have to wait. I needed to get Wills to school.

The minute I got home I called Katherine. She recommended that we ease Wills into Cowboy's prognosis very slowly. "As long as there's no immediate threat of her dying, we should make sure he has the information he needs as we go along. So he's not surprised or completely shocked when she does pass away." I cringed. *When she does pass away.* The words hung in the air like a speech bubble—concrete, inevitable, unavoidable.

That afternoon, Cowboy patiently waited all day to play with Wills, but he was running around the front yard with Patrick playing robbers. Michael threw the ball for her instead. He'd only thrown about five tosses when she flopped down next to the sliding doors and fell asleep. This wasn't her ordinary "I've just spent the day hiking up Mount Wilson" kind of flop. Something was wrong. She was sleeping so heavily and deeply, that when I tried to wake her, I couldn't. She tried to open her eyes, but they'd roll shut again.

"I hate to move her," I told Michael.

"The kids are going to end up stepping on her," he said. "I'll lift her up." But when he slipped his hands under her side, she reluctantly got up on her own. I guided her into Wills's room, where she stood and waited for me to lift her onto his bed. *Cowboy, you're scaring me,* I whispered to her, kissing the top of her head. Michael sat down next to her.

"Are you feelin' bad, Cowboy?" he asked, as she rolled onto her side again. He stroked her fur.

"She looks terrible," I told Michael. He nodded.

"This is about the worst thing in the world," he said, leaning down to kiss her cheek, "especially for Wills."

On cue, Wills and Patrick came racing into his room. Cowboy lifted her head.

"Who's the girl?" Wills asked, stopping long enough to see if she was going to hop up and chase them.

"I think she's having a bad day," I said. "You guys go ahead and have fun." They grabbed walkie-talkies off his dresser and ran out.

That evening, Michael and Wills were playing chess on the coffee table while I read *People* magazine. They were talking about knights and kings and I was reading about Jessica Simpson.

Cowboy was lying just under Wills's feet. There was only about ten inches of carpet between the coffee table and the couch, but lately, she'd taken to squeezing herself into tight places. Maybe it made her feel safer and closer to us. "You're going to whoop my butt," Michael told Wills.

"I know," Wills said. "The trick is to bring your queen out right away."

"Oh, I see." Michael protected his queen as if she were the Holy Grail. He moved a rook instead.

"Oh, that was dastardly," Wills said, without cracking a smile. He stared at the board. "Is Cowboy going to die?"

Michael glanced up at Wills, who kept his eyes on the board. I didn't move.

Images from the past two years flooded me. The day we'd picked

Cowboy up from the Pet Chalet and Wills was so sick, yet he loved her right away. The first time she knocked him down and he laughed. The two of them sleeping in Wills's bed with paws and arms intertwined. How would we tell this boy, who'd already been through so much, that his best friend in the world was going to die? And that we didn't know when, but it would be sooner rather than later. How do you explain what's left after a loss like that? We couldn't tell him it was going to be all right because it certainly wasn't. Or that he'd move on, eventually, and always have the memories to cherish because, right now, that would have been unfair to him. "She'll always be with us" or "We'll never forget Cowboy" were phrases that weren't adequate—not even close.

"She'll die someday," Michael said. "I don't know when."

"But she's really sick, right?" he asked, capturing one of Michael's knights.

"She feels pretty bad today," Michael said. "And thanks for taking my knight."

It was Michael's turn to bob and weave through one of these crushing moments, and I didn't envy him one bit.

"Will she live to be five years old?" Wills asked. I could tell by the tone of his voice that he already knew the answer. We'd tried to prepare him along the way without just coming out and saying it.

"I hope so, sweet boy."

Wills looked up, his eyes filling with tears and his lips pursed. "I don't want her to be sick," he sobbed, climbing onto Michael's lap.

"Of course you don't," Michael said, hugging him close. "Nobody wants Cowboy to be sick."

Wills slid down beside Cowboy and cradled her head in his hands. "Cowboy, we're going to take very good care of you," he said, crying even harder. "Don't be scared." He collapsed on top of her, rubbing his tear-stained face into her blond curly coat. She turned and licked the top of his head.

The guilt I felt over the whole thing was all-consuming. It was *my* fault. I'd read those warnings about "Don't buy a dog from a pet store," and I did it anyway. The "breeder" in Missouri where Cowboy came from was probably a puppy mill and now we had a critically ill dog. I'd broken my son's heart, not to mention my own. She was irreplaceable to all of us.

But who would Wills have been without her? And where would she have ended up? Maybe Cowboy's suffering had made Wills's challenges seem a little more manageable. I was so messed up about all of it.

The following weekend, Wills asked if he could shampoo Cowboy.

"Sure," I said. "You can shampoo her anytime."

"Let's go, girl," he said, holding onto her collar and leading her into the bathroom.

"Be careful with the hot water," I said. "Warm water is fine with her."

"Okay."

The two of them disappeared around the corner. Forty-five minutes later, they reemerged, Cowboy and Wills dripping wet.

"Doesn't that shampoo smell terrible?" I asked.

"It's not so bad," he said, as Cowboy shook water all over the bookshelves in the family room.

"Let me get a beach towel," I said.

"I want to start taking care of Cowboy." Wills sat on the edge of the couch. "I want to help her."

"She would love that!" I said. "Let's add some things to the Scheduler."

I draped the towel over my lap and she dove on it, wiping most of her body off on the carpet. Then she backed up; suddenly, I was a matador and the red-and-white polka dot towel was her signal to charge. "I think she liked getting a bath from you," I said.

"She's happy," Wills agreed.

"She's WILD," I laughed. "You really helped her out." Wills was bouncing up and down on the couch cushions.

"She's funny!" he said.

"Don't jump on the couch!" He did one last hop, landing on his butt with a satisfied grin. "Good job."

In early December, at one of our weekly appointments, Dr. Graham told me that he was adding steroid injections for Cowboy, twice a day. I stood straight up. Was there no end to this mess?

"I really think this will give her quite a bit of relief," he said. "I was hesitant to put her on such strong medicine, but I can see that she's suffering."

"Do I need to bring her here for the shots?" I asked, shaking my head in disbelief.

"No, you can give them to her at home," he said, matter-of-fact. "I'll show you exactly how to do it. There's no way you'll hurt her."

I looked down at Cowboy, who was lying on her side, snoring. Her lips were blowing in and out with a fluttering noise that was a cross between a snore and a sigh. I could have kissed her right on the mouth, she was so sweet and had put up with so much.

Dr. Graham showed me how to use the syringe as we helped Cowboy to her feet, and stuck the needle into the bunched scruff of skin between her shoulder blades. I felt nauseous about hurting her, but she didn't even glance back. She felt nothing. Thank God. After all she'd been through, I could not live with myself if I'd caused her any more pain.

I left his office with a bottle of Allergens that needed to be refrigerated immediately or they'd lose their potency. They were too expensive to ruin, so I sped home and put them next to the Miracle Whip, tossing the plastic container of syringes on a shelf above the kitchen sink.

With the addition of steroids, poor Cowboy needed lots of exercise to keep her from jumping out of her own skin. She was all over the place. Wills was keeping his promise of shampooing her on the weekends, and making sure she had enough food and water. He was also her personal trainer.

When she got too out of control, we took her to Santa Susana Park in Simi Valley, a small leafy park with plenty of places to run off-leash. There were also rocky boulders to climb and, best of all for Wills, railroad tracks that ran along the opposite side of the fence from the hiking trails. We could play *and* watch the trains plow through. Wills drew a map to show Cowboy.

It was November, so I packed our sweatshirts and we headed out. On the way there, Cowboy kept jumping from the front seat to the back so I pulled over and snapped the "doggie seat belt" on her for the third time. Wills kissed and hugged her tightly, which settled her down a little, then lowered the window halfway so she could stick her head out and enjoy the wind on her soft yellow face. I wondered how much hair was blowing onto Box Canyon Road as we sailed by.

Ten minutes later, Cowboy was (again) sitting next to me in the front seat.

"What happened, Wills?" I asked.

"She wants to be with you."

I glanced back and saw the seat belt in tatters. She'd managed to chew through the straps. I brushed my hand across the top of her head, her eyes closing with each stroke. *Don't be sick, little girl,* I thought, as she leaned against the center console, looking at me.

At Santa Susana, we all piled out and Wills ran for the rock formations. Since starting OT, he was getting so confident about climbing—and these weren't small rocks. Cowboy ran off-leash like a maniac coyote, ripping around one tree and then leaping on to a large rock at breakneck speed. The steroids were amping up her naturally elevated energy levels. I knelt down to grab a bottle of water out of my backpack and when I glanced up, Cowboy was standing on top of that huge bolder with Wills. I couldn't imagine how she scaled that rock, but she was there, her tail thwomping the back of Wills's legs.

"She loves it up here," he called down, waving.

"I can see that," I yelled, giving him the thumbs-up. One of the symptoms of canine lupus was how it affected the joints, making it difficult to maneuver smoothly. Sometimes I could see the disease in her so clearly—the way she limped along, but today it wasn't in her joints. She was climbing like her two-year-old self.

Those two spent the rest of the afternoon charging through dry creekbeds and climbing more craggy boulders. Wills even spotted two red-tailed hawks.

On the way home, I couldn't keep my eyes on the road because Cowboy was once again ricocheting all over the inside of the car.

"The drugs that Cowboy takes for her lupus are making her really hyper," I told Wills. "I hope she can settle down a little."

"She doesn't mind," he said, scruffing her ears. Cowboy was a trouper—just like Wills.

* * *

One day, a week before Christmas, I was in the kitchen when I heard Wills yelling, "HELP, MOMMY!"

Cowboy had knocked him out of the way and stolen a small plastic lawn jockey that stood at the gate of his Christmas tree village.

"Drop it!" I demanded. She assumed the front paws on the ground, ass in the air position. I stood there with my hands on my hips, grinning down at her. "Give me that jockey, you wild thing."

I knelt down to grab it, and she was off like a shot.

"I'm not chasing you!" I yelled. She was pacing back and forth on the patio, staring at me through the window. *"I'm not coming out there!"*

She didn't believe me, and ran off around the pool.

When I turned my back, I heard her paws pounding the tiles. She was heading my way. As she blew by, I grabbed her collar and spun her around to pry open her mouth—the lawn jockey was gone. I walked out to the pool to see where she'd dropped it.

I heard glass breaking, and Wills yelling, "MOOOOMM-MMYYYY!"

"What now?" I ran into the house.

In her excitement, Cowboy had knocked over Wills's little

Christmas tree, and the noise had frightened her so much that she took off running, her back paw caught in the lower string of lights.

Cowboy, the tree, and I tore down the hallway with bulbs breaking and pine needles flying as we squeezed by.

Over my shoulder, I was yelling to Wills, "Don't follow her. You'll step on glass. Don't follow us, honey."

I realized the medications had not only amped her up, making her manic, they'd also made her anxious—skittish. After finally untangling her paw from the string of lights, I could not calm her down. Her eyes were glassy and she wouldn't go anywhere near the family room.

I tried to sit with her, but she ran out to the pool and paced.

Wills was still standing on a chair.

"This is terrible," I said, lifting him off the chair and onto my lap.

"Cowboy went crazy," he said, watching her through the window, "and now, my tree is gone."

"The medications are causing her to be really rowdy right now," I said. "She can't help it."

"I'm mad at her," Wills said, his lip curling under just before the tears.

"I don't blame you," I said, "but she wouldn't tear up your tree or make you sad on purpose. Her paw got caught in the lights. That's what happened."

"She loves me." He tucked his face into my shirt.

"She loves you, all right," I said. "But it's okay to get mad, even if you love her."

He knew things had gotten worse. Where was the old Cowboy?

The steroids were wrecking her health or maybe it was the other drugs. I didn't know, but I was starting to wonder if we'd stopped helping her. She deserved a good life, a calm and happy one regardless of the length of it. I would call Dr. Graham in the morning and get her off this toxic stuff. She didn't deserve this.

She was lying on the cool tiles with her chin resting on top of her front paws, panting. We sat down next to her. Wills stroked her head.

"Who's my good girl?" he said in his Cowboy-loving voice. "Who's the best girl in the whole world?" Her tail thumped against his leg.

"I'll clean up that glass and then we'll get you another tree," I told him.

"Let's get the tree tomorrow," he said.

"Good idea," I told him. "Let's not leave Cowboy."

Before I cleaned up, I tucked Wills and Cowboy into the pink bed, and the three of us laid down together. Michael was still at work.

"I'm going to love on her," Wills said, stretching the entire length of his body on top of hers. She draped her front paw across his chest.

That night everyone slept in the pink bed.

* * *

The next morning Cowboy sidled into the kitchen as if she were Sir John Gielgud in a Noël Coward play—all dressing gown and slippers. She was sublime, not a hint of the mania. By Sunday night, she was doing much better.

The medications had somehow congealed and she was completely sane once more. Settled. And it lasted.

She pranced around the yard like a show puppy, and new baby hairs were springing up around her eyes. Of course, I took her straight to In-N-Out Burger for a Double-Double. It had been a while. *Maybe she* could *live a happy, energized life with lupus,* I thought as she raced me to the car. I knew better—the very idea registered "ridiculous"—but today, we would enjoy our Double-Doubles.

A few days later, Michael called me out to the yard, and pointed. There on the grass was a small plastic lawn jockey waist-deep in Cowboy poo.

"It looks like he's waving 'Happy New Year!' " I laughed.

"More like, 'Can you give me a hand down here?' " Michael said.

Wills came to see what all the fuss was about. "I don't want that back," he said. He saw Michael lean down with a grocery bag to pick it up. "I'm outta here before you disturb the outer crust." He ran back inside.

Michael and I had been monitoring Cowboy's poo with the intense focus of a forensic team, searching for scatological signs of improvement or decline in every bowel movement that graced our lawn.

One afternoon, I was on my way to pick up Wills from school when I saw a solid Cowboy poop lying in the backyard. I eyed the coiled hose in triumph, so happy that I wouldn't be needing it today—maybe her stomach was feeling better. I wanted to bronze that turd and save it forever.

I walked into the kitchen to get a plastic bag and when I returned to pick it up, there was a bright green praying mantis sitting on top of it. He was straddling it like Slim Pickens riding the H-bomb in *Dr. Strangelove.* I half expected to see a lasso in his tiny green hand and an itsy bitsy cowboy hat tilted at a jaunty angle atop his anvil-shaped head. I ran for the camera.

That picture totally killed Wills. He was laughing and holding his stomach.

That night, fresh out of the shower, Wills ran into the front yard in his pajamas. He stood on his swing as Cowboy circled the yard gathering plenty of speed for the leap into the trampoline. Wills jumped off the swing and made it in ahead of her.

Cowboy took a straight shot up the middle of the yard, hurling herself into the air and sliding through the slit in the black protective netting. While she took several victory laps around the inside of the trampoline, Wills grabbed her drool-soaked stuffed kitten and threw it over the net. In jubilation, Cowboy leapt out, scooped up the kitten without stopping, and circled the yard once more. Wills squealed with anticipation as Cowboy headed back toward the trampoline.

If only I could freeze-frame them both, just as they were—right then. Wills in his jammies giggling and Cowboy exuberant. There in our fenced-in yard, nothing bad could reach them. They were utterly protected and so happy.

CHAPTER SIXTEEN

Cowboy rode home from yet another Graham appointment with her head sticking out of the passenger window. She was feeling lousy again. Her skin was inflamed and covered in sores. She also had a fever, which meant another infection. This teeter-tottering back and forth was so hard on her.

I drove extra slow so she wouldn't lose more hair from her face. It had just grown back in. Cars on Ventura Boulevard honked at me. I didn't blame them. I remembered when I had places to rush to. Now I just wanted to slow everything down.

It was obvious to anyone who saw her that Cowboy was extremely ill. I knew it sounded dramatic when I told Michael one night that I "couldn't live without her." But I meant it. And worse than *my* loss was the unthinkable—that Wills would lose his right arm, his silly sister, his trampoline chum, the one who'd given him the confidence to sleep in a room of his own and swim in the ocean. The thought of losing her was unbearable.

Michael and I talked to Wills about Cowboy's condition every step of the way. If he had questions, we answered them; otherwise, we'd wait until she hit another health snag, and then we'd sit him down again.

Wills always responded by thinking of ways to make her life easier. He built a wooden ramp, for instance, to help her walk up to the couch or get to his bed. (We still had the gray stairs that led to nowhere, but her balance had gotten so bad, I worried she might fall off the side.) The ramp was about three feet wide with a very slight incline that she could negotiate just fine. He also cut up old T-shirts and sweatpants to make her a special extrasoft quilt, which he sewed together with large, loopy stitches. He even stuffed the insides with paper towels so that Cowboy would have a cushion for her head.

We added a Taking Care of Pets section to the Scheduler, which we were still using every day. This gave Wills a new sense of responsibility, and clearly showed how much he was helping his animals. He wrote the following cards himself:

- *Check Cowboy's food and water*
- *Shampoo Cowboy*
- *Feed fish*
- *Check hamsters' food and water*
- *Water the hermit crabs*

Halfway through second grade, and with Cowboy's health still careening all over the map, Wills was thriving at school. On his first day as class leader, he read all twenty of his classmates' names loudly, clearly, and without hesitation during roll call. It was the first time he'd managed to do that. He even had his story published in the school newspaper, about two spiders from New Jersey who take a train to D.C.

In OT, Wills had learned to balance himself on a Razor scooter. He could even go around corners without stopping. The only problem was, Cowboy couldn't keep up with her pal anymore.

"You go ahead, honey," I told him, "We can see you from here." Cowboy and I lagged behind, as he hurtled down the sidewalk. He looked like such a "guy" in his helmet and wrist guards, no longer protective of his body, thanks to Cowboy knocking him flat about a hundred times.

"I feel bad that Cowboy can't run," he said, circling back to where we were loping along.

"She's just happy to be out with us," I said. "The way her health goes up and down, she'll probably be running beside you before too long. Enjoy yourself."

Wills was also finally interested in getting a bicycle! Michael and I had prayed for the day we could walk into Pete's Bike Shop with Wills and watch him pick out his first bike. And with his ninth birthday only a few months away, that's exactly what we'd be doing.

That evening, Cowboy was asleep on the floor and Wills and I were on the couch trying to find that goofball Waldo in an enormous paperback called *Where's Waldo?: The Wonder Book*. All of a sudden, Cowboy's tail began thumping up and down on the carpet. I looked over and she was deep asleep.

"Look at Cowboy," I told Wills. "She's wagging her tail in her sleep."

"Only for a dog, though," Wills said.

"What's only for dogs?" I asked.

"Wagging your tail in your sleep. It's not for people because people don't have tails," he said, "only dogs have tails." He continued looking for Waldo, circling Wenda with a black Sharpie. "We could *never* be that happy," he added.

"We *could* be that happy, but our tails wouldn't wag," I said.

"Because we don't have tails," he reiterated.

"How do people show that they're happy?" I asked.

"They clap."

"That's right," I said, pleased that I had made my point.

Wills looked at Cowboy again. "We could never be that happy."

CHAPTER SEVENTEEN

The roof had still not been replaced, and there wasn't a thing I could do about it, but the bathroom cabinets, along with the rest of the paint and plaster in our 1951 ranch-style house, were starting to peel. And those I could do myself.

After sanding the doors, I was just starting to paint them when Wills ran in. "Richard's not in his house," he blurted out. Oh no, not the turtle, too.

"Are you sure?"

"I just looked," Wills said.

"He's outside in his pen," I told him. "He was banging his shell against the glass, so I put him outside in the grass." Wills looked skeptical. "Go look."

"HE'S GONE!!!" he yelled from the backyard. "RICHARD'S GONE!"

"I'm coming," I yelled, sticking my paintbrush into a pickle jar filled with turpentine and shutting the bathroom door so Cowboy wouldn't drink it.

Wills was inside Richard's wire pen pointing to a small freshly dug patch of dirt. Torn-up grass surrounded it like confetti.

"He's definitely been here," he reported.

"He was," I said, "I put him here myself."

He couldn't have gone far, thanks to the eight-foot fence surrounding the backyard. "He's here somewhere," I said, poking my head under the bushes.

Cowboy was running around in a frothy frenzy. She'd had two shots of steroids earlier that morning.

"Maybe Cowboy can find him," I said.

"I'll get his smell," Wills said, running inside to get Richard's hollowed-out coconut that served as his house.

Cowboy had rescued Richard before.

In a very Lassie moment, before she was sick, she'd rustled him out of the thick, overgrown ivy at the very back of our yard, rooting around like a warthog. Just as we were giving up hope, Richard's shell emerged, clamped securely between Cowboy's jaws.

"Good girl!" we cheered. Cowboy hopped around on her back feet as if she'd just gotten Bingo.

"Maybe Alex let him out," Wills said, eyes wide in panic.

Holy shit! I had left Richard in his pen when our gardener came to cut the grass. It was possible that Alex didn't see Richard in the pen because he hunkered down into the dirt just below grass level. The other problem was, Alex probably left the back gate open for about two hours while he worked.

"Let me call Alex and ask if he's seen him," I said.

We searched the neighborhood, and nailed posters with Richard's picture on it to telephone poles. I was sure that someone would find it odd seeing a turtle walking down Ventura Boulevard, and would pick him up, see our flyers, and return him to us. Only no one did.

Our menagerie was shrinking.

In March, Cowboy's health rallied. Her eyes were brighter, and she was digging up my new box shrubs I'd just had the courage to replant.

"She seems so well all of a sudden," I told Dr. Graham, who'd called to check on Cowboy's progress.

"Sounds like she's in remission."

"She's swimming again," I said, "and chasing balls around the yard."

"It's March twenty-first, maybe she's welcoming the vernal equinox."

"I'll take it," I said, hanging up.

Our relief was short-lived.

In April, Dr. Graham gave us terrible news. Cowboy's organs weren't strong enough to sustain the strong medications anymore.

"I'd hoped she'd be better, and we'd be able to take her down off these large doses of the medications," Dr. Graham told me, leaning down to pet Cowboy, "but she's not better, and now the drugs are affecting her liver." He kissed her nose.

"What do we do now?" I asked.

"We have to back off," he said. "We have to let her recover from some of the effects of these toxic drugs. I'm not taking her off everything, though."

"Will she get worse?" I asked.

"She'll lose her hair again. I imagine you can expect exactly what we had before: flaky skin, sores, and ear infections."

"Is this the beginning of the end?" I asked.

"Do I think she'll recover from the effects of the lupus? No," he said. "Do I think she's dying? No, I don't." I sat there stunned. What *was* he saying?

"What will we do when she starts going downhill again?" I asked.

"We'll treat the symptoms."

"Will she still get her shots?"

"We'll keep the shots going," he said, "but I'm going to be bringing her down off the steroids."

I sat on the floor and pulled her onto my lap. "Is there anyone who specializes in canine lupus? Anyone we could call?" I'd asked him this about twelve times already, and he always answered patiently.

"I wish I knew of someone or something," he said. "The reality is, she came to you with all of this. There's no other way this was going to go for her."

Cowboy and I drove through In-N-Out Burger to get her a Double-Double. I ordered a Coke to see if it would help my mounting nausea. It didn't.

I put off going home right away. Instead, Cowboy and I rode around in my denial for a while listening to AC/DC at top volume. As long as Dr. Graham and I were the only ones who knew about Cowboy's failing liver, maybe it wouldn't be true.

Eventually, the CD ended, night fell, and we went home to Wills and Michael to face what was surely coming.

* * *

Cowboy didn't decline as I'd expected after she was taken off the steroids. Who knew how long it would last, but for now she seemed comfortable.

The first of May, Wills and I were walking in from the grocery store, when I noticed that Ruby wasn't thumping for attention in the unsoiled side of her double-wide. She was lying on her stomach, her back legs spread out behind her, flat against the floor, the heft of her black-and-white body oddly crooked. She lifted her head and looked at me as if to say, "What the hell happened to my legs?"

"Wills, something's wrong with Ruby," I said. He walked over, and bent down, pulling the brim of his Western Pacific Railroad hat around to the back of his head.

"She looks good," he said, readjusting the hat.

"She looks 'wrong,' " I told him.

Evelyn, our babysitter, had stopped by to pick up a sweater she'd left earlier in the week and I asked her if she could stay with Wills while I rushed Ruby to the emergency animal hospital.

I opened the hutch and stroked Ruby's head. She lifted her double chins toward me, the bottom of her floppy ears dragging in the hay.

"What's wrong, Ruby?" I asked her. She wore an expression that I'd only seen in nursing homes: a lost, faraway stare.

"I'm going to get you fixed up," I told her, lifting her gently. Her back legs hung down and her front paws followed suit. From the neck up she was fine, but the rest of her was paralyzed.

On the way to the hospital, I held her on my lap, wrapped loosely in a green-and-yellow beach towel. Her face peered out, sleepy and relaxed. I offered a few bites of lettuce and she managed to eat them, which was a good sign.

Traffic was worse than usual, so I sang an old World War II song. "Nights are long since you went away, I think about you all through the day, my buddy, my buddy, nobody quite so true. Miss your voice, the touch of your hand. Just long to know that you understand. My buddy. My buddy. Your buddy misses you."

This was clearly the worst possible song I could have picked and by the end of it, Ruby and I were both sobbing. Okay, *I* was sobbing, but if a rabbit could cry, she'd have needed a tiny hanky because I sang the hell out of that song.

I walked into the waiting room of the animal hospital with Ruby hugged tight against my chest.

"Can I help you?" a gentleman asked.

"I think my rabbit might have had a stroke," I told him, holding her up so he could see.

"Lady, that rabbit is deceased."

I looked at Ruby. Her black eyes were glazed over, the upside-down U that had been her constantly munching mouth was slack, open. She'd died in the car, and I didn't even notice. What in the hell was wrong with me, and how could I have sent her out with such a depressing song? Why hadn't I chosen "Put on a Happy Face" or "Blue Skies"?

I slowly handed her over to a nurse and signed papers confirming that after cremation, she'd be mailed back to us in a small cedar box.

"Keep the towel," I said, to no one in particular, as I wandered out into the empty parking lot in a haze. No more burrowing. No more round black nuggets rolling around on our patio for Cowboy to gobble up. The leporine queen was dead.

I thought Wills would fall apart, but he took the news with a solemn nod of the head and continued rolling a plastic pickup truck, with two hermit crabs in the back, along the masking-tape road he'd constructed that led to the Lego Village. Was I the only one of us who was sad?

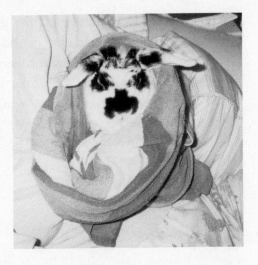

I had to face the truth, Ruby was mean to everyone but me. Still, I'd miss holding her every night during the eleven o'clock news while she chewed through the expensive linen throw we'd gotten as a wedding gift that was big enough to wrap around the both of us. I'd even miss her jackhammering back leg, letting me (and the neighborhood) know that she was pissed off.

Four weeks later, her ashes *did* arrive in a small cedar box. Whoever packed her placed a light pink grosgrain ribbon around the outside of it with a note card attached.

> *The joy they brought us, is the gift they leave behind.*
> *We're sorry for your loss.*

I appreciated the extra effort and the fact that someone was sorry she was gone. Michael attacked that hutch like a human wrecking ball, stuffing it into our trash barrel with maniacal delight. She'd treated him especially harshly, biting all the way through his thumbnail on two separate occasions.

I spread her ashes in the garden she'd always been intent on destroying. Next to squeezing her thick, overly fed body into her burrow under the back shed, Wills's garden was Ruby's favorite place.

There was something about the grainy feel of the dust, her bones. And such a small amount, considering her girth. The powder blew up and around the beefsteak tomatoes, some of it teetering on top of the blond hair on my arms. Like the stringy remains of Wills's friend Olivia's stuffed rabbit, that was all I had left of her—and then she was gone, with a gust of wind.

Chapter Eighteen

Second grade ended with—yes, another loud and spirited Sing, and when I met with Neal at the end of the year, it was decided that, with Wills pushing for more independence, he wouldn't need a full-time aide in the classroom next year.

He'd be staring third grade without Lynn! It was a moment I could never have imagined even a year earlier. She would be staying at CCS, so he would see her every day, she just wouldn't be working with him.

I had mixed emotions—thrilled that he'd achieved social and academic autonomy, but also worried that if he needed Lynn in the middle of the school year, she'd already be assigned to another student.

"I think he's going to be fine," Lynn said. "There are children much more in need of an aide than Wills."

I would miss her weekly (and sometimes daily) reports. With Lynn in the classroom, I never missed a beat. But now, he needed Mommy to step back. What happened in the classroom was *his* business, not mine. And he would always have Katherine to talk to if anything came up that he didn't want to share with Michael or me.

But, oh my God, I'd miss knowing that Lynn was right beside him, like a security blanket.

Wills was on summer vacation and the following Saturday

morning, I went to buy bagels. When I got home, I was greeted with a "Hamster Warning!" note stuck onto the door leading out of the garage:

DANGER:

Do not come here!

If you get Booner mad, he will bite you and that is 100% BAD.

It was written in Michael's handwriting, but these were clearly Wills's words. He'd drawn a picture of Booner with a big X through it.

When I got to the back door there was another sign written on blue construction paper:

PLEASE!

When you come into this house,
DO NOT COME HERE.

Because if you build a Booner House, and if he comes to a point
where he doesn't know where to go, you might have to help him.
You might just have to wave a piece of paper to blow him away
from that spot so he won't come back there. And that is a true thing.

Once inside, I saw Wills and Michael working on an elaborate Booner setup, complete with his new Bachman HO scale Santa Fe diesel freight engine with the classic *Warbonnet* paint scheme, sitting in the wooden roundhouse.

"Can I come in?" I asked. "I have bagels."

"Mommy, stay away from danger," Wills warned.

"Did Booner grow one hundred feet tall and sprout fangs while I was gone?" I asked.

"Wills is making Booner scary today," Michael said.

"Why is Booner scary?" I asked.

"Booner doesn't want any more animals to die," Wills said. "He's crazy mad."

"About Ruby?" I asked. Wills shrugged. "Is he mad that Ruby died?"

Wills burst into tears. "He's mad that breathers die."

Wills curled onto my lap and I wrapped my arms around him. I should have realized that losing Ruby would set off all kinds of concerns in Wills. We'd lost hamsters, hermit crabs, fish, and, of course, wandering Richard (the turtle), but Ruby was different. We'd had her for more than four years, and even though she was a pistol, her brash personality had embedded itself into our lives. She was always *there*—and now she wasn't.

A sign taped to the center of the television screen read:

NO MORE GOODBYES!

* * *

Dr. Graham suggested that we take Cowboy in for a puppy cut so that her hair loss wouldn't be so traumatic for Wills.

"What's a puppy cut?" I asked. "A haircut?"

"They trim the hair but leave about half an inch instead of shaving her," he said. "It's really cute, actually. The cut will also cool her down a little," he said, "letting her skin breathe."

"I'll take her in."

"It's not a rush," he said. "I just think it might be easier on Wills."

When Wills got back from a playdate at Cole's I announced, "Cowboy needs a haircut! If we take her to Camp Happy Dog, they can also cut her nails, which she *really* needs."

"How short will her hair be?" he asked.

"It'll look like it did when she was about this old." I pointed to a picture taped on the fridge of an adolescent Cowboy with a stuffed heart in her mouth.

"She'll look like a puppy again," he said, smiling.

"It'll be adorable," I agreed.

And it was! When we picked up Cowboy from Camp Happy Dog, she really did look like that picture, only taller. There were no bald patches on her sides or back, and her tail was sleek, not scraggly. She looked healthy, except for her face and the crusty eyes, which weren't crusty too often because I was constantly wiping them with a warm washcloth.

But looks can be deceiving. During the next month or so, Cowboy's health began spiraling downward. She was too ill to swim or dive, so she drifted around the pool on her very own pink mesh *Hawaii Five-O* float. She slept through the kiddie cannonballs off the side of the pool, the water guns, and all of us yelling, "Marco Polo." The familiar sounds of her family must have been comforting, plus all of the kisses and head rubs she received as she glided by, her front paw making a small wake in the water.

Anytime Michael was preparing for a belly flop, one of us would steer Cowboy's float to the shallow end, protecting her from the ensuing wave, which was often high enough to clear our neighbor's eight-foot fence. Michael's a big man.

I worried that Cowboy felt left out, like a kid cooped up with the chicken pox watching her friends having fun outside. But at two and a half, she looked more like Benjamin Button, her soulful brown eyes taking in the action with the kind of wisdom and peaceful resignation you only see in old dogs.

Regardless of how painful it'd become dragging her stiff, aching body up off the carpet to follow us, she made it a point always to be in the same room with us, just like old times. We made adjustments, too. We took her on car rides with all of the windows down so that, even though she wasn't steady enough to stand up and poke her head out the passenger window, the breeze still blew against her face. Wills sat with her as she raised her chin, eyes partially closed.

That summer, Wills decided to go to an arts day camp three days a week, which was huge. He never wanted to be away from home (or Cowboy) during the summer, but now that he was older, he wanted to be with his friends. Plus, there was this funky, multicolored woodworking bus that pulled into camp in the morning, and Wills spent hours in there building small bridges and houses for his hermit crabs. Each day he came home with a painting, a haiku poem, or a clay ashtray that he'd made especially for Cowboy. He'd present them to her in the car as the three of us headed to Wienerschnitzel for hot dogs and root beer floats. I missed having Wills home, but I realized that he was undeniably, unequivocally happy for the first time!

Lynn was at the same camp teaching yoga. We'd decided that it was a good way to ease Wills into starting third grade without relying on her. She'd be nearby, but he was in charge of himself.

The first class of the day was Cowboy Breakfast, where they taught kids to cook breakfast on an open grill. We know why Wills picked Cowboy Breakfast as his first activity, but what we didn't realize was what a difference it would make in his eating habits. He'd refused to eat anything but white food for as long as I could remember. But before camp was over, Wills was whipping up scrambled eggs (with a dash of seasoned salt), turkey sausage, smoked apple bacon, and French toast. And not only was he cooking, he was eating it, too.

He ended each afternoon in Lynn's yoga class with soothing music and candles. I walked in early one day to find him lying in the center of the yoga studio with cucumber slices over both eyes, his hands, soft and relaxed, folded across his chest.

★ ★ ★

In August, Michael, Wills, and I took a trip to New Jersey for Michael's father's eightieth birthday bash. Pop was the best of the best, Wills's namesake—he'd taken care of all of us at one time or another. There was no way we were missing his big day. Still, we hated to leave Cowboy.

It wasn't as if she were in any immediate danger, and Dr. Graham thought she'd be okay. But I felt guilty that I was looking forward to a vacation. It would be a relief to not be in charge for a while.

Cowboy was in the care of our dear friend Cara, who was a self-proclaimed hermit. She moved into our house the morning we said our tearful good-byes, and promised not to leave Cowboy alone until our return, six days later.

I stocked up the fridge and left a stack of DVDs, along with instructions on when to give Cowboy her medications, how to administer shots, and where to reach both Dr. Burke and Dr. Graham. Michael gave her enough cash to cover any possible Cowboy emergency.

Two days after the party, Cara called my cell phone. "Cowboy's really bad," she said. "I hate to call you because you're with your family, but she's lying on her side, and I can't get her up."

"Can you take her to Dr. Burke's?" I asked, cursing myself for not being home.

"I'll take her right now," Cara said.

I pulled Michael aside. "We have to get home. Cowboy's on her side and Cara can't get her to stand up. She's taking her to Dr. Burke's."

"Oh, Monica, no," Michael said, both of us in tears. "I'll call Burke right now and let him know they're on their way."

I sat down beside Wills at Pop's patio table and said, "Cowboy's feeling a little lonely and sick, so I'd like to go home."

"Let's go," he said, standing up. "Is she okay?"

"She's not feeling good," I said.

"She never feels good anymore. She'll be okay, Mommy."

Michael changed our plane tickets. The next flight out of Newark was in three hours.

Cara called, asking us to call Dr. Burke.

"Will she make it until we get there?" Michael asked him.

"I can't promise you that," Dr. Burke said.

"We're taking an earlier flight back," Michael said. "We'll be there tonight."

"I hate to interrupt your vacation and then have her rebound," he said, "but, I have to be honest, this is the worst I've seen her."

"Does Dr. Graham need to see her?" he asked.

"I already called him," Dr. Burke said.

"Does he have any suggestions?"

"I think this is out of his jurisdiction," he said, "and mine."

"Meaning?"

"She's dying, Michael; there's nothing either of us can do to prevent that from happening," Dr. Burke said gently. "It's just a matter of when. In the meantime, it's my job to keep her as comfortable as possible."

We packed our unused clothes and headed to the airport. A terrible lightning storm broke out while we were on the New Jersey Turnpike, backing up traffic for miles. We missed our flight to L.A. I was unsuccessful at reining in my hysteria, as Wills sat next to me in the backseat.

"Mommy, are you worried about Cowboy?" he asked.

"I *am* worried about Cowboy," I said. "And I'm not good at sitting in this kind of traffic. It makes me really anxious."

He looked out the window. "It's a parking lot."

"It sure is," I said.

"We'll get another flight, Monica," Michael said, already on hold with Continental Airlines. I was starting to cry.

"We could get out and walk faster than this," I said, infuriated. "How could it take two and a half hours to drive twenty miles?" All I could think of was getting my arms around Cowboy.

"It's because of that lightning storm," Wills said.

"That's right," I said, trying to sound calm. He was so sweet and patient, sitting in his booster seat. I felt like a raging lunatic. Cowboy was probably dying, and I was sitting behind a Dunkin' Donuts truck at Exit 12.

I called Cara.

"We're home from Dr. Burke's now," she said, "and Cowboy's sleeping. I called Jeremy to come sit with us." Jeremy was her boyfriend.

"I'm sorry to be putting you through this," I said. "I can't believe it."

"Don't worry," she said. "I'm okay. And really, she seems more peaceful right now."

"We're trying to get there," I told her, which was code for *Please tell me she's not going to die while I'm sitting on the New Jersey Turnpike,* because I couldn't say any such thing in front of Wills.

"You'll make it," she said.

When we finally got home, we were shocked by what awaited us. Happy as Cowboy was to see us, she could not pull herself up on her own to greet us. She was emaciated, her eyes rimmed in runny, green mucus. We'd been gone only five days.

"There's something on her leg," Wills said, leaning in to get a closer look. Both of her front legs were shaved and there was a shunt wrapped in red medical tape on her front left.

"Looks like Dr. Burke gave her an IV," I said. "I've had one of those before."

"In your leg?"

"My arm," I said. "Daddy, you've had an IV, haven't you?"

"Yes," Michael said. "When I was in the hospital once."

"It hurts her," Wills said.

"It looks like it hurts," I said, "but once the doctor puts it in, you don't really feel it anymore."

"She looks good," Wills said, stepping back. I wasn't sure if he really felt that way or if he just didn't want to admit what was happening. I didn't want to pretend, only to have him shocked and hurt later if she passed away soon.

"She looks bad to me, honey," I said, "very sick."

Katherine had told us a few weeks ago to make sure Wills knew that Cowboy had *some* time left, but we weren't sure how much.

I cradled Cowboy's head in my lap, grateful to see her chest moving up and down in a steady rhythm. Wills ran to his room and came back with the striped comforter off his bed.

"Here, Cowboy, let's snuggle in." Holding two ends at the same time, he shook it out, letting it float down on top of her. He crawled underneath it, too, spooning against Cowboy's back. It was eighty-five degrees outside. Wills closed his eyes and rubbed his nose in the fur on the back of her neck.

When she began panting, I told Wills, "Honey, she's too hot under the blanket." He sat up. "You can still lie with her. Just toss this blanket off."

"She likes it," he said.

"She's too hot," I told him. "She needs some water." He ran to get her bowl. "The medicine makes her thirsty, too."

Everyone was tired—us from the flight and Cowboy from being so frail—so we spent the rest of the afternoon drawing, reading, and eating popcorn with Cowboy on the family room floor. That evening, Wills cooked us a Cowboy breakfast—cheese omelettes and turkey sausages.

At bedtime, Wills asked, "Can you bring in Cowboy?" He was strumming his old red guitar. Cowboy was lying peacefully on the cool hardwood floors outside his bedroom door.

"I'm a little worried about her being in the bed," I said. "Her fever is making her really hot, and she's more fragile now. I wouldn't want you to roll over on her."

He threw down the guitar and began crying.

"This is what I want for her birthday," he sobbed. "A cake shaped like a Cowboy hat from Bones Bakery and Murphy for her to play with."

Wills and I unearthed the old AeroBed, and I slept in his room that night lying next to Cowboy.

Within two days, Cowboy could barely walk. She needed to be carried outside to go to the bathroom, but could still stagger from room to room. There was blood in her urine. We called Dr. Burke.

"I'd like to examine her again," he said, "but it sounds like she's suffering."

"Maybe there's something we can do," I said, trying to stay hopeful. "She's rallied before."

"Bring her in, Monica. I'll take a look."

As Michael and I lifted her into the car, she groaned. She *was* suffering.

"Mon, I think we need to let her go," Michael said. I climbed into the backseat and wrapped my arms around her. It was rush hour and the ride from Sherman Oaks to Santa Monica took fifty minutes. Cowboy slept, I cried, and Michael drove.

Dr. Burke took the shunt out of her leg and covered the small opening with gauze. She was lying on her side, but her tail still managed to thump against the floor as he attended to her.

"She's a fighter," he said, smiling and running his hand along her side. Michael stood to the side with his hand against his mouth, and I sat next to Cowboy, weepy.

She began struggling to stand up. Dr. Burke helped her to her feet and she wobbled over and scratched at the door.

"She has to pee," I said. "She'd never do it on the floor if she could help it."

"I'll walk outside with you and see how she does," Dr. Burke said.

Cowboy walked on her own to the grassy strip in front of his office, where about thirty dogs a day relieved themselves. The aroma perked her up. She began pulling us toward the sidewalk with renewed strength. A brown Labrador was brought out for a bathroom break and Cowboy barked at him, tail wagging. We laughed. She was looking for a playmate.

"I haven't heard her bark all summer," I said, my throat tightening. "She sounds so hoarse."

"I don't know what to tell you, guys," he said. "There's little doubt she won't be coming back from this, but it looks like she's not quite ready to give up the ghost just yet."

"We'll take her home," I said, quickly.

"Definitely," Michael echoed. "We'll take her home."

"You know, there's a doctor who's supposedly very good with severe cases like this. I sincerely doubt that he'll be able to do much, but he might know how to keep her comfortable," Dr. Burke said. "He's a canine cancer specialist, and when I called him about Cowboy after the lupus diagnosis, he didn't seem to think he had the expertise to help her. But he knows a lot about maintaining quality of life at the end of a long illness."

"I'll take her," I said.

"He's part of a practice in West Hollywood," Dr. Burke said. "He's not cheap."

"That's okay," Michael said.

When Michael carried Cowboy back in so we could pay the bill, China, Cowboy's favorite, was just coming in to work. The shock from seeing just how bad Cowboy had gotten was clear from the way her face dropped as she knelt down to wrap her arms around her. "What happened, little girl?" she asked, rubbing the top of her head. "What happened to you? She's only two, right?" she asked.

"Her third birthday's in a month and a half," I managed.

"I'm so sorry." She took two Kleenex from her pocket and handed one to me.

"I know." I shook my head. "It's so unfair."

I wouldn't have put her through it, but I had my eye on Wills starting third grade in less than three weeks. I didn't want him to lose his beloved Cowboy right as he was getting used to a new teacher, a bigger class, and no Lynn. I didn't want his grief over Cowboy to jeopardize how far he'd come.

"Let's try to make it until September," I pleaded with Cowboy, which wasn't fair at all. "Let's get Wills on his feet, girl." She looked up at me with those exhausted, endearing, droopy brown eyes. I was no longer sure if I was asking her to hold on for Wills or for me.

I took Cowboy to the cancer specialist, preparing myself for the worst, but when I carried her inside, she struggled to get out of my arms and onto the floor. There was a sexy bulldog over by the Science Diet display and she needed to smell his butt. By the time the vet came into the examining room, Cowboy was practically doing the high kicks from *A Chorus Line*. She was standing on her own and wagging her bedraggled tail.

"When you called, you thought perhaps she needed to be put down," Dr. Miller said, evenly. "She looks ill, but I wouldn't say there's no hope for this dog."

"Dr. Burke didn't seem to think so," I said. "He was more concerned about making sure she ends her life comfortably."

"So you don't want to put her down?" He looked over the top of his glasses.

"Why would I drive all the way over here if I wanted to put her down?" I asked. "Dr. Burke could have done that if we'd wanted it."

"She looks like she has plenty of energy," he noted.

"She hasn't been like this," I told him. "I carry her almost everywhere now. When she tries to walk on her own, she usually stumbles to the left and falls. I'm worried that she's in pain."

He looked at me with disdain. "If she were my dog, I'd believe in her a little."

"Is there something else we can do?" I asked, cutting to the chase. Maybe there was a miracle in this shitty place. Cowboy fell onto her side, and I sat beside her on the floor.

"I'd start with chemo, for one thing. Have you tried that?" he asked, checking his cell phone.

"Have you tried caring for a critically ill dog for two years?" I asked. He didn't look at me. "Aren't the drugs she's been on for lupus chemo-class?"

"Chemo-class drugs are not *'chemo,'*" he said, snapping his phone shut.

"No one told me to put her on chemo," I said, worried now that I hadn't done enough for her.

"Well, that's your first problem," he said. "I'll start a chemo regimen and see how that goes."

"What are the side effects?" I asked. "She's been through so much already—she has sores in her mouth and her skin is terribly infected. She's feverish."

"Well, if you'd rather relieve yourself of the obligation," he said, "that's up to you."

"What?" I snapped.

"If you're intent on putting her down, nothing I say is going to change anything."

"Do you just not like people or is it me?" I quipped. "You are without a doubt the coldest person I've ever met in my life. You aren't even listening to me!" He turned his back on me. "I would *never* put Cowboy in your care. I wouldn't even let you near my goldfish." I was starting to sob, which was pissing me off more.

"We're done here," he said, one eyebrow raised in a haughty display of all that he knew and all that I didn't. He walked out of the examining room.

I was outraged, hysterical. I followed him. "I want to see another doctor, NOW."

"Fine," he said, not turning to look at me.

"You shouldn't be working with families," I told him after he'd already gone into another examination room.

I walked back to get Cowboy. I carefully bundled her up in the beach towel and struggled to carry her out of there. We were going home with no answers, no way to ease the pain. I made it to the door that led to the waiting room, when a tall, absolutely flawless woman in a white doctor's coat reached to open the door for me.

"You look terrible," she said. All I could do was blubber, and Cowboy was getting so heavy.

"Dr. Miller thinks I want to kill my dog," I said, "but she has lupus and has gotten so ill. I don't know what to do for her." I was hysterical.

She moved the towel back and looked at Cowboy's balding face and crusty eyes. "Come with me," she said, reaching underneath to help support Cowboy's weight. "I'm Dr. Grier."

"Monica Holloway." She smiled. We moved Cowboy into another examining room. "My son has high-functioning autism," I explained to her, wiping Cowboy's eyes with a corner of the towel. "Cowboy means everything in this world to him. We were hoping she'd make it until the middle of September so he could begin third grade without this huge loss hanging over him," I said. "But now, it seems cruel to let her suffer like this."

"Why don't I start a type of chemo that might relieve some of her pain and possibly give her a little more time: a month at the most. Would that be something you'd want to do, to get yourselves more prepared for her passing?"

I looked at Cowboy, who was asleep on the linoleum, her paws stuck straight out in front of her, like Superman flying.

"Let's try it," I said.

"It's very costly," she warned.

We'd spent so much already, it had gotten so out of hand—but what was one more ridiculous expense when Cowboy's life hung in the balance? When the Graham MasterCard was maxed out, which would be very soon, then we'd have to finally stop all of this.

"Can we start today?" I asked.

"Absolutely."

I put my forehead against Cowboy's side.

"Monica? I don't think you want to kill your dog. I'm really sorry about Dr. Miller. It's truly unforgivable, what he said to you."

"Thank you," I said, kissing the side of Cowboy's face. "Thank you so much."

* * *

Cowboy was given chemotherapy through a permanent shunt inserted into the front of her leg. It relieved the pain a little, but that was all. Her walking was still unsteady and she began coughing up yellowish, thick mucus. Mostly she slept, and when she woke up, I carried her outside to pee. I slept on the floor next to her and Wills dragged the air mattress into the family room to be with us.

In the middle of the night, I'd listen to Cowboy's labored breathing. No one could turn this around.

September came, and Wills started third grade without Cowboy riding along with us or Lynn waiting at the gate. In his new Nike sneakers (that he could tie himself), he sprinted down the sidewalk and was inside the gate before I could even kiss him good-bye.

He came home that afternoon bubbling with news about the model of a Chumash Indian village he would be building "out of clay and leather," and the report he'd be working on to read at the all-school meeting.

"In front of everyone?" I asked.

"I'll be holding a microphone."

"No way! I'm so proud of you, Wills." I was already picturing it, every hair on my arms standing straight up.

"Cole's in my class. And Wyatt, too." He walked over and sat down next to Cowboy, who was asleep on her blanket. "Did she miss me?" he asked. "She was devastated, right?"

"Devastated," I said.

"I thought so."

The phone rang. It was Kyle, a new kid in Wills's class. "The phone's for you," I called out for the first time in my life.

"Who is it?" he asked, peeking around the corner of his bedroom, unsure about picking it up.

"Kyle."

He answered a series of questions on the phone with two-word responses. It was worthy of a ticker-tape parade down Ventura Boulevard—my son was getting calls from his peers!

The next morning, I took Cowboy to Dr. Grier for her second round of chemo.

"Does she seem more comfortable?" she asked.

"She mostly sleeps," I said, "and she's so thirsty."

"That's the medication," she said.

"This is going to sound crazy," I said, "but the top of her head feels a little pointy—like it's changing shape."

"That's a side effect of the steroids," she said. "All my patients have these little coneheads." She rubbed the top of Cowboy's head. "Yep, she's pointy all right."

Dr. Grier drew blood and administered the chemo. Cowboy, who was lying on her blanket, didn't even wake up.

"Is she eating?" Dr. Grier asked.

"She mostly drinks tons of water."

She nodded, listening to Cowboy's chest and back. "She looks thinner to me, but I don't want to wake her up to lift her onto the scale."

"Are we being cruel, keeping her alive like this?" I asked.

"Here's the thing that's been true in every case I've ever had," she said. "When Cowboy's ready to go, there will be no doubt in your mind that it's time. Either her health will decline rapidly or she'll stop drinking her water. Since she's already given up eating, I think she's winding down."

My mascara began running down my tear-stained face, but Dr. Grier was used to that. We carried her out to the car. "I don't know how we got so lucky," I said, "having you taking care of Cowboy."

"Look at these eyes," she said, lifting Cowboy's chin. "How could I not take care of this little soul—and this one, too." She tapped my chest.

That night, sleeping next to Cowboy, Wills woke me up. "Mommy, you're snoring."

"I am?"

"Loudly."

"Do you want to go into your room where you can't hear it?" I asked.

"Can you just stop snoring?" he wondered.

"I didn't know I was doing it."

Cowboy's breathing was deep and quiet tonight, which, oddly enough, seemed even more unsettling.

"Mommy, I'm scared about Cowboy," Wills said. I could make out his profile in the dark, one arm folded behind his head.

"I'm scared, too," I said. "But she seems peaceful right now."

"I'm afraid she'll die," he said, staring at the ceiling.

"She is going to die, Wills," I said, quietly. "I would give anything to stop it from happening, but I can't."

He turned over, pressing his face into his pillow.

Pretty soon I heard Michael's footsteps coming out of the bedroom. "Is he crying?"

"He's afraid Cowboy's going to die, and I had to tell him that she *was* going to die." Michael lay down on the floor beside us, and all four of us slept in the family room that night.

Third grade was indeed turning out to be the year of independence for Wills. His teacher, Corinne, had told us at the end of last year that Group Three was a time when children "begin to move away from their parents and step more solidly into the world."

Katherine backed this up, encouraging me to "give him the space and time he needs to make his own decisions." This would be the equivalent of walking backward or climbing into a completely new skin.

I'd pondered that possibility all summer, and now it was here. Wills had some new rules for me to follow: no more hugs or kisses allowed near campus, no embarrassing him at school by wearing sloppy sweats that "look exactly like pajamas," and no climbing over the other kids on the play pyramid to see how his day went.

In keeping with his new, autonomous self, I'd made a conscious effort to stay out of Wills's business. If he needed me, I was there, probably way too fast, but if he didn't need me, I let him go about his daily life without a lot of questions.

The third week of classes, I volunteered to come up with an article for the *Three O'clock News,* the all-school newspaper. I knew precious little about what was going on in the classroom, so when he sauntered by I said, "Hey, Wills, come here for a second."

He sat down next to sleeping Cowboy and me. He was curious about my new Apple computer, which he hadn't had a chance to use yet. "What's going on in third grade?" I asked. "What are you guys working on?"

He looked at the blank screen, and then at me. "Are you going to type what I say?"

"Absolutely," I responded, snapping to attention, fingers poised over the keys. I didn't expect such an enthusiastic response.

"There were old people who were in Mexico before the Spanish came," he told me. "They were the Maya and Aztec people." (Thankfully, I was a fast typist.) "There was the Toltec and the Incas." He stopped, looking closer at the screen. "New paragraph," he said.

"We're learning Spanish words, too. Lauren's mom comes in and teaches us Spanish, like how to tell somebody your name or 'I have beans.' " He began fiddling with the strings of his hooded sweat-shirt. "We're doing reports about things in Mexico. Like I'm doing a report on Mexican volcanoes. I'm going to draw a picture, write the name of the volcanoes, and say whether it's active or not."

"Maybe you could build a model of a volcano to go along with your report," I offered, enthusiastically. There was a pause.

"I'm trying to tell you what's going on," he said. I'd overstepped his newly drawn boundaries.

"Ignore me," I said, and he did.

"My favorite volcano in Mexico is Paricutin. Everyone gets to report on something different."

Wills gave Cowboy a kiss on the side of her face, and headed outside.

"Is that all you want me to write about Group Three?" I asked.

"Math with dice," he added. "Oh, and Kathleen's back. She's not sick anymore." He grinned and headed out the front door. Ironically, Kathleen, who'd encouraged him to dance, was recovering from cancer. I couldn't wait for Wills to reconnect with her.

I sat on the couch, trying to format what he'd said into an article. Five minutes later I heard, "MOMMY?" I got up and walked out the front door. Wills was swinging.

"What's up?" I asked.

"I also made a stamp of a hermit crab and a fish out of a linoleum block. I drew it first and then carved it out." He pumped his legs until he was going almost as high as the bar above him. I sat down on the front steps. It was getting dark. "I'm bringing it home soon," he smiled.

"I can't wait," I told him, and I couldn't.

Cowboy hobbled out to the stoop. She leaned against me. "Look who's here," I said.

"COWBOY!" Wills shouted. Her tail began swishing against my leg. "Who's my girl?" he asked her. "Who's the best girl in the whole world? You are. Yes, you're the best." He jumped off mid-swing, landing on his feet. Cowboy wagged her tail again, and then lay down on her side, her energy gone.

That night, with Wills doing so well, and Cowboy's quality of life so deteriorated, Michael and I decided to stop the chemotherapy. No more medical interventions.

In the middle of the night, as if on cue, Cowboy turned away from her water.

The next morning, Michael and I headed to Dr. Grier's. "She hasn't had anything to drink since about nine thirty last night," I told her.

"I think it's time to let her go," she said, placing her hand on my arm. "We can do it here," she said, "or you can have Dr. Burke do it. It's up to you."

This was no surprise, of course. It was the antisurprise. So why was the finality of it so overwhelmingly shocking?

"We'll take her to Dr. Burke's," I said. "We need to prepare Wills when he gets home from school tonight."

"Without water or food, she's going to dehydrate very quickly," she said. "I want to give her some fluids to make her feel better." Dr. Grier injected saline solution under her skin, creating an enormous asymmetrical bulge on her left side.

"Is that permanent?" Michael asked.

"Her body will slowly absorb it," she said. "It'll be gone in an hour or so."

In the parking lot, I turned to Dr. Grier, "Thank you for treating her with so much love."

"She's a lucky dog," she said.

"Well, she's the *best* dog." I'd spent the last few weeks weeping nonstop, and here it came again.

Michael lifted Cowboy into the car, and I sat in the backseat snuggling against her all the way home. We rolled down the windows and let the wind blow through, just the way Cowboy liked it.

Michael and I decided we'd take Cowboy to Dr. Burke's the next morning. Katherine suggested telling Wills no more than a day or so in advance, unless, of course, she passed away on her own.

It was dusk on Cowboy's last day. Michael was working late, so I sat down alone with Wills. Cowboy was lying on his lap, belly up, his arms wrapped around her, like he was holding a baby. Ironically, her hair looked fuller, but I knew that meant nothing. The skin on her stomach had become so infected that it was covered in a thin layer of yellowish liquid.

"She's tired," Wills said.

"She's really sick now."

"Like bad sick?" he asked. "Worse than before sick?"

"She doesn't want to eat or drink anymore," I told him. "She can't live without water."

"But she's living now," he said.

"The doctor gave her a lot of water today," I said, "to make her more comfortable."

"Will she get more water tomorrow?" he asked.

"We're going to have to let Cowboy go very soon," I told Wills, tucking his hair behind his ears. He hugged her so tightly that her face was all scrunched up. He broke down into loud, throaty sobs. "I'm so sorry, sweet boy."

"Cowboy's third birthday is almost here," he cried. He was right, she wouldn't make it to three. "What about her birthday cake from Bones Bakery?" He was hiccupping and crying at the same time.

"I don't think she's going to make it that long," I said.

"OH NO," he sobbed. "Oh, Cowboy, don't go. Please don't, Cowboy."

"It feels horrible, unthinkable, that Cowboy will die," I said. And then using Katherine's words, I told him, "It might even feel like you can't live through it, but you will."

He wailed even louder.

I was inadequate. There was nothing I could do to help my son. Nothing I could say to make this any easier. I had run out of words.

"Can you hold her, Mommy?" he asked. He went to the garage to collect his toolbox and some wood, but when he came back, he was also hauling Cowboy's doghouse—the one he'd made out of the Kenmore dishwasher box when Cowboy first arrived. While Wills began working, Cowboy struggled to get down off my lap and, with great effort, took her rightful place inside the cardboard home that he'd designed and decorated especially for her.

Wordlessly, Wills spent the next two hours building a small, crooked bookcase with three shelves and silver hooks sticking out all over the right side. After that, he painted it a mishmash of different colors—not neatly, like he usually did, but messy with huge blotches of green, yellow, and blue overlapping each other.

I couldn't figure out what he was making this for, but I watched as he worked and wiped his nose on the sleeve of his shirt.

"Do you want to talk?" I asked. He didn't.

When Wills was done building, he left the paint to dry and went into the bathroom and ran the water. He'd never started his own

bath. He was in there for more than twenty minutes, when finally I knocked on the door.

"Wills, are you okay in there?"

"I'm not coming out," he said.

"Okay, but it's getting a little late, and I want to give you some dinner."

"I can't eat."

"Could we snuggle with Cowboy? Or just us?"

I stood with my ear against the door, but that was it—silence.

I walked back into the family room and sat on the floor beside Cowboy, who didn't even hear me come in.

After ten minutes, with no sound coming from inside the bathroom, I opened the door with an Allen wrench. Wills was sound asleep on the bath mat.

CHAPTER NINETEEN

The next morning, Michael took Wills to school so I could stay with Cowboy. Wills didn't know that today was the day, but he knew it would be very soon. We didn't know how to tell him that we were putting her to sleep that very morning. How could we? He loved her most of all.

I sat with Cowboy on the carpet, my back leaning against the yellow-and-white–striped chair. She was so thin, her head resting on my lap. I stroked the sides of her face, and remembered all of the hair that had come and gone, what a brave puppy she was.

She got up carefully and wandered into the kitchen to get a drink of water, but couldn't make it and fell onto her side. Picking her up, I carried her to her water bowl. Holding it up to her mouth, covered in sores inside and out, she lapped up every drop. I could tell she was in pain. It must have been excruciating.

I thought back to all the firsts. Wills, who could barely say hello to a person, proudly leading her around the school so the kids could pet her; Wills's first swim in the pool; him sleeping in his own bed with Cowboy spooning him; Cowboy sitting outside the restaurant so that Wills could sit inside, tolerating the noise and the people; the red-and-white doggie pajamas we'd ordered her from the Hanna Andersson catalog that matched Wills's pajamas exactly.

* * *

On her final day with us, I sat on the rug and held Cowboy in my arms, her tummy up, legs limp. I was careful to steady her head with my hand. I quietly rocked her, my hands shaking. I had to admit that I was exhausted from the shots, the specialists, the anxiety and sadness, but at that moment, I would have given anything for one more day with my girl.

Michael came into the kitchen. It was time to go to Dr. Burke's. Michael's eyes were red and swollen. I had decided that I couldn't go with them—that I wouldn't have the courage, that I would have backed out and taken Cowboy home with me. So I had to say my good-bye here at home.

Before I got up, I held Cowboy as tightly and gently as I could and cried into her soft ears, just as Wills had done through endless hurts and worries.

Michael walked down the front walkway, turned around and called for her. "Cowboy, come." I couldn't understand why he was calling her. He knew she couldn't walk down the front steps. But when she saw him heading toward the front door, she stood on four wobbly legs and headed out right behind him.

I helped her down the steps, but she was actually tottering along by herself, dignified. I was sobbing so hard I could barely see her. Michael walked out of the gate and opened the car door. She loved him; she would have followed him anywhere.

Cowboy looked back at me expectantly. I'm sure she was wondering, *Are we going for a ride together?* I knelt down beside her, kissed both sides of her pointy head, and slicked her ears back with both my hands until she looked like a seal.

"I love you, precious girl," I whispered into her ear flaps.

We'd already packed her soft blue doggie bed, her beloved stuffed buffalo with the nose chewed off, and her yellow quilt. When she got to the gate, she turned to look directly at me, right on cue, tail wagging.

"Don't do it," I yelled to Michael. "She's not ready. Let's don't."
I felt frantic, something irreversible was happening, and I had no
control over it. She'd been suffering for months now.

Michael gingerly picked up Cowboy, carefully placing her on the
bed in the backseat.

I just stood there beside the car, my face soaking wet.

"She's so ill, Monica," Michael said, giving me a tight squeeze.
"We've let her suffer long enough."

Over his shoulder I could see her face lifted toward the window
and I knew I'd never see her again. As they drove away, I could see
her tiny head poking above the seat. She loved riding in that car.

Once inside, the house was still. Cowboy's purple leash was still
coiled on top of the washer and dryer. We hadn't needed it since July.
Her toys were in the same white broken basket we'd used since her
first night with us, when Michael stood in the rain begging, "Potty
outside?" I sat on the floor and squeezed what was left of one of her
favorites: the plushy pink kitten skin with the thick tail that she'd
gutted two hours after we'd given it to her. I sat there in grief for all
of us—for Michael, who had to witness her passing; for Wills, who
would be destroyed by the news; and for myself, who didn't have the
courage to sit with her while she died.

The phone was lying on the rug beside me awaiting Michael's
call. I wondered if it was worth it—loving with such fierceness, only
to suffer an incomparable loss. It was unfair to put Wills through
that—worse—it was cruel.

Two hours and ten minutes later the phone rang:

"She's gone," Michael said. I somehow managed to cry even
harder than I'd been crying before. I couldn't speak, I could only
sob. "It was very peaceful, and she was in her own bed. Everyone in
Burke's office was a mess. They felt terrible." He waited for some
kind of response but I couldn't speak. "I have her collar and tags. We
wrapped her in the quilt."

I wish I could say we had the kind of yard that would have

allowed us to bring her home and bury her here with us. My childhood dog, Sugar, was sixteen years old when we buried her under
the small maple tree in the only backyard she'd ever known. But
here in L.A., we had concrete all around us, and a small backyard.

We reluctantly agreed to have her cremated, which felt wrong.
But then, nothing would have felt right—she was gone.

CHAPTER TWENTY

When I picked Wills up from school that day, he took one look at me and said, "She died, right?"

I nodded.

He burst into tears, dropped his backpack on the grass, and ran toward the car. He didn't pause at the four-way stop or look to see if cars were coming. He stood in the street, pulling on the back door.

I was right behind him, hands in the air waving off traffic. Holy shit, he was scaring the hell out of me. "Hang on, Wills," I yelled, fumbling with my keys, "I have to unlock the doors."

He was silent in the car, staring out the window all the whole way home.

"I'm so sorry, Wills."

When we got home, we sat on the family room floor facing each other, our foreheads touching, his hands, palms up, lying on my knees. He lifted his head and looked me straight in the eye for the longest time.

We collected Cowboy's chew toys, the shorts with the tail hole cut out, her mesh flowered pool float, and her food bowls. Wills put all of it inside the cardboard doghouse.

He decorated a large shoebox with COWBOY printed in blue glitter on the lid, and pasted pictures of the two of them all over it.

When he finally broke down, it was the hardest I'd ever seen him cry—crushing grief. I held him on my lap and stroked his hair.

We called Katherine to tell her it was over. She asked to speak to Wills, who carried the phone into his bedroom and slammed the door.

Five minutes later, he came out and handed it to me. "Hi, Katherine," I said.

"I'm sorry, Monica, I know how hard this must be."

"It's terrible."

"Wills said you're gonna let him stay home from school tomorrow," she said.

"He's a mess," I told her.

"I completely understand your impulse to keep him home," she said, "but I think he should definitely go."

"Why?" I asked.

"Because he needs to know that when he feels very, very sad, he doesn't have to stay home and hide it," she said. "He needs to talk about what happened and see that his friends will support him."

"But he's inconsolable," I insisted.

"He needs to know that there are other kids in his class who have also survived loss," she said. "Plus, all of his classmates know Cowboy."

I paused and finally said, "Okay, I'll send him."

"I know you don't want to," she said, "but you'll see it's the best thing for him."

That night, Wills lay on his side, and ran his Bachman trains across the hardwood floor. He held his hamster, Brownie Black Ears, around the waist, and I didn't care when it peed on the floor. We ate macaroni and cheese sitting at the coffee table, made popcorn, and watched *Lady and the Tramp* until his swollen eyes finally gave way to sleep. Hopefully, Cowboy would be there in his dreams.

Michael called from his cell phone. "I'm outside the gate. I have

Cowboy's bed," he said, "and her collar, and tags. Should I bring them in?"

"Not tonight," I told him. "Wills is asleep, and I don't think I can face them."

After reheating him some dinner, I fell asleep with Michael on the couch, my head resting against his. We woke up the next morning in the exact same position—the lights on, music playing. It was the first full night of sleep I'd had in months. I hadn't realized how exhausted I was.

When Wills went to school that morning, he dropped his backpack on the floor near his cubby and looked at books in the classroom library until the class gathered for morning circle time.

When Corinne asked if anyone had something they'd like to share with the group, Wills's hand shot straight up.

"Wills," Corinne said. "Go ahead."

He stood up and shoved his hands into his pockets. "Cowboy died," he said, as fast as he could, and sat back down. This set off a chain reaction in the classroom, as everyone spoke up at once.

"Maybe we could go around the circle and if some of you would like to say something to Wills, you can."

Sacha, who was sitting directly across from Wills leaned in. "First of all, I just want to say"—she was wiping her nose with the back of her hand—"that Cowboy was Murphy's best friend." She scooted forward a little. "I'm so sorry, Wills." She broke into sobs, which made Lauren start crying and the next thing Corinne knew, the girls were huddled around Wills, hanging off his shoulders and weeping right along with him.

Corinne let them have a minute, surprised that Wills was allowing himself to be squeezed and touched like that.

Justin Lambert stood up. "My dog died this past summer," he said. There was a huge intake of air, as if the entire class was holding their breath, and maybe they were, but Justin sat back down and looked at the floor.

"Do you want to tell us what happened?" Corinne asked.

"He got hit by a car," he said, "right in front of my dad and me."

Now all the girls ran to Justin, dragging Wills along with them. Justin was okay with a little hugging, but then he waved everybody off. He was a pretty cool customer for an eight-year-old.

Corinne brought over a box of Kleenex and placed it in the center of the circle that wasn't exactly shaped like a circle anymore. She handed two tissues to Wills, who badly needed them.

"My grandfather died," Grace said. "He was a farmer so when he died, we got to take in all of his animals. But I'd rather have *him* back. But if he came back, I'd ask him if I could keep the tortoise."

"I haven't lost anyone," Patrick said, a little huffy. "Not one person or animal has ever died in my entire life."

"We all experience loss, Patrick, and it's not always due to a death. Remember when you had to move into a new house?" Patrick nodded, confused. "Remember how much you missed your old room and the yard with the climbing tree?" He nodded again. "You experienced loss right then." He looked relieved, and then really sad. "See, you're feeling it right now." She asked everyone to sit down. "Wills, what could we do to support you today? What would make you feel comforted?"

Wills shrugged, trying to compose himself.

"Why don't we go around the circle and say the one thing that we liked most about Cowboy." Wills pressed the tissues against his eyes. "See if you can bear hearing about all of her happy times, Wills."

"When I was over at your house, Cowboy took my tennis shoe and we couldn't find it when my dad came to get me."

"Cowboy swam in our pool."

"Cowboy only wanted to be with Wills. She wouldn't come to me."

"I saw Cowboy hanging out the window of your car—twice."

"Cowboy makes me laugh."

"I didn't know Cowboy very well."

"Cowboy goes crazy during car pool."

"She was really soft."

"Cowboy did not want to be sick."

"Cowboy knocked me onto the pyramid once and I bruised my ankle."

"You let me hold Cowboy's leash one time and she dragged me down the sidewalk all the way to the stop sign. Remember that?"

"Here's one thing I know," Corinne said. "Cowboy loved you, Wills, and even though you're going to miss her a lot, you're going to find yourself surprised by all the things she's left behind for you." Wills didn't understand this at all. "Not actual things you can touch or pick up," Corinne said, "things you know now, that you wouldn't have known if you hadn't had Cowboy in your life."

All the tearstained faces just stared at her, blankly. "Wait and see." She smiled.

The rest of the day, Wills was front and center, allowing whatever feelings he had to wash over him. Helen heard the news and rushed out to the playground to give him a big hug. "I'm sorry, pal," she said. Wills hugged her back

When Neal walked by, Wills told him, "Helen was her grandma."

"Whose grandma?" he asked.

"Cowboy," Wills said, and fell completely apart.

"Cowboy died yesterday," Helen told him.

"Oh, Wills, I'm really sorry to hear that," he said, putting his hand on Wills's shoulder. "That's just terribly sad, isn't it?" Wills nodded.

When it was almost time to go home, Terri patted his back and told him how sorry she was. "I remember when you first got Cowboy," she said. "Remember how tiny she was when you brought her to kindergarten?"

"She was little," Wills said.

"And so were you," Terri told him. "And now, look how you've grown. I'm really proud of you, Wills."

* * *

When I picked Wills up that afternoon, he walked out of his class-room with at least seven children surrounding him, their arms wrapped around his waist and Sacha's head resting on his shoulder.

His eyes were bright as he looked up at me. In the car he said, "I told everyone during circle time this morning that Cowboy died."

"What did they say?"

"Some people started crying when I told them."

"I'll bet they did," I said.

"And then *I* cried, too." He was squeezing his hands together.

"I'm glad you were able to tell your friends," I said.

"No big deal." He shrugged, his eyes welling up with tears. "These things happen." He ran his hands down the length of his thighs, as if his palms were wet and needed drying off.

"But it doesn't make it easy or okay."

He nodded. "It's pretty terrible." He took off his shoes and socks, flinging them into the way back.

"Let's go home," I said, patting his leg.

"I'm hungry, Mommy."

"Where do you want to go?"

"In-N-Out Burger."

I flinched. That was Cowboy's place. We couldn't go there with-out her, could we? "In-N-Out Burger?" I asked.

"I want a chocolate shake," he confirmed.

EPILOGUE

We spent the following weeks ridding the house of anything that reminded us of Cowboy's absence. We replaced the pee-stained wool carpet in the family room, bought new underpants to replace the ones Cowboy had chewed through, reseeded the yard, even replanted all the flower beds Cowboy had been so intent on digging up. There were no squeaky-toy steaks to step on or hairballs the size of tumbleweeds to sweep up. No one even drank the pond water, so I never needed to fill it up. Things were just too neat and tidy . . . not to mention quiet.

On Halloween, Wills went over to his friend Cole's house to trick-or-treat. We packed his scary zombie costume, the one with the plastic guts and white rubber exposed ribs sticking out the front of the chest. His mask was just a black scrim covering his face, topped off with a gray fright wig. A whole group of his friends gathered at Cole's because his neighborhood was by far the best for trick-or-treating—the houses were always elaborately decorated, as hundreds of kids ran screaming up and down the streets.

Wills left a witch's cauldron of assorted candy all mixed together in one bowl beside our front door with a sign that read, BOO LADS!! PLEASE LEAVE SOME CANDY FOR THE GHOULS BEHIND YOU!

Michael and I spent the evening, same as the other parents, racing around behind the kids, counting and recounting heads as they streaked from yard to yard.

After about two hours, exhausted and overheated underneath their sticky masks, they meandered back to Cole's house, where they spread their candy out on the living room floor to trade with each other, like the NFL draft, only with Smarties.

On the way home, I sat in the backseat with Wills.

"Pretty great," I said, patting his leg.

"Pretty great," he repeated. He put his head on my shoulder.

"Are you pooped?" I asked. He didn't respond. "Are you sleepy?" He shook his head and I realized he was crying. "What's wrong, Wills?" I wrapped my arm around his shoulders.

"Cowboy missed Halloween," he sobbed.

"I know," I said, pulling him close.

The rubber bones on his chest jiggled up and down with each gasp, and his hair, still wet from the sweat that had gathered under his wig, was slicked back against his head, making him look so much younger. "She would be glad you had a good time," I said, which was just about the lamest thing I could have offered.

"But she's not here."

No, she wasn't . . . and yet, she was still with us in so many ways. Wills could never have trick-or-treated among that many children, or tolerated that level of noise, or even stepped one foot into a stranger's house if he hadn't known Cowboy. She dragged him toward children and all the new places he didn't want to go. She even sat beside a urinal at Beeman Park while he kicked and screamed about going to the potty all those years ago. But when Wills saw her sitting there, looking almost irritated that he was wasting her playtime, he laughed. "Just a minute, Cowboy," he'd said. Turning to me he pointed. "You're gonna flush, though."

All I could do to comfort him now was to rub his head while he cried and tell him, "I'm so sorry about Cowboy."

Michael carried him into the house and put him to bed still in his zombie suit.

My impulse, of course, was to run out and get a new dog right away, but Katherine said that Wills needed time to grieve. So we compromised—two months, at least, before I'd go anywhere near a breeder website or a dog adoption shelter. Obviously, I'd *never* go anywhere near another pet store.

Wills wasn't even close to being ready, and maybe he never would be.

A month or so later, I saw Wills reading *Dog Fancy* magazine, which we still subscribed to. He hadn't touched a copy since Cowboy died, but I left them in the magazine pile anyway. I could have sworn he was lingering over the puppy pictures. I waited.

Weeks later, when the new grass in the yard was thick and lush, Wills walked in from school and said, "Can we get a new puppy?"

I thought he'd *never* ask.

Two months later, another series was launched:

BUDDY AND WILLS

My new puppy was born on October 21, 2006, with 11 other puppies—3 females and 9 males. I'm getting a female.

This weekend we are going to visit the puppy at the farm.

The most important thing about my new puppy is that she is very healthy. Her dad is named Cowboy. Just like my Cowboy. Her mom is named Wendy.

This book is not finished but I'm getting a new puppy and there will be a story called Buddy and Wills.

Wills was right; there would never be another Cowboy. She was his first love and his first love lost. Heaven knows, she left an indelible mark on all of us. But with that unimaginable loss came an incalculable lesson: we all have to learn to say good-bye. It doesn't mean we don't miss her or that she could ever be replaced—of course, she never could. It means that Buddy is the next generation—not the original, but unique just the same—to teach Wills that nothing, not even cancer, can destroy love.

ACKNOWLEDGMENTS

Trish Boczkowski, my astute, generous, brilliant and way-cooler-than-me editor, deserves all praise for this book. You believed in me when I had no confidence, when I quit bathing in the final rewrites, and my ass resembled Dom DeLuise's from sitting at my computer for so many hours. For never seeking the limelight or asking for credit for any of your hilarious lines, your supreme editing skills, or your ability to shoulder (with aplomb) any difficulty thrown your way (and yes, I'm speaking of my anxieties and late-night phone calls)—YOU are a shining star. I can't imagine who I'd be without you.

Jen Bergstrom, you're beautiful in every way, and so damn smart. Your fierce loyalty and sharp sense of humor has buoyed me through all kinds of shit storms (and you know what I'm talking about). You're the best—one of a kind.

Hope Edelman, my dear friend (also my very first writing teacher), you rock! Thank you for being outrageously talented and for generously sharing that with me. This year goes down in history, right?

Liz Berman, you are a gem in every way. You have my undying love and affection. I would never want to roll through these days without you.

Laurie Fox, your generosity and outpouring of love is unmatched.

I am so grateful for your kind heart. Thank you for knowing what I need even before I do.

Linda Chester, you gorgeous wonder. Thank you for believing in me and for the most glamorous cocktail hour I've ever experienced.

Edward, you're the man. Period.

To the Simon & Schuster team of extraordinarily smart and innovative women who have supported this book beyond the call of duty: Louise Burke, Jen Robinson, Lisa Keim, Kerrie Loyd, Carly Sommerstein, Paula Amendolara, and Cara Bedick. How did I get so lucky?

Michael Nagin, many thanks for my beautiful book cover.

Eric Rayman, this book was way easier for us, but if I ever need someone to plug the boat, there's no doubt that you're the guy.

Melissa Cistaro, Christine Schwab, Deborah Lott, and Samantha Robson, you have taught me so much through your talented, brave writing. Thank you for being such loyal and honest comrades.

Barbara Abercrombie, you are an inspiration. When I lose my literary footing, I come barreling back to you. Thank you for your open arms.

Leslie Morgan Steiner, you have such strength and talent. I'm so proud to call you a friend.

Jennifer Lauck—I'm so glad to have you back!

David Murphy, your beautiful music inspires us all. Thank you for creating "Cowboy's Waltz," the music composed especially for the book trailer. Thanks also to Turn Here Video for doing such an amazing job on the book trailer.

Tama and Joy and all of the wonderful staff from The Early Years School, who were the first to guide Wills into a more social world. I can't thank you enough for taking such good care of us.

The Children's' Community School family: Neal Wrightson, Helen Stevenson, Heather McPherson, Robyn Lawrence, Ruth Belonsky, Berta DeLeon, Carlos Garcia, Terri Agbodike, Daniel Casanova, Seth Shteir, LaKetta Winbush, Cynthia Roldan, Corrine Biggs, Zach Wyner, Coleen Erdmann-Orkin, and Carol Ouimette. You are an indelible part of our lives.

To the CCS families who believe in their children and love to BBQ.

In special memory of Kathleen Zundell, Wills's dance teacher. Her storytelling and extraordinary ability to include everyone, especially those who were shy to express themselves, changed so many lives—Wills's included. You are so missed.

Lynn, you are beloved, and Vanessa, you are a pillar of strength and support for all of us. Your are both officially part of our family.

"Katherine," you've never let us down—never once in eleven-plus years. Your dedication to Wills has changed his life *forever*, and my gratitude to you is boundless. We're not supposed to tell therapists that we love them, but I'm going to embarrass you now and tell you that we unequivocally and undeniably love you.

Thanks also to my dear friend Barrie Gillies, who thought of the Part One title, "It Takes a Zoo" and pushed me to write this book. To Amy and Tom Dugan, for sticking by my family through thick and thin. Thank you to Mary Schakel, an Indiana girl, who keeps me laughing, and Jennifer McRoberts, who's been with me since the beginning of time—or so it seems. Mary Chaisson, you are *always* there for me.

Rebecca Scribner, thank you for giving us our healthy, happy, three-year-old golden retriever, Buddy Rose, who heals us all.

Michael, thank you for reading the book, and then reading the book, and then reading it again. Your enthusiasm for my writing is unmatched.

JoAnn, the keeper of my past and the one I always turn to. I'm pretty sure I can dial your phone number in under two seconds. I love you.

Wills, you are my heart. You are changing the world.

Cowboy & Wills

A REMARKABLE LITTLE BOY

AND THE DOG THAT CHANGED HIS LIFE

Monica Holloway

READING GROUP GUIDE

INTRODUCTION

Wills is a bright young boy whose developmental difficulties reveal a diagnosis of high-functioning autism. Wills and his parents, Monica and Michael, are almost entirely alone in dealing with this upsetting news—with the exception of Monica's sister—and so they build their support system from a different place: the pet store. Soon the house is filled with fish, hermit crabs, turtles—even a rabbit. Finally, there is only one pet missing: a puppy. After years of promising Wills a dog, one Christmas a gorgeous golden retriever named Cowboy comes home to the Price family. Cowboy's presence by Wills's side begins to make the world feel safe to him, and he progresses with a speed his parents only imagined. Within a year, however, Monica and Michael realize that their beautiful and supportive puppy is terminally ill with lupus. And soon Wills will have to cope with the thought of losing his very best friend.

Cowboy & Wills is a heartwarming memoir about the unique relationship between a struggling young boy and the puppy that made it possible for him to embrace the outside world—and a fragile reminder that the loving relationships we form with our pets are always deeper than we imagine.

QUESTIONS FOR DISCUSSION

1. Wills's diagnosis rocks his parents' world, even though they are almost expecting to hear the news. How do they deal with this startling realization? How is it complicated in the beginning by Michael living in Chicago? How does Monica deal with not only Wills's autism, but the fact that she feels that she is dealing with it alone?

2. From the start, Monica and Wills compensate for bad days and bad moods by visiting the pet store and taking home a new family member, even though it gets to the point where they can barely afford it. What do you think drives them to find comfort in small creatures? How does it help them cope? Why don't you think Monica can make herself stop?

3. Monica, Michael, and those around them refer to Wills's exceptionalism and extraordinary talents, but yet these are also the qualities that define his autism. How do they reconcile these two extremes? How do Monica and Michael deal with things that are both a blessing and a curse?

4. The Prices, Monica especially, feel an urge to fit in, to belong—something that is increasingly difficult for them as Wills enters preschool and then kindergarten. Why is this so important to them? How does being perceived as "different" or an "outsider" make life more difficult for Monica and Wills? Do other parents have the same anxieties?

5. Michael and Monica's relationship is at times a struggle and at times a saving grace. How can difficult life situations both strain and enhance a relationship? Has there been a time when a tragedy has affected a relationship of yours? How can stress test a relationship? And at the same time, how can stress bring two people closer?

6. Some of Monica and Wills's proudest moments come when Wills is forced to try something new, even if the idea of doing so paralyzes him with fear. Discuss moments in your or your children's lives when the two of you were rewarded after completing a task that petrified you. How difficult must it be to force a loved one to take such a leap? How does this make everyone involved stronger in the long run?

7. Monica has an obsession with being in control, whether it is orchestrating a perfect home visit with a friend or aide or cleaning compulsively. How does Wills's autism threaten her feelings of being in control? How does she cope with this, and how does she progress as Wills does?

8. Monica and Michael sometimes have to deal with criticism from naïve parents of Wills's peers. How does their attitude develop over time? Why do you suppose that other parents feel it necessary to judge a situation that they know nothing about? How does Monica react when receiving advice from parents who seem to know too much, for example, when Chelsea claims to have "cured" her son of his autism simply by changing his diet? Or with Amanda, who accuses Monica of being neglectful and unloving in her home?

9. Wills can't tell his parents that he loves them, because of his difficulty expressing himself. How do Monica and Michael handle this? Why does this make his first "I love you" to Cowboy that much more powerful? Do you think his parents were hurt by this, or overjoyed that he expressed himself at all?

10. Over and over again, we see the innate kindness of children as they reach out to Wills. How do these children spur Wills's progress in school and in his social life? Why do you think that children have this bold power to reach out to people without seeing and judging their differences?

11. How does Cowboy's entrance into Wills's life change him from the very beginning? Discuss how even Cowboy's presence pushes Wills to try new things and enhances his bravery in facing the world. Cowboy gives Wills the confidence to move more freely within the social realm at school, and to even request a bubble bath at home. Wills now giggles and laughs uproariously. Why do you think this puppy has such an effect on the small boy?

12. When Wills begins to form close friendships, Monica does, as well. What does Monica's friendship with Sacha's mom, Bethany, offer her that she's been missing? What does Bethany show her that she has been isolated from since Wills was born? How does Bethany temporarily relieve some of Monica's anxieties about parenting? How does Sacha help Wills in similar ways, without even realizing it?

13. Monica's sister, JoAnn, develops a deep and steadfast friendship with her nephew; how does she influence Wills? She is almost as important to him as Cowboy is. How so? Why do you think that she is one of the only adults with whom Wills forms such a close bond?

14. Monica explodes at an elderly woman in a parking lot for accidentally honking her car horn and scaring Wills. Instead of being upset, Wills finds the whole situation hysterical, and Monica finds the humor in it, as well. How does this incident help Monica to understand that it is okay for Wills to see her express a variety of emotions, including anger? How might her holding back hinder Wills's development? Where else do we see Monica having to force herself not to protect Wills from the world?

15. At the end of Chapter 10, when Wills dances with his class in a performance for the parents, Monica feels that they finally belong, after so much waiting. Why do you think that this is such a relief for Monica? Discuss the weight that is lifted off her shoulders.

16. After months of testing with Dr. Bauman, he delivers a crushing report of Wills's development to the Prices, even after Wills has made so much progress at school and home. Lynn, his school aide, dismisses the report as wrong and Vanessa, his new educational therapist, refuses to let the report define the way in which she can help Wills learn. Discuss these dramatically differing opinions and the "validity" of the report. How can Dr. Bauman's test be so conclusive when he has only seen Wills in testing circumstances, and knows so little of how he interacts with the world outside the office?

17. By the end of Chapter 11, Monica has become comfortable enough with herself and in Wills's development that Amanda's comments about her parenting roll right off her back. How has Monica progressed along with Wills? How has she changed in her attitudes since the beginning of her story? What are some of the things that have made her more confident in herself and her son?

18. In Part 3, Cowboy starts to get sick, and Monica is stretched thin again, coping with another diagnosis. How does Cowboy's diagnosis mirror Wills's early autism diagnosis? How is Monica better prepared now? How does Cowboy's illness temper Wills's?

19. Now the story is reversed: Wills rapidly progresses, just as Cowboy's health starts to decline—but Cowboy's illness begins to threaten his development. Cowboy is the only one to whom he has ever said "I love you." How does Wills cope with his puppy's lupus? How does Monica handle the fact that Cowboy's passing may affect who Wills has become?

20. As the family prepares for Cowboy's death, Monica thinks back over her decision to bring Cowboy home. She feels guilty that they made a sick puppy a part of their family, and that now her little boy has to watch his beloved dog die. But at the same time,

in a few short years, Cowboy helped Wills progress faster than he ever would have alone. How do you think that Monica can reconcile this internal conflict? How would you feel if it were you? Would you turn back time to save your little boy grief?

21. As Cowboy gets sicker and sicker, first Richard the turtle runs away and then Ruby the rabbit has a stroke and dies on the way to the vet. How do these two losses help Wills prepare for the death of Cowboy, if at all? How does Wills cope with Ruby's death?

22. As Monica cares for Cowboy in her dying days, she comes to realize that it was not only Wills that needed their puppy so much—it was her, as well. How has Cowboy supported Monica over the past few years? How does she cope with the thought of losing Cowboy?

23. Cowboy helped Wills make his social debut and make his first friends. When Cowboy dies, how does that support group and those friends help him cope with his loss? In a way, has Cowboy prepared her replacements? How has she helped Wills come full circle?

ENHANCING YOUR BOOK CLUB

1. In Monica Holloway's memoir, we come to know Wills's autism quite intimately, but autism is a varied and far-reaching disorder. Research autism more thoroughly and share your findings with your book group to expand your discussion.

2. Wills's parents make a conscious effort to send their son to a mainstream school, a decision that not all parents (and schools) would have made. Discuss the benefits and disadvantages of doing so, from the perspective of both special needs families and families that are fortunate not to have to deal with autism or other developmental disorders.

3. The relationships that people have with their dogs are always more powerful than we can ever imagine. Rent a movie with your book group that explores those relationships, such as *Marley & Me* or *Old Yeller*.

A CONVERSATION WITH MONICA HOLLOWAY

What a powerful, moving story. How is Wills doing now? Are he and his new dog, Buddy, as close as he and Cowboy were? How does Wills remember Cowboy?

Wills is twelve now, and he's doing very well. Socially, he keeps making enormous strides. He would never need a puppy or a mommy to stand in front of him now. He handles social situations with aplomb. That isn't to say that he still doesn't work on his social skills, but it comes much more naturally now and remains, of course, completely "Wills." He has his own, unique way of approaching people and things.

Wills and Buddy go everywhere together, too. Buddy is two and a half years old now, and healthy as a horse. She weighs a whopping ninety-eight pounds and is so gorgeous. I look at her and realize how ill Cowboy must have been from the beginning, because Cowboy was so much smaller than Buddy.

Wills's heart is still broken over the loss of Cowboy and I don't think that's something that will ever truly go away. As I wrote in the book, Cowboy was his "first love and his first love lost." You never outgrow feelings for the "firsts" in your life. When Cowboy comes up, Wills still gets quite emotional.

Having said that, Wills is very excited about this book, and has found quite a lot of comfort in the stories he's read from it—in recalling all the fun. (He was a good resource when I had questions about some of the events that took place.)

He and I sat down to go through our pictures of the two of them for the book and the video, and Wills cried at first, but then we found ourselves laughing really hard.

It seems that the book has brought about healing for Wills. He talks about the book quite openly and seems to be proud of all that he's accomplished and his first dog. This was my most hopeful wish, of course, when I wrote the book.

Now that your family is more comfortable with Wills's diagnosis and progress, and you have Buddy as a companion, do you still find yourself at the pet store after a bad day? Or is that stage of your life in the past?

I thought maybe I was past the "animal addiction" phase of my life, but apparently not. This summer, I was dealing with a fairly difficult personal loss and adopted two beautiful white rabbits from LA's The Bunny Foundation. A boy bunny, whom Wills named Niege (French for "snow"), and a girl named Liza Minnelli in Rabbit Form because of her gorgeous black eyes and long eyelashes. The bunnies are domesticated and very friendly. Liza will let Buddy lick her fur until she's soaking wet but Niege prefers to bathe himself.

Three days ago, August 16, 2009, we bought another golden retriever puppy from Buddy's breeder, Artistry Golden Retrievers in Simi Valley. Wills named him Leo Henry, and he's only eight weeks old. We're over the moon with him, and Wills is having a blast. Now he has two dogs sleeping in his bed.

Buddy is very gentle with Leo and the two of them have been happily playing in the sand under Wills's fort. Wills strolls Leo around in an orange and gray puppy stroller while Buddy trots along beside them.

We also have one hamster, three hermit crabs, and two fire-bellied frogs among others.

So no, I wouldn't say that my animal addiction is under control. But we have a pretty happy, if not hairy, house.

Raising a child is always difficult, made only more complex in your case with an autism diagnosis. Looking back, is there anything you would have done differently?

I wish I could have relaxed more. Not knowing what the future holds for a child is difficult for any parent, but when there's a diagnosis involved, it spins you off in all kinds of bad scenarios. Some days are better than others. But over all, if I'd known he'd improve this much and lead such a happy life, I might have cleaned the house less obsessively and spent that time focused on the moment at hand—on the present.

Having said that, Wills is going into middle school in a few weeks, and I found myself scrubbing the bathtub with renewed intensity the other day while recalling how difficult junior high was for me—for most of us. So I still worry about him, but now Wills reminds me, "Mom, don't be so overprotective!" And it makes me laugh. He can handle it himself.

How did your childhood, as described in your first book, influence how you see yourself as a parent? What sort of perspective did it offer you? Was there anything that you felt you were missing, or were unprepared for?

I in no way wanted to emulate my own parents, and so that left me with precious little to go on in terms of role models. I read tons of books and felt quite alone, actually. Ultimately, I think I was too overprotective of Wills because I did not want to be neglectful. I was unclear about the boundaries—what was helpful and loving to Wills and what might have been suffocating to him.

Cowboy teaches Wills so many things, and introduces him to a much wider world while giving him the confidence to venture out in that world. What did Cowboy teach you? What life lesson from your puppy do you hold most dear?

Cowboy never whimpered or showed her discomfort in any way. Given how sick she became, I could only admire her determination to keep up with Wills as he ran through the yard or seeing her wagging her scraggly tail while she stood by the garage door, hoping to go for a ride with us. (Of course, we always took her.)

She was in pain, but being with us meant more to her than lying still or sleeping. She taught me to get up off my butt even when I didn't want to.

Her loyalty and fierce love for all of us was an honor to behold. It was so pure and came so naturally for her. We were lucky.

In the book, one of the mothers you meet claims to have cured autism in her son by changing his diet. You note, however, that the boy developed autism after receiving a vaccine. How do you feel about the very public media debate over the causes of autism, and about the decision some mothers make not to vaccinate their children, out of fear of their developing autism?

I feel very strongly that there must be something to this. I have seen too many children who were developing "normally" until the vaccines were administered, and then they began to regress, to lose language, to "disappear" inside themselves. This was not Wills. He had early-onset autism, as I discuss in the book, and I did not notice a change in him after his vaccinations.

I'm not a scientist, but from what I've read, it seems plausible to me that something (perhaps the large dose of metals in those vaccines) could possibly trigger autism if the gene is already there. I have no proof of this, I don't even know if there is an autism gene, I'm just a mom. But there are too many cases out there for me to dismiss it. Research needs to continue and increase.

Wills and Cowboy were incredibly close, but you and Cowboy also developed an amazingly deep relationship. How do you cope with the fact that she, who changed you and your son's life so dramatically, is no longer there? Has writing this book been a way for you to mourn and move on?

I wear a silver chain with a sterling silver cowboy hat hanging from it in memory of Cowboy. Just like Wills, I'll never move on from Cowboy completely, but days go by when I don't think of her and then there's that moment, that dog at the beach who looks exactly like her (she was smaller than most goldens) when my stomach clutches and I feel that pang of emptiness.

This is your second memoir. How, in your incredibly full life, have you managed to have time to write? How do you juggle being a mother and a writer, along with everything else?

One thing I do that cracks up my other writer friends is I write in my Jeep. I sit at a park or beside a lake and I type away. That way, I'm really close to Wills's school so I can take him in the morning and pick him up at 3:00 p.m. (Wills is at a new school forty minutes from our house. He's in middle school now.) Most days, Buddy is with me and we run through the park or sit on a quilt where she chews on bones or naps while I type.

Buddy goes on hikes three days a week with my friend Michael Blaser (also known as "the Dog Runner"), which gives me even more time to write while Wills is in school and it gives Buddy social time with the other dogs Michael walks.

That's why we waited for a new puppy until I was in between books. Now I have to be on top of Leo Henry all day.

We just built a little office for me at home, so let's see if I can work there. I think part of me feels less pressure when I'm writing "out in the world" and not sitting at my desk. Too much pressure. We'll see.

Writing a memoir is such an intimate form of communication. What motivated you to tell your story? Do you ever feel that you are revealing too much of yourself, or exposing your family, through your writing?

I heard Joan Didion speak two years ago, and she said (and I'm paraphrasing) that when you write nonfiction, you always "sell someone out." And when I heard that, I thought it was such a negative way to look at writing memoir, but since hearing that, I've come to realize that she was probably right. I can tell my story, but someone will inevitably be caught in the crosshairs—intentional or not. I can change a name or move something to a new setting, but someone will still feel the prick. On the other hand, Anne Lamott says in *Bird by Bird* that if someone wanted a better story, they "should have treated you better." This was much more true for my first book.

Cowboy & Wills was such a relief and a joy to write because Wills is the absolute love of my life and to tell the world how brave he is and how important it is to recognize the power of healing through animals was an incredible honor.

What is next for you as a writer? Do you think that you will ever move away from essays and memoir and write fiction?

I'm working on a book of essays right now that are also nonfiction. I can't see myself moving into fiction, but I wouldn't say never. Life speeds along and there's always something to wonder about, so I imagine I'll end up writing nonfiction for a while longer.

About the Author

MONICA HOLLOWAY is the critically acclaimed author of the memoir *Driving with Dead People*. She has contributed to the anthology *Mommy Wars,* from which her essay "Red Boots and Cole Haans" was described by *Newsday* as "brilliant, grimly hilarious." She lives in Los Angeles with her family and can be found online at www.MonicaHolloway.com.